Shintō and the State,
1868–1988

Studies in Church and State

JOHN F. WILSON, EDITOR

The Restructuring of American Religion: Society and Faith Since World War II
by Robert Wuthnow

Shintō and the State, 1868–1988
by Helen Hardacre

Shintō and the State, 1868-1988

Helen Hardacre

PRINCETON
UNIVERSITY
PRESS

Published by Princeton University Press, 41 William Street,
Princeton, New Jersey 08540
In the United Kingdom: Princeton University Press, Oxford

This book has been composed in Linotron Galliard text
and Optima Bold Display type

On the title page: The Gate of the Yasukuni Shrine

Printed in the United States of America by Princeton
University Press, Princeton, New Jersey

Library of Congress Cataloging-in-Publication Data
Hardacre, Helen, 1949–
Shintō and the state, 1868-1988 / Helen Hardacre.
    p.   cm.—(Studies in church and state)
        Bibliography: p.
        Includes index
    ISBN 0–691–07348–1 (alk. paper)
1. Shinto and state. 2. Shinto—History—1868–1945.
    3. Shinto—History—1945–   I. Title.   II. Series.
        BL2223.S8H36 1989
    322'.1—dc19   88-35665

For Yōko

Contents

CONTENTS

CONTENTS

Tables

Foreword

Shintō and the State, 1868–1988 is the second volume in the series "Studies in Church and State" sponsored by the Project on Church and State at Princeton University and funded by the Lilly Endowment. The Project has two goals: to sponsor scholarly publications on the interaction of religion and its political environment, primarily but not exclusively in the United States, and to draw on disciplines beyond those traditionally concerned with church-state issues to investigate that interaction. These goals flow from the conviction that religion and politics interact in many settings other than the institutional and the conventional. In consequence, as earlier scholarly emphasis on the organized life of religious bodies is superseded by inquiry into the broader role of religion in culture, particularly political culture, insights of sociologists and anthropologists are necessarily added to those of historians of religion, law, and society. The present volume was written by a historian of religions who teaches in the Department of Religion at Princeton University.

A number of books have already been published under Project sponsorship. A two-volume bibliographical guide to literature on the church-state question in American history was followed by a casebook on church-state law compiled by John T. Noonan, Jr. The first of the Studies in Church and State was *The Restructuring of American Religion: Society and Faith Since World War II*, by Robert Wuthnow of Princeton University's Department of Sociology. Wuthnow analyzes the general forces that have been redefining the role of religion in this country over the past four decades.*

In *Shintō and the State, 1868–1988* we have an examination of what is so frequently thought to be a "state" religion. However, as Hardacre points out, Western definitions of religion are of limited relevance to Japan. In addition, local practices have decisively affected Shintō's role as a "state" religion. Hardacre's work is important for its investigation of a modernizing nation-state's relationship with religion and for its exemplification of the general goals of the Project.

The books by Wuthnow and Hardacre inaugurate a series of approximately ten studies that will explore the interrelationship of church and state in America and in India, Latin America, and Europe as well as Japan. The authors of these books, all well known in their fields, share the view that the role of religion in society today is best understood by means of many disciplines and comparative perspectives. Obviously the project cannot publish studies on all the topics that deserve scholarly treatment, but by demonstrating, as this volume does, the potential for new work on the church-state issue, we hope to broaden current discussion and stimulate further scholarship.

Throughout the life of the Project we have been guided and supported by Robert Wood Lynn of the Lilly Endowment. Yoma Ullman has coordinated our work from the start, and her many skills, high standards, and great dedication have left their mark. Further, we are grateful to the Princeton University Press and especially Walter H. Lippincott, its director, and Gail M. Ullman, history editor, for their interest, encouragement, and support.

John F. Wilson
Robert T. Handy
Stanley N. Katz
Albert J. Raboteau

* John F. Wilson, ed., *Church and State in America; A Bibliographical Guide*, Vol. 1, *The Colonial and Early National Periods*; Vol. 2, *The Civil War to the Present Day* (Westport, CT: Greenwood Press, 1986, 1987). John T. Noonan, Jr., *The Believer and the Powers That Are* (New York: Macmillan, 1987). Robert Wuthnow, *The Restructuring of American Religion* (Princeton: Princeton University Press, 1988).

Acknowledgments

THIS STUDY was generously supported by the Lilly Endowment, the Japan Foundation, the Social Science Research Council, and the Committee on Research in the Social Sciences and Humanities of Princeton University. That support is gratefully acknowledged. The Lilly Endowment's Project on Church and State, directed by Professor John F. Wilson, has provided a climate conducive to research, and a meeting of series authors held at Princeton in 1986 generated many ideas important to this book. The wealth of substantive suggestions received from the Steering Committee of the project, and especially from Professor Wilson, has been invaluable. The superb editorial assistance of Yoma Ullman, also of the Project on Church and State, coupled with her ironic humor, has resulted in important improvements.

In Japan, a Professional Fellowship from the Japan Foundation enabled me to spend a year at the Institute for the Study of Classics of Kokugakuin University. Takao Hirota of the Japan Foundation greatly assisted me in securing access to rare sources vital to this research, as well as providing many enjoyable social occasions. At Kokugakuin University I received gracious assistance from Professors Naofusa Hirai, Nobutaka Inoue, Koremaru Sakamoto, Minoru Sonoda, and Masato Uno, all of whom discussed my research with me at length and gave me access to documents in their private collections. I am particularly indebted to Professors Hirai and Inoue, both of whom in addition gave me the benefit of their encyclopedic knowledge of the Shintō tradition. At Kōgakkan University Professors Seigo Tani, Igashirō Ban, and Emeritus Professor Junji Nishikawa offered valuable assistance. Professor Nishikawa in particular was most generous with his time and shared his great knowledge of Shintō history with me, both in person and by correspondence. The president of the university, Takashi Tanaka, extended much-welcomed friendship and hospitality. The staff at the Okayama Prefectural Library offered valuable assistance in researching the history of Kurozumikyō and Konkōkyō. Researchers at the headquarters and Tokyo offices of Konkōkyō were very helpful in providing access to unpublished materials, and in this connection I was particularly assisted by Reverends Motoo Tanaka, Kiyoshi Yamane, Setsuaki Fujio, Futoshi Nishikawa, Yoshitsugu Fukushima, Satō Mitsutoshi, Yoshikazu Matsuda, and Yoshio Miura. In researching the history of Kurozumikyō, I was fortunate to be aided by Patriarch Muneharu Kurozumi and the head priest of the Munetada Shrine, Tadaaki Kurozumi. Professor Masato Miyachi of the University of Tokyo and Professor Daikichi Irokawa taught me a great deal about the interpretation of Meiji-period documents. I am particularly grateful to Professor Irokawa for extended discussions in both Princeton and Tokyo.

James Foard, Anne Walthall, and Sheldon Garon read portions of the manuscript in draft and generously gave advice and suggestions. Both Marius Jansen and my father, Paul H. Hardacre, provided useful information.

This book is dedicated to Yōko Suemoto, who spent hundreds of hours assisting in its creation over a period of five years. She traveled to Yokohama, Okayama, Niigata, Tokyo, and Princeton to cull hundreds of local histories, shrine documents, and many thousands of feet of microfilm of Meiji period newspapers for evidence of popular participation in Shintō. This book owes its existence to her, not only for the research work she contributed with such tenacity, but for her unstinting enthusiasm for and belief in the project, and, most importantly, for her support and encouragement.

Shintō and the State,
1868–1988

Introduction

One of the most striking changes in modern societies is the increase in the power and authority of the center over its own periphery and in the simultaneous increase in the power and authority of the periphery over the center of its own society. This diminishes the distance between center and periphery. One of the phenomena of this narrowing of the distance between center and periphery is the change in the substance of tradition.

When the center expands in its powers, it dominates the situation of the periphery. . . . The combination of the power of the expanding center and the incapacity of the leaders of the subcenters and peripheries to maintain their autonomy increases the persuasiveness of the tradition associated with the newly ascendant center.—Shils, *Tradition*

THIS STUDY examines the relation between Shintō and the Japanese state from 1868 to 1988. The interest of this subject for the historian of religions lies in its significance as a case study of modern relations between religion and state. It illustrates the effects upon popular religious life of that relationship, and the complicated motivations of the state, the Shintō priesthood, and the populace as they created, maintained, dismantled, and then, after World War II, attempted to reconstruct it. Nowhere else in modern history do we find so pronounced an example of state sponsorship of a religion—in some respects the state can be said to have created Shintō as its official "tradition," but in the process Shintō was irrevocably changed, as Shils's remarks quoted above would lead us to expect.[1] In the end, Shintō, as adopted by the modern Japanese state, was largely an invented tradition, as Chapter 2 will show.

The term *State Shintō*, as used here, designates the relationship of state patronage and advocacy existing between the Japanese state and the religious practice known as Shintō between 1868 and 1945. The present study limits the term to the period 1868 to 1945 because active state patronage, as opposed to covert sponsorship concealed from the populace, was confined to those years. This was a period in which the power, authority, and prestige of the Japanese state greatly expanded, and in which its direct influence over many aspects of the lives of the populace increased markedly. Through both ritual and influence within the educational system and local civil administrations, the Shintō priesthood contributed to this expansion of the power of the center over the periphery, and, although since 1945 Shintō's sphere of influence has greatly contracted, nevertheless, the state has sought to reestablish elements of its former patronage. The populace now demonstrates a range of views on this attempt that reflect varied religious and secular interests. Thus, the legacy of State Shintō has persisted to the present, and church-state relations of interest to this study remain important in Japan. This introduction discusses the nature of Shintō before 1868 as a means of setting the stage for a history of the relation between Shintō and the state in the modern period (an overview of which is presented in Chapter 1), and in order to demonstrate how radically State Shintō departed from anything in the country's previous religious history.

The study of Shintō's relations with the state provides many examples of the invention of tradition to unite disparate elements into a modern nation.[2] Japan before 1868 represented a collectivity of persons whose sense of identity was focused not upon the state but upon local communities. In the process of unification, many of the rites and symbols of Shintō were appropriated, assembled in new forms, and given new meanings. Like European nations, Japan in the period of State Shintō created its first national ceremonial calendar, flag, national anthem, and rites of state accessible to all subjects. The emperor acquired, quite literally, new clothes and began to appear publicly in military uniform rather than the flowing robes of the ancient court; in the twentieth century his new image was circulated for public veneration to all public schools. While none of these state-sponsored symbolic innovations was specifically Shintō in the sense of being created by the priesthood, all were supported consistently by priests and have been associated in popular consciousness with Shintō. Furthermore, while all these innovations were the creations of the late nineteenth and early twentieth centuries, many were presented as emerging from hoary tradition, supposedly preserved intact from remotest antiquity, and the association with Shintō lent credibility to this claim.[3]

Shintō is a word with a long academic history and a remarkable variety of meanings. Kuroda Toshio has reviewed the range of meanings that have, at one time or another in Japanese history, been attached to the word, and he has shown, as this introduction will, though in a different way, that for much of its history Shintō has had no independent, autonomous existence. Instead, the practice of Shintō has existed as a mere appendage to Buddhist institutions or as the localized cults of community tutelary deities, with no comprehensive organizational structure to unite the whole.[4] This information comes as something of a surprise precisely because of the successful efforts of the state and the Shintō priesthood during the late nineteenth and early twentieth centuries to rewrite the past in order to provide a continuous history for Shintō from antiquity, one that included a particularly close relation to the state.

The meanings attached to Shintō have proved both maddeningly vague to the scholar and conveniently vague to the politician seeking to appeal to tradition, however recently invented.[5] Shintō has been said to be "the way of the gods," and "the indigenous religion of the Japanese people." At the same time it has been said to be nonreligious in character, or a suprareligious entity expressing the essence of the cultural identity of the Japanese people. The idea that a nation of 120 million persons has a single spiritual essence uniting them and wiping out all divisions of gender, class, and ethnicity is of course a convenient fiction that itself constitutes a political appeal or tool.

The creation of even the semblance of a comprehensive, national organization for Shintō dates to 1900. Before that the worship of its deities, the *kami*, was carried out on a localized basis, and its priests were organized not in a national priesthood with unified ranks conferred by agreed-upon criteria of ordination, but in independent sacerdotal lineages managed by a small number of the largest shrines (described below as Shintō's second layer), or by purely local arrangement and on a rotating basis among male members of a community. Thus in an institutional sense, Shintō has no legitimate claim to antiquity as Japan's "indigenous religion," however frequently the claim is made.

Shintō's ties with the state before 1868 were obscure and limited for the most part to the rites of the imperial or shogunal courts, always coordinated with, and usually subordinated to, Buddhist ritual. After 1868 Buddhism lost its former state patronage, and Shintō was elevated and patronized by the state. This patronage did not come about immediately or without misgivings and negotiations in government and among Shintō priests. Nevertheless, by the early decades of the twentieth century, Shintō was providing the rites of empire and claiming (falsely) always to have done so, from time immemorial.

STUDIES OF STATE SHINTŌ

The term *State Shintō* has been employed in two main ways in previous studies. Shintō scholars apply it only after the establishment of a Shrine Office (Jinja kyoku) within the Home Ministry in 1900, restricting its use to administrative measures regulating Shintō shrines and priests.[6] For these scholars, State Shintō came to an end in 1945. Historians and historians of religions have tended to use the term in a broader way, thinking of State Shintō as a systemic phenomenon that encompassed government support of and regulation of shrines, the emperor's sacerdotal roles, state creation and sponsorship of Shintō rites, construction of Shintō shrines in Japan and in overseas colonies, education for schoolchildren in Shintō mythology plus their compulsory participation in Shintō rituals, and persecution of other religious groups on the grounds of their exhibiting disrespect for some aspect of authorized mythology. These historians also see State Shintō as a pervasive coloration of the thought and beliefs of the people by Shintō ideology.[7] They are likely to speak of a resurgence of State Shintō in the postwar era.

Among Western scholars, Daniel C. Holtom was the first to give serious attention to State Shintō, and his work concentrated on the link between State Shintō and Japanese nationalism and imperialism, tending to accept the wartime rhetoric of Shintō as the "engine of war."[8] More recent studies by Ernst Lokowandt have concentrated on aspects of legal history, studying government documents without delving into questions of the manner of their implementation.[9]

Virtually all Japanese Shintō scholars are Shintō priests, descended by blood or academic lineage from the creators and administrators of State Shintō.[10] Their approach is decidedly apologetic, and the aspects of coercion and persecution central to the studies by secular scholars are rarely even mentioned. Discussion of the concrete actions of specific persons is avoided. Japanese historians and historians of religions dealing with Shintō, on the other hand, tend to view State Shintō as a monolithic entity that indoctrinated the people in Shintō ideology, thus stifling the development of free thought and democratic social movements.[11]

Like studies by secular historians in Japan, this study has sought to identify key personalities in Shintō's modern history and to document their actions, but the task has proved difficult. Too often scholars—of any ideological persuasion—have written only of the activities of "the state" or certain agencies ("the Department of Divinity then set about . . ."), leaving the impression that nearly a century of religious history passed without any particular person taking any identifiable action. The reasons for this faceless quality of research on State Shintō are not far to seek. The primary texts consist principally of government directives and laws regulating shrines and their rites, or curtailing the activities of other religions. It is seldom possible to determine the author of a given document, or the circumstances to which it was meant as a response. Diaries and other private papers of the principals rarely shed much light on such issues. It is rumored that at the end of the war, before the American occupying forces arrived, Shintō officials realized that their activities would be scrutinized and, in an effort to forestall a purge, hastily destroyed many documents that would have made it possible to assign personal responsibility for acts of religious persecution.

The problem of giving "faces" to State Shintō cannot be fully solved at this stage of research. We may never know as much as we would like about the personalities and motivations of the state in its relations with Shintō. Nevertheless, we may gain fresh insights by asking new questions. Whereas most scholarship on State Shintō focuses upon the state and its activities, one can ask instead how the character of religion in Japan was changed as a result of the state's involvement with Shintō.

ISSUES, THEMES, AND GOALS

A major aim of this study is to explore the significance for popular religious life of the state's involvement in Shintō between 1868 and 1945. This inquiry requires a shift of focus from the center to the periphery, looking more to the documents of rural areas than to government directives, more at the manner of implementation of government orders than at the orders themselves and the puzzles of their authorship. It is here that we see the expanding influence of the periphery over the center and the decreasing distance between the two relative to the situation in pre-Meiji Japan.

Whereas previous studies have emphasized actions originating with the state bureaucracy responsible for the administration of Shintō, this study examines the motives that led the priesthood to seek ever-stronger ties to the state, and the populace to become involved in Shintō. The activities of the priesthood throughout the modern period have been dominated by attempts to build, maintain, and strengthen ties to the state as a means of raising its own prestige. We shall see that leaders and adherents of popular religious movements, as well as independent religious entrepreneurs, women seeking to raise the prestige of their households, and men with political ambitions all found an association with Shintō either felicitous in their efforts at self-promotion and self-aggrandizement, or unavoidable as the power of the state extended further into all areas of life. Shintō was useful to them precisely because of its relation to the state. In addition, local-level civil administrations and parish organizations have consistently patronized Shintō as a way to raise the prospects of provincial communities. In these various ways Shintō has served as a conduit for access to the prestige of the state, connecting the periphery to the center, and increasing the ability of the periphery to exert influence over the center.

A topic bearing directly upon the changes wrought in popular religious life by the state's appropriation of Shintō symbolism and ritual is the Great Promulgation Campaign of 1870 to 1884. For the first time in history, the state attempted to author a religious doctrine and undertook to promulgate it systematically by enlisting as National Evangelists members of every religious organization except those refusing to be so co-opted. The priesthood became involved for the first time in the systematic inculcation of state-sponsored values, a role it has tried to preserve down to the present. The campaign offered the first of many opportunities for the leaders of popular religious movements to enhance their prestige in the eyes of their adherents by forging a relation to the state, though the price paid was frequently the falsification of their founders' original messages. Meanwhile, the populace did not receive this new state-authored message passively but instead appropriated it selectively and in line with local interests. The campaign is the subject of Chapter 2.

The Shintō priesthood, the subject of Chapter 3, evolved slowly from the highly localized situation existing before 1868. Its members were often deeply immersed in other religious traditions and highly resistant to state efforts to systematize kami-worship. Priests varied greatly, and this accounted for much of the diversity, at the local level, in the way state policy on Shintō was understood and implemented (or, equally frequently, not understood and not implemented). When seen from the perspective of the local level, the story of the Shintō priesthood demonstrates the need for serious qualification of the view, so prominent in Western and secular Japanese scholarship on State Shintō, of its supposedly monolithic character.

Chapters 4 and 5 discuss the creation of a nationally ranked hierarchy of shrines of several types and the performance of ritual that affected the religious life of virtually the entire nation by the early decades of the twentieth century. In particular, the creation of a cult of fallen military combatants—apotheosized as "glorious war dead"—its center in the Yasukuni Shrine, has, of all the invented traditions of State Shintō, most profoundly colored the character of popular religious life and remains an issue at the end of the twentieth century. The maintenance of such a cult could only have occurred in an increasingly closed political culture marked by the stifling of opposition. Creation of this culture was greatly assisted by Shintō ritual. As ritual, it had no contrary and hence could not be contradicted. It could thus prevail in popular consciousness as long as alternative views of the nation, its proper symbolization, and its proper relation to religion were suppressed.[12]

The decade of the 1930s and wartime Japan have been extensively treated in Western scholarship as the era of thought manipulation and maximized control of the state over individual liberties. Partly because this era has been so thoroughly debated in recent scholarship, the present study has not given it sustained attention. That decision was made not because the period 1930 to 1945 is unimportant in the history of Shintō—it certainly was significant—but to allow more extensive coverage of topics that have received virtually no discussion in either Japanese or Western scholarship, such as the priesthood, shrines as religious institutions, and shrine rites as appropriated by the state.[13]

A theme that runs throughout the modern history of Shintō concerns its clashes with Western, especially Protestant, ideas of religion. Much modern Shintō thought is devoted to this subject, and upon it hinges a century of Japanese jurisprudence and constitutional philosophy treating religious freedom and religion's relation to the state. The issue of Shintō's religiosity remains a vital issue in contemporary Japanese politics. Important challenges to the postwar constitution's provisions for religious freedom and the separation of religion and state have repeatedly illustrated the incompatibility between indigenous constructions of religious life and Western definitions of religion. The modern history of Shintō's relation to the state demonstrates the difficulty in Japan, as elsewhere, of resolving the conflicting claims of individual liberties and a political regime's drive for symbolic legitimation. Chapter 6 discusses the issue of religious freedom under the Meiji Constitution.

The final chapter of this study treats the dissolution of State Shintō by the Allied Occupation following World War II and recent attempts by the Japanese government to revive the symbolism of Shintō in the service of several goals. One of these would seem to be to present the history of the prewar political regime in a benign light, to whitewash domestic acts of suppression of individual liberties, the persecution of religious groups outside the umbrella of orthodoxy, and the suppression of dissent at home and in the colonies. Revival of Shintō symbolism is but one part of a broader campaign to rewrite the past; equally important is the censoring of history texts used in public schools. Another goal is the creation of a compelling myth of cultural identity encompassing a formula for the legitimation of the state, one that will again submerge the divisions of gender, class, and ethnicity in the cozy, penumbral illusion of spiritual unity, articulated in the characteristically vague and incontrovertible rites and symbols of Shintō, with special use of the Yasukuni Shrine. The difference in the postwar era is, however, that opposition is no longer stifled, even if it does not speak with a single voice. Contemporary Japanese political culture is now irrevocably pluralistic, and hence the state no longer enjoys hegemony in its manipulation of Shintō rites and symbols, though the priesthood may well wish that it did.[14]

SHINTŌ IN THE TOKUGAWA ERA (1600–1868)

The extent to which State Shintō represented a departure from previous religious history cannot be fully appreciated without discussing the character of Shintō in relation to Japanese understandings of religion before its creation. Throughout its modern history, there has been much discussion of whether it is appropriate to consider Shintō a religion. In fact, this sort of question has often been raised about Taoism, Confucianism, and the sacred traditions of nonliterate peoples as well. The question becomes one of "religion by whose definition?" The sociologist of religions Joachim Wach divided religion into three components: doctrine, rites, and communal observances.[15] Western scholarship's Christian, especially Protestant, heritage entails a predisposition to give most weight to doctrine (and the related attitudes of faith and belief), so much so that doctrine is commonly assumed to constitute the universal essence of religion. By comparison, rites and communal observances seem to be gratuitous appendages to the core of religious life. These complex assumptions about religion do not accord well, however, with indigenous constructions of religious life found outside the purview of Judaism, Christianity, and Islam. Certainly they do not accurately describe the traditional religious life of Japan, and they are especially unhelpful in attempting to understand Shintō.

As noted earlier, Shintō has often been called the "indigenous religion of Japan." It is an ancient cult directed to native deities called kami, and included among these are deified emperors and heroes, spirits of nature, and deities of Japanese mythology. For the greater part of its history, Shintō has been highly localized—as in the cults of clan or territorial tutelary deities. Functioning for the most part as the communal cult of small-scale social groupings, it assumes the values of society but does not (except in the case of its sectarian varieties, a nineteenth- and twentieth-century phenomenon) promulgate doctrine. It is primarily a liturgical practice.[16]

Until the end of the nineteenth century, Shintō knew no comprehensive organizational structure. Japanese Buddhism was divided into separate schools, the priests and temples of which were organized hierarchically. Shintō had no comparable organization for its cult centers, called shrines by convention, to distinguish them from Buddhist temples. Shintō had no central figure analogous to a pope, nor were its priests trained in any unified doctrine or practice. Instead, we may think of Shintō during the Tokugawa period, which immediately preceded the creation of State Shintō, as existing in three layers, all of which were crosscut by Shintō's relation to Buddhism.[17]

Known in some way to the greatest number of people, Shintō's first layer was constituted by the ritual practice of the imperial court, which maintained a formal schedule of elaborate ritual for both Buddhas and kami. The emperor presided over rites of the harvest, the equinoxes, worship of the four directions, New Year's, and a host of other rites.[18] One type of imperial enthronement ritual (the *daijōe* or *daijōsai*), which consisted of the new emperor offering firstfruits to, and symbolically sharing a

meal with, the imperial ancestors, was held in a Shintō style.[19] The calendar
of imperial court rites was inherited from the *ritsuryō* system of rites and
government (seventh to tenth centuries), when an elaborate ritual calendar
was codified in the *Engishiki* (927), an important Shintō liturgical text.[20]

During the Tokugawa era, emperors were assisted in carrying out a
much reduced version of *ritsuryō* rites by members of the court (nobility
itself constituting their qualification), especially by priests of the Yoshida
and Shirakawa houses, who filled the office of Jingihaku, Councillor of
Divinities. By an edict of 1665,[21] the Yoshida and Shirakawa were granted
the authority to rank all shrines and priests (mainly on the basis of antiquity, lineage, and payments made to the two houses by the shrine or priest
desiring an increase in rank). The Shirakawa had charge of those shrines
linked directly to the imperial house, while the Yoshida supervised the
remainder, the great majority. Both maintained separate cults of the eight
tutelary deities of the imperial house,[22] and this gave them special priestly
authority in the conduct of imperial rites.[23]

While there were many Shintō ceremonies, the rites of the court were
by no means exclusively Shintō in character. The emperor and members of
the court also performed many Buddhist rites. The imperial family were
officially parishioners of the Shingon school of Buddhism and were cre-
mated according to Buddhist funeral rites. Many members of both the
court and the imperial family joined Buddhist monasteries, and Buddhist
memorial rites for the spirits of the imperial ancestors were a major part of
court rites. In addition to Shintō rites of accession to the throne, the new
emperor received "accession ordination" (*sokui kanjō*), a rite that paralleled
the rite of taking the tonsure to become a Buddhist priest. To make matters
still more complicated, Masters of Yin and Yang (*on'yōshi*) were also employed at court to supervise other imperial rites.[24]

Scarcity of funds prohibited fulfilling the entire ritual schedule because
the shogun's government (the actual ruling body of the country and holder
of imperial purse strings) was intent upon establishing the cult of its founder Tokugawa Ieyasu. Accordingly, it was little interested in permitting
imperial ritual to be carried out on a comparable scale. The court's income,
a rice stipend received from the shogunate, did not exceed that of a middle-
ranking feudal lord.[25]

While imperial ritual continued to be performed on a diminishing
scale at the court in Kyoto, the sacerdotal roles of the emperor were widely
known to exist, but probably not understood in any detail by the rest of the
populace. Feudal lords, who were frequently related to the court by marriage, were aware of the court and its ritual life. Many artisans and merchants were linked to various aristocratic houses as suppliers of goods used
in ritual, and so they also were conscious of court rites. The people as a
whole were required to observe mourning for deaths at court and therefore

knew of imperial funeral and memorial rites. Ise pilgrimage, discussed below, had an indirect influence on popular awareness of the court and its affairs because a connection between the deities enshrined there and the imperial court was generally known.[26]

The second layer of Tokugawa Shintō was constituted by the practice of those great shrines of the nation large enough to have their own hereditary priesthoods, branch shrines, and extensive landholdings. In addition, the extensive development of pilgrimages further popularized the cults of transregionally known kami. Such shrines can be discussed as a group for the purposes of this chapter, even though they had no organizational connections and no common rites and doctrine, because they were alike in that their rites and deities were known to people in more than one domain.

The phenomenon of branch shrines first developed in the medieval period in three main ways: (1) when clans or their subgroupings migrated to a new area and established a new shrine of the clan deity; (2) through the dedication of fiefs to shrines; and (3) through the appearance of worshipers of the original shrine's deities in a distant area. A branch shrine was officially linked to the original shrine through a ceremony in which the new shrine installed as its object of worship the "divided spirit" (*bunrei*) of the original shrine.[27] The result was a main shrine that received tribute and pilgrims from its distant branch shrines. Priests from the branch shrines in some cases were trained at the main shrine and then spread the word of the virtues of the main shrine's deities, and of pilgrimage to it, among the people living on the shrine's detached landholdings.

Consider, for example, the case of the Usa Hachiman Shrine in Usa City on the island of Kyushu, which enshrines, inter alia, the spirit of the deified Emperor Ojin as the deity Hachiman. This shrine, long the recipient of imperial patronage, is considered second in prestige only to the Ise Shrines. In 859 a branch of the Usa Shrine was built in Kyoto by a Buddhist monk and named the Iwashimizu Hachiman Shrine. The Minamoto house (of the Kamakura shogunate) regarded Hachiman as their clan deity, and when Minamoto Yoritomo, first of the Kamakura shoguns, moved his government to Kamakura, he founded a branch of the Iwashimizu Shrine, called the Tsurugaoka Hachiman Shrine in 1063, thus linking the new shrine to its immediate parent in Kyoto as well as to the Usa Shrine. Many more shrines dedicated to Hachiman were founded around the nation, and now the Usa Hachiman Shrine serves as the central shrine for some twenty-five thousand Hachiman shrines throughout Japan.[28]

This phenomenon of branch shrine construction and, thereby, of proliferation of the cult of the main shrine's deities throughout Japan can be seen also in the case of the Inari, Kasuga, Tenjin, Konpira, Munakata, Suwa, and Izumo shrines. The priesthoods of these shrines were generally organized as a sacerdotal lineage; their teachings were transmitted for the most part in rather esoteric ways, in texts that were closely guarded and not made available outside the priestly lines. Thus we can think of them as developing lineage theologies that were not widely known outside a particular lineage even among priests, to say nothing of the populace as a whole, which probably remained unaware of their existence.

Branch shrines constituted a vehicle for the transmission of the cult of their kami to large numbers of people across a wide geographical area. In addition to venerable shrines and their branches, another type of Shintō cult center emerged as an important part of popular religious life. There were shrines that developed as pilgrimage centers during the Tokugawa period, the Ise Shrines,[29] the Konpira Shrine on Shikoku, or the Kanda Myōjin or Nezu Gongen in Edo being important examples. These shrines were also important in drawing pilgrims from a wide geographical area, not only through advertising the boons available from their deities, but also through large markets held in connection with shrine festivals.[30]

It is important to note that Buddhist priests participated widely in shrine rites, often leading villagers on pilgrimage or journeying to shrines to undertake austerities for their own spiritual practice. Even large shrines of this layer generally existed as one component of a temple-shrine complex, performing their rites side by side with a temple, generally for the same audience as the temple's rites. In such a complex, the Shintō priests were subordinate to their Buddhist colleagues, but at the popular level there was no thoroughgoing distinction between the cults of Buddhas and kami.[31]

The third layer of Tokugawa Shintō encompassed by far the greatest number of shrines during the period, the local tutelary shrines of agrarian villages, the *ujigami* and *ubusuna* shrines (these terms are basically interchangeable, both connoting the idea of a territorial protective deity). Whereas the main shrines of the second layer of shrines might be called *jinja* ("shrines"), village tutelary shrines were generally known by the simpler title of "the *ubusuna* or *ujigami* ('tutelary deity') of such-and-such a place."[32]

In most cases village shrines did not have a professional priest but were served by adult men of the village on a rotating basis or their cults monopolized by village elites who formed a shrine guild (*miyaza* and other terms). While for the most part any villager might observe the festival of the village deity, actual participation was most frequently restricted in a manner mirroring the social hierarchy of the village, the most prestigious roles automatically accorded to those with the highest social standing. The status of parishioner (*ujiko*) of the village shrine was not accorded to all villagers but was usually reserved for those of wealth and/or long residence in the area.[33]

13

THE RELATION BETWEEN BUDDHISM AND SHINTŌ

Having introduced these three layers of Tokugawa Shintō, we must examine how they were related to Buddhism. At the time of the Meiji Restoration (1868), it is estimated that there were 74,642 shrines and 87,558 temples in Japan.[34] The shrines were administered under the jurisdiction of the Councillor of Divinities, and most were small, lacked full-time priests, and performed worship of local tutelary gods. The great majority existed as one component within a temple-shrine complex, in which temple and shrine functioned together as a single cultic center. The complex was generally controlled by the Buddhist clergy.[35]

The relation between the cults of Buddhas and kami was expressed doctrinally in the theory holding that kami were the protectors and phenomenal appearances (*suijaku*) of Buddhist divinities, who represented the purest, original form of divinity (*honji*). Implied was the idea that kami were beings of lower spiritual attainments than the Buddhas.[36]

This combination of Buddhism and Shintō was pervasive and included even such large and venerable shrines as those discussed above as constituting Shintō's second layer, exceptions being the Ise and Izumo Shrines and shrines of the Mito domain after the rule of Tokugawa Mitsukuni (1628–1700). Even at Ise, however, while there was a nominal ban on Buddhist observances, it was ignored. In 1868 there were nearly three hundred temples at Ise. Recitation of Buddhist sutras before the altars of the kami, on the theory that the kami needed these Buddhist rites in order to attain salvation, was common, and many Buddhist priests journeyed to Ise as pilgrims and to perform austerities there.[37]

The legacy of the *honji-suijaku* theory, the institutional combination of temples and shrines, and the long-lived idea of the "unity of the three creeds" together constituted a popular religion that seldom made the thoroughgoing distinctions between Buddhism and Shintō that most present-day scholarship takes for granted. If anything, the populace at the end of the Tokugawa period probably perceived shrine priests as minor functionaries compared to Buddhist clerics, since in terms of relative status shrine priests' standing was at its nadir.

Shrine priests were subject to the temple registration system (*tera-uke*), according to which they had to become temple parishioners regardless of their beliefs, and they were almost always forced to have Buddhist funerals, a cause of considerable resentment. The temple registration system was Tokugawa Japan's nearest equivalent to a census system; in effect the Buddhist priesthood was charged with keeping records of all births, marriages, deaths, travel, and changes in residence or occupation. Shintō priests were not exempt by virtue of different religious beliefs.

Buddhist priests inevitably held higher positions and commanded greater administrative authority than shrine priests. Shrine priests were seated lower than Buddhist clerics at village assemblies, and in the minutiae of diurnal etiquette, the lower status of the Shintō priesthood was made abundantly and humiliatingly clear. This situation did not pass entirely without protest, but organized resistance among Shintō priests transcending domain boundaries was virtually unknown before the Meiji Restoration. Priests of Iwami (present-day Shimane Prefecture) provided an example of protest by petitioning for seven years for exemption from the temple registration system, with but limited success.[38]

All forms of Tokugawa Shintō were pervasively influenced and restricted by Shintō's relation to Buddhism. As one might expect, there was considerable ill-feeling against Buddhism among the Shintō priesthood, but until the advent of National Learning (discussed below) as a grassroots nativist movement at the end of the period, there was little to be done.

The priesthood was unorganized and manifestly incapable of resisting Buddhist control. Almost all shrines of the second level were attached in a subordinate status to temples, and shrines of the third level most frequently were only informally staffed. Tutelary shrines confirmed communal ties, underwrote local status hierarchies, and affirmed popular values originating in communal life. To fulfill those functions, shrines required no special doctrines nor a professional priesthood. The role of the priest here, as in all levels of Tokugawa Shintō, was liturgical, not pastoral or theological.

Popular worship of kami could and did exist, as in the mushrooming popular pilgrimage that so conspicuously characterized the period, quite independent of the priesthood and its interest in National Learning. Popular faith in the kami (except for three new religions founded at the end of the period and discussed in Chapter 2) was concerned with this-worldly benefits such as bountiful crops and personal well-being. A popular form of kami-worship, transcending domain boundaries and extending throughout the nation, developed around the Ise Shrines.

ISE PILGRIMAGE

Ise pilgrimage, especially during the later Tokugawa period, was a phenomenon that involved vast numbers of people in worship of the kami. Probably no single religious practice of the period rivaled these pilgrimages in scale and extent of influence. They were managed by an informal order of the Ise priesthood called *oshi* who controlled networks of confraternities that by the end of the period extended nationwide except for the Northeast. Between 80 and 90 percent of the nation maintained a confraternity membership, and thus powerful oshi might have as many as four to ten thousand households in their control.[39]

Oshi traveled to their confraternities once or twice a year to distribute almanacs, talismans, and purifying wands. In return they received "first-fruits" (*hatsuho*) in cash, in amounts calculated in proportion to the rice tax.[40] Village confraternities sent their members on pilgrimage to the Ise Shrines annually if they were financially able to do so. Pilgrims were met at the city limits and escorted to their oshi's lodge where they were royally hosted, sacred dance (*kagura*) was performed for them, and their prayers were transmitted to shrine deities. Upon completion of the trip's religious business, pilgrims (at least male pilgrims) could take in the secular delights of Ise. These were innumerable, and not all were of a religious nature—there were mammoth brothels employing more than a thousand women.[41]

The people viewed the Ise deities as harvest gods or as deities who could protect the faithful, and they visited the shrines to pray for abundant crops and personal well-being. In addition, there were areas of Japan in which Ise pilgrimage was part of the coming-of-age rites for both men and women, without which they could not be considered adult, hence ready to marry and shoulder civic responsibility.[42]

While Ise pilgrimage during the Tokugawa period became in large part a popular phenomenon, many Shintō theologies were also produced during that era by various sacerdotal lineages, though mainly restricted to their shrines as esoteric knowledge. Since these had little impact upon popular religious life or upon the formation of State Shintō, however, they have not been treated here.[43] There was, however, one variety of Shintō thought that exerted a direct influence upon State Shintō and hence must be discussed.

THE INFLUENCE OF NATIONAL LEARNING

It is impossible to understand State Shintō's origins without examining the school of thought known as National Learning (*kokugaku*). National Learning began as a type and method of philological study associated most prominently with Kada no Azumamaro (1669–1739), Kamo Mabuchi (1697–1769), and Motoori Norinaga (1730–1801). Particularly with Motoori, National Learning strove to "recover" an idealized, pure mentality and world view ascribed to the ancient Japanese, to return to the thought and consciousness of the ancients before the country became (as these writers understood the situation) "polluted" by contact with foreign culture and religion. Buddhism was attacked as the agency most to blame for Japan's loss of its original way of life.[44]

It was the National Learning of the end of the Tokugawa period that most influenced the formation of State Shintō, and in many ways nineteenth-century National Learning had moved great distances from its beginnings. Its most influential nineteenth-century figure was Hirata Atsutane (1776–1843), who had many followers among Shintō priests, to whom National Learning seemed to offer a way out of Shintō's centuries-old enforced subordination to Buddhism. After Hirata's time, National Learning ceased to be a type of scholarship and instead acquired the rudiments of a nativist movement.[45] This nativist character was particularly evident among the followers of Ōkuni Takamasa (1792–1871), and for them National Learning and Shintō were completely merged into a spirituality centering upon worship of the kami.

As this movement impinged most directly on Shintō, its goals were the separation of Buddhism from Shintō, freedom for Shintō priests to hold Shintō funerals, reestablishment of the Department of Divinity (Jingikan, an organ of state under the ritsuryō system) as a formal department of government, and standardized worship of local tutelary deities as a means for the common people to regain the spirit of early Japan.[46]

National Learning was able eventually to gain a hearing with those who were to become the leaders of the new Meiji state because at the end of the Tokugawa period it had broad affinities with restorationist ideals and was supported by personal ties to the future leaders of the Restoration. Western Japan, a stronghold of restorationist sentiment, was an important center of the movement, and there it became permeated with the ideal of restoring imperial rule, and of the repudiation of foreign influence.

Two domains of western Japan, Hamada and Tsuwano, provided concrete examples of National Learning in action. Hamada broke the tradition of temple registration and made Shintō funerals the official practice of the domain in 1838. Tsuwano followed suit. There the National Learning of Ōkuni Takamasa, its last great pre-Meiji leader, was the official ideology of the realm. Tsuwano carried out its own separation of Buddhism from Shintō in 1867, under the direction of Ōkuni's disciple Fukuba Bisei (1831–1907), who later became a high administrator of Shintō affairs in the Meiji government, being the principal architect of the Great Promulgation Campaign, the subject of Chapter 2.[47]

The advent of Perry's fleet in 1853 posed the threat of foreign invasion, and the shogunate's inability to make an effective response polarized the country. Those against the shogunate rallied to the call of "revere the emperor and expel the barbarian" (sonnō jōi). The idea of restoring imperial rule implied toppling the shogunate, but beyond that there was a wide spectrum of opinion on what "restoration" might mean in terms of practical politics.

National Learning figures hoped to restore the Department of Divinity to unify the populace through common worship of national deities, as opposed to the prevailing localized cults. In their vision of a unified national cultus, National Learning leaders assumed that the Department of Divinity would administer the resulting religious system and that it would be an autonomous organ of government. They were aided by the future statesman Iwakura Tomomi (1825–1883), who, under the influence of his National Learning mentor Tamamatsu Misao (1810–1872),[48] wrote draft proposals on the department's operation. Many National Learning figures joined the call for the department's reestablishment, including Ōkuni Takamasa, Yano Harumichi (1823–1887), an influential National Learning figure of late Tokugawa and early Meiji, and Mutobe Yoshika (1806–1863), Shintō priest and National Learning scholar.[49]

These Shintō figures desired that the Department of Divinity be simultaneously the highest administrative organ of government and a religious entity. Besides the business of administering all religious affairs, the department would enshrine the eight tutelary deities of the imperial house, the exclusive prerogative of the Yoshida and Shirakawa houses from the fifteenth to the nineteenth centuries. Taking over the cult of these deities, the department would assume the status of highest religious authority in the land, issuing proclamations in the name, as it were, of those deities. In addition, the department would enshrine the spirits of the imperial ancestors and the gods of heaven and earth (*tenjin chigi*), and the emperor would conduct ritual there.[50]

SUMMARY

The cultic life of shrines as described in this introduction constituted a major part of Japanese religious life in the era immediately preceding the creation of State Shintō. The center of shrine life lay in the observance of rites and such communal observances as festivals and pilgrimage. Thus the character of pre-Meiji Shintō was liturgical and closely integrated with social life. By comparison, doctrinal or ethical questions were peripheral to shrine life as experienced by most people. That is not to deny the importance of faith in the kami to aid or support a devotee, but this faith did not exclude similar devotion to Buddhas and ancestors, nor were the faithful called upon to proclaim their devotion in formal creedal statements.

In pre-Meiji Japan there existed no concept of religion as a general phenomenon, of which there would be variants like Christianity, Buddhism, and Shintō. People spoke of having faith (*shinkō*) in particular kami and Buddhas, but no word existed to designate a separate sphere of life that could be called "religious," as opposed to the rest of one's existence. This may indicate that religious themes and concerns were deeply integrated in popular consciousness and social life in a way fundamentally at odds with modern Christocentric notions of religion as a private matter of an individual's relation to a deity.

Furthermore, especially before the advent of National Learning as a nativist movement, the word *Shintō* was not widely used in ordinary speech. Although it is used now to indicate any or all cults of kami and everything relating to them, including shrines and their priests, it was not widely used with that meaning in the Tokugawa period. Not even the shrine priesthood universally used the word, probably because shrine life was either so localized or so preoccupied with the cult of particular divinities that priests had little sense of being involved in a common undertaking that could appropriately be named with a single term. Probably no one but priests devoted to National Learning regarded themselves as exclusively Shintōist, in the sense of being entirely independent of Buddhism, and not even they used the word *Shintō* exclusively. Thus the idea of Shintō as an independent religion scarcely existed before the Meiji Restoration; that sense of the word is purely a modern, post-Meiji invention. Thus when the term came to be more widely used in the Meiji period, there was considerable confusion and disagreement about its meaning.[51]

Japan in the Tokugawa era had an indigenous construction of religion that was centered in liturgical and communal life. It undergirded a vigorous and flourishing religious life, of which shrines were a central part. There was much in Japanese cultic life that was fundamentally at odds with the Western notions of religion that entered Japan after the Meiji Restoration. Those same notions of religion underwrote Western judicial philosophy about the place of religion in a modern nation, the principle of religious freedom, and the separation of religion and state. While Western ideas of religion grew out of centuries of Western religious life and experience, those ideas and the jurisprudence based upon them could not be easily assimilated by a nation like Japan, with its vastly different religious heritage. Nowhere was the incompatibility more evident than in the history of Shintō's relations with the state after the Meiji Restoration.

1. The Modern History of Relations between Shintō and the State

THIS CHAPTER provides a narrative history of the relations between Shintō and the state between 1868 and 1988. Succeeding chapters treat specific aspects of that history in greater detail.

In addition to the periodization to be introduced immediately below, running through the entire modern history of Shintō is a thematic issue: Is Shintō properly considered a religion? The early Meiji period was characterized by a rapid influx of Western culture, and among the many new ideas were those dealing with religion. Western, especially Protestant, ideas about religion were absorbed by Japanese intellectuals, but, for the reasons examined in the introduction, they did not produce immediate changes in popular religious life, nor were they widely accepted by shrine priests, many of whom came to believe that Shintō was not a religion but a suprareligious entity. This clash between indigenous and Western notions of religion has provided one focus for debate about Shintō down to the present.

CHRONOLOGICAL OVERVIEW

Several periods in the relation between Shintō and the state can be demarcated for the years 1868 to 1988. Each is characterized by a distinctive attitude of the state toward Shintō, of the Shintō priesthood toward the state, and a particular mode of involvement of the populace and of popular religious movements in Shintō.

21

1868–1880: Experimentation and Disillusion. The years 1868 to roughly 1880 were characterized by state experimentation with Shintō. Beginning in 1868, the state unceremoniously dropped its former patronage of Buddhism and turned a blind eye when Shintō priests used the occasion to pillage Buddhist temples. At the same time, as part of the Great Promulgation Campaign, state officials wrote doctrine and empowered a bureaucracy headed by Shintō priests to promulgate it and to create accompanying ritual appropriating the symbols, vestments, and rituals of the shrines. When the campaign proved unable to unite the populace in support of a unified creed, however, Shintō bureaucrats fell from favor, and state support, as measured by bureaucratic rank of priests in government service or by monetary grants to shrines, fell sharply.

In the heyday of the campaign, Shintō priests briefly occupied high bureaucratic office and began efforts to overcome the fragmentation and lack of unity that had characterized their history before the Meiji Restoration. The priesthood developed a conviction, still prevalent at the end of the twentieth century, that Shintō was a nonreligious or suprareligious entity with the political function of establishing the spiritual unity of the populace. A component of this attitude was a scornful, elitist view of popular religious life and a conception of themselves as teachers of the populace through ritual, rather than as religious leaders with a pastoral role.

Leaders of many popular religious movements were drawn into the state's attempt to create a religion out of Shintō through their participation in the Great Promulgation Campaign, with the result that these movements traded their independence and autonomy for the prestige of a connection with the state. This habit became ingrained in many religious movements. Popular religious life—with the exception of the new movements—began to incorporate a national, unified ritual calendar revolving around newly created imperial ritual superimposed upon preexisting local festival calendars. This acceptance was, however, spotty and not fully achieved until perhaps 1900.

1880–1905: Declining State Support. The years 1880 to 1905 represented a low in Shintō's relation to the state. The bureaucratic offices governing Shintō affairs were ranked lower than in the preceding period. The trend in financial support for the shrines from public funds was to assign ever greater responsibility to local parishes.

This tendency was alarming to the priesthood. Priests understood that if they had to answer to local supporters they would be required to provide such religious services as rites of healing and blessing, as well as funerals, while they were concerned to preserve for themselves a distinctly nonreligious status affiliated in some way with the state. The priesthood during this period saw itself an an embattled minority, misunderstood by government and seeking to reinstate the positions of prestige enjoyed briefly in the preceding period.

Nevertheless, during these years many important shrines were constructed and linked in a national hierarchy. The cult of the war dead was begun in earnest, and the populace was drawn into the cult and into shrine life generally by conscription and by an alliance at the local level between the educational system and shrine priests. Popular religious movements remained supporters of Shintō for the most part.

1905–1930: Expansion and Increased Influence.
Much of the expansion of relations between Shintō and the state that took place from the end of the Russo-Japanese War to 1945 had been set in motion much earlier and represented simply a hardening or universalization of earlier policy. For example, Shintō mythology had long been used to explain the origins of the imperial house, but the idea of the imperium's divine origins received new support in this period, and stricter sanctions were applied to anyone who denied it.

The Russo-Japanese War marked the beginning of many social policies, such as the shrine merger program, designed to increase social control more generally. The war, the annexation of Korea (1910), and the colonization of Manchuria produced a heightened mood of patriotism that the priesthood enthusiastically supported. Shrines and their priests were expected to serve the nation in fostering patriotism, and the state proved willing to pay for their services. From around 1910, a program for the training of Shintō priests was underwritten by the state, and its appropriations increased steadily. National budgetary appropriations for shrines rose in absolute terms, though their share of the total annual budget fluctuated considerably (see Table 1).

The priesthood increased its influence in public life during this period through an increased presence in the educational system. Priests were more numerous and better trained, thanks largely to the expanded program of government support. Graduates of Shintō schools such as Kokugakuin University and Kōgakkan University, as well as those holding even a second-grade rank as a priest, were automatically qualified, without further training at normal school, to teach in the public schools, which many did to supplement their meager income as priests. Priests were a great asset in universalizing such practices as formal veneration of the imperial portrait and the Imperial Rescript on Education, as well as periodic visits to shrines by school pupils for labor or formal worship.

Another source of the priesthood's increasing strength was the creation of a national organization and prefectural branches. The national organization was created in 1900, and by the end of this period it was fully

1. Government Support for Shrines as Percentage of Total
Annual National Budget, 1902–1944 (in yen)

	Total Budget	Shrine Payments	Percent
1902	249,596,131	1,071,727	0.43
1907	602,400,959	510,432	0.08
1912	593,596,444	358,012	0.06
1917	735,024,251	877,063	0.11
1922	1,429,689,621	4,191,009	0.29
1927	1,765,723,000[a]	1,774,000	0.10
1932	1,950,141,000	1,373,000	0.07
1937	2,709,157,000	2,297,000	0.08
1942	8,276,476,000	2,081,000	0.02
1943	14,459,908,000	6,633,000	0.05
1944	20,173,076,000	1,331,000	0.01

SOURCES: *Meiji Taishō zaiseishi* (Tokyo: Keizai ōraisha, 1956), Vol. 4; *Diamond Keizai tōkei nenkan* (Tokyo: Diamondsha, 1939); *Tōyō keizai nenkan* (Tokyo: Tōyō Keizai shinpōsha, 1926); Naikaku tōkei kyoku, *Nihon teikoku tōkei nenkan*, 59 vols. (Tokyo: Naimushō, 1882–1940).
[a] Figures from 1927 to 1944 only available in thousands of yen.

operational. It was supported by branches in every prefecture and made its activities known by a national publication.

In this era, popular religious life became profoundly influenced by the state's relation with Shintō. The Russo-Japanese War produced many apotheosized "glorious war dead," and the death of so many in war, followed by their public worship, both at the Yasukuni Shrine and in its prefectural branches, the Nation-Protecting Shrines, brought state-sponsored shrine rites into popular consciousness in a new and deeper way (see Table 2). Observance of shrine rites began to take on a semiobligatory character, and local administrations routinely assessed residents for shrine support.

Popular religious life was also influenced by state intimidation, which itself utilized Shintō elements. Most striking was the suppression of the rapidly growing independent sect, Ōmotokyō, in 1921, when many of its leaders were jailed. Other religious movements were suppressed on charges of lèse majesté if their doctrines were deemed vulgar or somehow slighting to the orthodox view of Shintō mythology.[1]

1930–1945: Maximized Influence. The years 1930 to 1945 saw a major expansion of shrine administration, culminating in the establishment of the Board of Rites (Jingiin) in 1940, to the gratification of all priests. Appropriations for shrines and priests' training continued at high levels. Priests

2. Souls Enshrined at Yasukuni, by Wars
or Military Engagement

Meiji Restoration	7,751	World War I and	
Seinan War	6,971	Siberian Invasion	4,850
Sino-Japanese War	13,619	Saishin Incident	185
Taiwan Annexation	1,130	Manchurian	
Hokushin Incident	1,256	Incident	17,161
Russo-Japanese War and		War with China	188,196
Korean Annexation	88,429	World War II	2,123,651
		TOTAL	2,453,199

SOURCE: Ōe Shinobu, *Yasukuni Jinja* (Tokyo: Iwanami shoten, 1984), 16–17.

continued to occupy positions of prestige in local administrations and in the educational system. These trends represented the expansion and continuation of trends established earlier.

Shintō's sphere of influence widened during this period less through any new exertion of the state on its behalf or through new initiatives on the part of the priesthood than as a result of an increasingly closed political culture. Dissent of any kind was suppressed, and political opposition of any kind was so intimidated that those players left in the ring, including the priesthood, could operate with great freedom and without fear of contradiction. In 1932, for example, national outrage followed when Christian students from Sophia University refused to pay tribute at the Yasukuni Shrine. Their refusal to bow before the national shrine for the war dead confirmed suspicions that Christians were unpatriotic and Christianity incompatible with Japanese sensibilities.

During this period the influence of Shintō upon popular religious life increased as more households enshrined talismans of the Ise Shrines (see Table 3), more school trips to the Ise Shrines and other shrines were carried out, and as the general populace traveled to Ise on pilgrimage by the millions (see Table 4). Suppression of popular religious movements continued, most spectacularly in the destruction of Ōmotokyō's headquarters

3. Ise Talismans Distributed per Year, 1919–1943 (Approximate Figures)

1919	5,000,000	1937	8,000,000	1941	11,000,000
1927	6,000,000	1938	9,000,000	1942	12,000,000
1935	7,000,000	1939	10,000,000	1943	13,000,000

SOURCE: Gomazuru Hiroyuki, "Jingū hyakunen no ayumi," in *Meiji ishin Shintō hyakunenshi*, ed. Shintō bunkakai (Tokyo: Shintō bunkakai, 1966), 1: 471ff.

4. Persons Paying Tribute at the Ise Shrines, 1904–1944

1904	1,299,360	1923	2,520,631[a]	1937	5,541,367
1905	1,430,006	1926	2,914,132	1938	6,558,616
1912	1,614,781	1929	3,846,120	1939	7,326,623
1918	3,339,245	1933	3,642,386[b]	1940	7,982,533
1919	3,642,386	1934	3,783,412	1944	4,391,570
		1936	4,373,626		

SOURCE: Gomazuru Hiroyuki, "Jingū hyakunen no ayumi," in *Meiji ishin Shintō hyakunenshi*, ed. Shintō bunkakai (Tokyo: Shintō bunkakai, 1966), 1: 492.
[a] The Tokyo earthquake of 1923 may account for the decrease of that year.
[b] Gomazuru lists identical figures for 1919 and 1933.

in 1935. In 1937 the religion Hitonomichi was disbanded by state order on charges of lèse majesté. In 1941 a branch of the Nichiren sect of Buddhism was suppressed for its calligraphic mandala, used as an object of worship, in which Buddhist figures were ranked higher than Shintō divinities. In 1943 the Seventh-day Adventists were outlawed for preaching the second coming. Passage of the Religious Organizations Law in 1940 gave the state sweeping powers to regulate the activities of all religious associations.

1945–1988: Dissolution and Partial Reconstruction. State Shintō came to an end with the Shintō Directive of 1945 (see Appendix 2). This administrative directive, which remained in force until the end of the Allied Occupation, prohibited all state support for and patronage of Shintō and directed that all Shintō influence be removed from the public schools. All bureaucratic mechanisms for the administration of shrines were dismantled, and many Shintō figures were purged. The priesthood as a whole suffered an immediate and seemingly irreversible loss of prestige. In the years since 1945, Shintō has, in addition, been dealt a heavy blow by the same demographic changes that have undermined the economic base of temple Buddhism.

Although all official relations between Shintō and the state were severed, various forms of covert support have quietly been reinstated, such as provision of official information about the death of combatants to the Yasukuni Shrine on an exclusive basis while denying the same service to other religious groups that have requested it (see Chapter 7). It is notable that the state seeks to expand its connection only with Shintō religious bodies, not with Buddhist or other institutions. Meanwhile, the Supreme Court has gradually expanded the scope of religious activity deemed permissible to the state under the constitution.

The Yasukuni Shrine remains the center of much controversy, and the state has staked and lost much prestige on five failed efforts to reestablish state support for this shrine. So eager is the state to reappropriate Shintō symbolism in articulating a myth of cultural identity that it has supported several judicial decisions that seem to move toward a reestablishment of the former alliance of Shintō and the state, even when a curtailment of individual religious liberties is involved.

The general populace remains unaware of, and unconcerned with, these postwar developments for the most part. While some citizens, mainly Christians and members of those religious movements persecuted before 1945, monitor the state's actions in this area closely and protest vigorously, they are a minority. The academic intelligentsia has consistently opposed all state efforts to revive Shintō symbolism, whether it be the attempt to give legal status to the national flag, anthem, or reign-names as the official form of dating,* or the question of state support for the Yasukuni Shrine. Because of the postwar era's open and pluralistic political culture, the state must answer these vocal critics and is not free to reestablish its former patronage of Shintō without debate, though the priesthood overwhelmingly favors a return to the prewar situation.

With this brief overview complete, we can proceed now to a fuller narrative of the relation between Shintō and the state in the modern period as it was established shortly after the Meiji Restoration.

THE MEIJI RESTORATION AND THE BEGINNING OF STATE SHINTŌ

With the coup d'état of 3 January 1868, a chain of political struggles and changes known as the Meiji Restoration was inaugurated. In addition to dismantling the rule of the shogunate and replacing it with the limited representational system of the Meiji Constitution (1889), the Restoration accomplished the political unification of the country, brought an end to hereditary social status, and gave the people freedom of residence and occupation. Trade and diplomatic relations with the West began, and sweeping social reforms, including universal compulsory education and military conscription, changed the country drastically. It was at this point that the state's involvement in Shintō affairs increased in a way that would affect Japanese religious life as a whole. State Shintō begins with the Restoration.

THE SEPARATION OF BUDDHISM FROM SHINTŌ

In 1868 an order calling for the complete separation of Buddhism from Shintō (*shinbutsu bunri*), intended to raise the status of Shintō and to secure its independence from Buddhism, was issued. Shintō objects of

* For example, the reign of the present emperor is officially known as the Heisei era, and all government documents use this system, so that 1988, for example, is referred to in all government documents, from interoffice memos to national legislation, as the first year of the Heisei era.

27

worship were to be removed from Buddhist temples and Buddhist appurtenances were to be stripped from shrines. Shrines and temples were to be set up independently. All shrine priests and their families would henceforth have Shintō funerals. The order for the separation of Buddhism and Shintō was accompanied by the unauthorized plundering of everything Buddhist, collectively known as *haibutsu kishaku*, in which the pent-up resentment of the Shintō priesthood was unleashed in ferocious, vindictive destruction. Buddhist priests were defrocked, lands confiscated, statuary and ritual implements melted down for cannon. The extent of the damage varied regionally, but Buddhism suffered significant material loss as well as the loss of the state patronage it had enjoyed in the previous era.[2]

This maneuvering did not, however, seriously undermine the attachment of the populace to Buddhism. As before, the people largely continued to maintain temple affiliations, based on funerals, grave sites, and ancestral memorial rites performed by temple priests. While statues could be removed, Buddhist influence upon Shintō was too deep to be expunged with a single stroke. Shintō still lacked doctrines capable of filling the void left by the separation. Thus the separation of Buddhism from Shintō did not immediately result in the establishment of Shintō as a fully independent religion.

Shintō gained ground, however, in an attempt to co-opt the cult centers of Shugendō, the cult of sacred mountains combining the worship of *gongen* (mountain deities), Buddhas, and kami with ascetic pilgrimages to the mountains. Shugendō's mountain ascetics, called *yamabushi*, were outlawed in 1871, and required to become Buddhist priests, Shintō priests, or return to lay life. It was declared that the *gongen* were really Shintō kami, although believers had not previously distinguished them as such. In this way, it was hoped, such pilgrimage sites as Mt. Fuji, Yoshino, Haguro, Gassan, and Yudono could be made into Shintō establishments, and thus their revenues would accrue to Shintō.[3]

BUILDING INSTITUTIONS

Because each Shintō shrine had been so autonomous before Meiji, it was necessary to organize them in their new setting to insure smooth administration. The state attempted to bring all shrines in the nation under the umbrella of the Ise Shrines by ranking them according to a single hierarchy in 1868, with Ise at the top.

Thereafter all shrines held a certain rank or received the designation of "Unranked Shrine" (*mukakusha*). Whereas large shrines had previously been great landholders, shrine lands were confiscated in 1871 and replaced with limited compensation or promises of support. The state pledged to support those shrines with the rank of National or Imperial Shrine (*kokuheisha, kanpeisha*).[4]

Once the shrines had been ranked, the state turned to the people themselves, and organized them as "parishioners" (*ujiko*) of shrines, a status previously restricted to those of high social status. In place of the former Buddhist temple registration system, shrine registration (*ujiko shirabe*) was instituted. According to the new system, every subject at birth became a parishioner by receiving a talisman from a local shrine. Everyone was to register with a new shrine upon a change of residence, and at death the talisman was returned. In addition, subjects were to enshrine a talisman of the Ise Shrines in their homes. In this way, each household would be installing the "divided spirit" of the Ise deities in its domestic altar for the kami, as opposed to the simple purification instrument oshi—abolished in 1871—had formerly distributed.[5] Symbolically speaking then, each household became a "branch shrine" of the Ise Shrines, thus linking all the populace to this cult center.

Shrine registration was clearly intended to transfer from Buddhism to Shintō the census functions formerly undertaken by the temples, and the intent of talisman distribution was to unify the nation in the worship of the Ise deities. In fact, however, shrine registration was not carried out systematically, and the system soon fell into disuse.[6] Nevertheless, the status of "parishioner" remained and operated as an important element of local government down to 1945.

DISUNITY IN THE DEPARTMENT OF DIVINITY

In 1868 the Department of Divinity (Jingikan) was established as the highest organ of government, even surpassing the Council of State (Dajōkan). Secular politicians hoped that it would provide a symbolic legitimation for the new political regime. The department's establishment represented a victory for Shintō activists of the Restoration such as Fukuba Bisei. At last a central institution for the administration of religious affairs and conduct of state rites had become a reality. The Department of Divinity conducted rites for the spirits of the imperial ancestors, harvest and New Year's rites, as well as maintaining the imperial tombs, the cult of the gods of heaven and earth, and the eight tutelary gods of the imperial house. Its rites were performed as rites of state, and the other shrines of the nation were expected to make corresponding observances in concert.[7]

While the establishment of the Department of Divinity was a partial victory for those National Learning figures claiming to speak for all the shrines, however, they were unable immediately to displace the Yoshida and Shirakawa houses, which between them previously had controlled most such shrines. Whereas followers of National Learning had hoped to consolidate all rites on a single basis, the Yoshida and Shirakawa were not to be so easily dislodged from their customary prerogatives in relation to the imperial house. Fukuba was able to keep them out of the Department of Divinity itself, but he was not able to wrest from them the title of Councillor of Divinities, and on this basis they retained control of a separate cult of the eight imperial tutelary deities within the palace. Therefore the Department of Divinity and the palace remained two distinct ritual centers, and thus there arose a double character in national ritual at odds with the original ideal of those behind the department.[8]

The department aimed for complete, central control of the priesthood and shrines, thus abrogating the former Yoshida and Shirakawa prerogatives to appoint priests to certain ranks in exchange for "contributions." In actuality, however, the Department of Divinity retained direct control only of larger shrines of higher ranks: the Ise, Imperial, and National Shrines. The administration of smaller shrines, the great majority, was turned over to the prefectural governments. The national survey and ranking of shrines was supposed to concentrate control of shrines in the priesthood, but instead it gave the prefectures considerable autonomy in shrine administration. In these ways the desired central control of the Department of Divinity slipped away even before it was firmly established—to the Yoshida and Shirakawa in the case of imperial rites, and to the prefectures in the case of many of the shrines discussed in the introduction as Shintō's third layer.[9]

To make matters worse, Department of Divinity administrators were divided among themselves on a host of theological and policy matters, the followers of Hirata constantly pitted against those of Ōkuni. The Hirata faction held that the department should be concerned exclusively with state rites, while the followers of Ōkuni, particularly Fukuba, emphasized its function of uniting the people in a common creed. Internally divided itself, the Department of Divinity could not command the full commitment of the Shintō priesthood, who were still not linked in any national organization.[10]

On 8 August 1871 the Department of Divinity was demoted to the status of a ministry and renamed the Ministry of Divinity (Jingishō), then on 14 March 1872 it was abolished and reconstituted in the Ministry of Education (Kyōbushō). The reasons for this precipitous demotion after such grand beginnings lay in secular politicians' decreasing faith in the ability of Shintō administrators to fulfill the original mission of the Department of Divinity. Politicians were increasingly preoccupied with the question of treaty revision, and Shintō figures seemed to have no appreciation of the political realities of Japan's situation.

For example, Iwakura Tomomi, a court noble and an important political figure, had accepted the guidance of the National Learning figure Tamamatsu Misao and had been an advocate of the Department of Divinity. Iwakura's enthusiasm for Shintō causes began to fade as it became apparent how little Shintō leaders understood contemporary political issues. Tamamatsu Misao quarreled with Iwakura and left the government in high dudgeon when Iwakura refused to relent in his plan to move the imperial court to Tokyo so that there would be a single seat of government. Tamamatsu believed that any involvement of the throne in such mundane affairs would impugn the imperial dignity. Powerful politicians like Iwakura could hardly be expected to take such arguments seriously.[11]

Upon the forcible opening of the country, Japan had been required to sign a number of unequal trade treaties. Revising these became the government's most important political issue. Iwakura headed a mission to negotiate revision of the treaties, and everywhere he went he encountered the demand for freedom for Christian missionaries to proselytize freely within Japan as a precondition for negotiation. Toleration in religious matters was clearly one of the accoutrements of a modern nation Japan needed to gain recognition as such by her trading partners. It was evident that some compromise with Christianity was inevitable, but Shintō leaders remained adamantly opposed.

In the face of this harsh reality of international politics, the preoccupations of those at the Department of Divinity, who were still talking about revering the emperor and expelling the barbarian, must have seemed hopelessly antiquated, obscurantist, and unrealistic.

Another aspect of the mission of the Department of Divinity concerned the goal of unifying state rites. It will be recalled that during the Tokugawa period the Yoshida and Shirakawa houses exercised great influence over shrine priests and over the performance of imperial ritual. For the Department of Divinity to gain control of the entire priesthood and state rites, it would have had to unseat the Yoshida and the Shirakawa houses, but that proved to be a difficult task. The new Shintō administrators in government were unable to oust them from the palace, and thus it was principally under Yoshida and Shirakawa influence that the religious significance of the emperor and of the imperial rites took shape.

REFORM OF IMPERIAL RITUAL

Prior to Meiji, it was traditional for the emperor to send a proxy with offerings to major shrines on the occasion of their festivals. Following the example of the last days of his predecessor Emperor Kōmei, the young Emperor Meiji broke with tradition and began to visit shrines in person. When the palace was moved to Tokyo in 1868, he sent deputies with offerings to the most venerable shrines along his route from Kyoto, and he personally visited the Atsuta Shrine where one object of the imperial regalia, the sword, was kept. Arriving in Tokyo, he journeyed to the Hikawa Shrine, where he proclaimed the unification of rites and government (*saisei itchi*). In 1869 Emperor Meiji personally paid tribute at the Ise Shrines, which no reigning emperor had visited since the reign of Jitō (686–697), a gap of more than a millennium.[12]

The palace itself was a religious institution as well as the emperor's residence, and it enshrined the same deities as the Department of Divinity.[13] Unlike premodern times, however, the Emperor Meiji's performance of palace rites was systematically made known to the populace. Thus when he performed the harvest rite Niinamesai in 1868, the whole population was ordered to worship the kami.[14] An annual calendar of thirteen rites, replacing the traditional one, was created for imperial performance. These rites were observed as national holidays. Of these, only the Niinamesai had customarily been performed by emperors before the Restoration.[15]

It was not only at the palace that these rites were observed. Under State Shintō the emperor's religious authority was based upon his unity with the imperial ancestors, collectively symbolized by the deity Amaterasu Ōmikami, whose principal seat of worship was at the Ise Shrines. This union guaranteed and manifested one of the symbolic hallmarks of State Shintō: the idea of an "imperial line unbroken for ages eternal," stretching back to the age of the gods and forward forever. Thus the emperor's rites and the rites of the Ise Shrines were carried out in tandem.[16]

The rites of the imperial palace and other rites performed by the emperor in concert with political officials, the military, and the populace constituted an important element of the state's symbolic legitimation. State rites, the heightened prominence of the emperor's religious roles, and a new relation between the state and the Ise Shrines became pillars of State Shintō.

THE CREATION OF NATIONAL RITES AND CEREMONIES

While imperial and Ise shrine rites were coordinated, the rest of the populace was not forgotten. Ranked in a hierarchy below Ise, the shrines were all expected to align their rites with Ise's. Many built small worship facilities facing Ise so that they could symbolically participate in Ise rites from a distance. These altars were known as "places to worship from afar" (*yōhaisho*). Shrines assembled their parishioners on the new national holidays and had them participate in the worship of Ise deities. This time it was the Buddhist priests who were obliged to participate in rites regardless of their beliefs.[17]

This smoothly articulated coordination of rites by ruler and subject was duplicated later at the Yasukuni Shrine. The emperor and politicians, the military and the general populace simultaneously observed rites at this shrine and its prefectural branches, the Nation-Protecting Shrines (*gokoku jinja*). This nationwide orchestration of ritual was an attempt at the most daring social engineering. Here was a plan to use religion to unify the people in a single cult, headed by the emperor as head priest, focused upon his ancestors (and later the war dead), who had also been declared national deities.

But real life proved much more complicated than this brilliant vision. While this plan might have worked in a nation where the idea of freedom of religion was entirely unknown, many Japanese went abroad in the Meiji period, or studied Western societies, and Japan was under growing pressure from foreign nations to establish the right to religious freedom. Buddhists also could see plainly that the destruction of their religion was one of the covert goals of Shintō Department of Divinity administrators, and they were quick to protest.[18]

The establishment of the new imperial calendar of rites meant the end of the schedule of five annual national observances (*gosekku*) that had preceded it. The new calendar did not, however, instantly replace the old. Some prefectures tried to institute the new one, but not all. More were concerned to put an end to the Buddhist All Souls' Festival (*bon*), probably to ensure that workdays not be lost in its observance in addition to the days lost to the new rites. The diary of Edwin von Balz (1849–1939), a doctor teaching medicine in Meiji Japan, shows that in 1880 police coercion had to be used to persuade people to fly the national flag on the new holidays. Diaries of Meiji Japanese showed no awareness of the new rites until 1900. It was not, in fact, until 1910 that the new holidays came to be generally observed. In other words, the declaration of the new temporal order did not immediately bring it into reality. As in so many aspects of State Shintō, it was the Sino-Japanese and Russo-Japanese Wars that finally brought about the acceptance of these new rites.[19]

THE SLUMP OF MIDDLE MEIJI (1880–1905)

The shrine priesthood attempted during the years 1880 to 1905 to regain the political favor Shintō had enjoyed so briefly at the beginning of the period. In this attempt, the phrase describing Shintō as "the nation's rites and creed" (*kokka no sōshi*) served as a rallying cry.[20]

The priesthood interpreted Shintō according to this slogan in a way that distinguished Shintō and "religion" as two separate categories. According to this understanding, if shrines had the official, governmental function of providing the nation's rites, then they should be formally and administratively distinguished from religious institutions. Shintō priests, in this view, should be treated differently from Buddhist priests, whose rites had no significance for the nation as a whole.[21]

The priesthood considered it a matter of course that all the priests and shrines of the country would be supported with public funds. Priests received the title *shinkan*, a term meaning "priest" in which *-kan* denoted official, bureaucratic status, and priests of Imperial and National Shrines received salaries as national civil servants. But the proposal that all shrines should be publicly supported was probably a fiscal impossibility from the beginning.

While the Ise, Imperial, and National Shrines received state support, those below that level (the Prefectural, District, Village, and Unranked Shrines) were entrusted to the "faith" (*shinkō*) of the people; in other words, they had to depend on the contributions of their parishioners.[22]

While the Shintō priesthood promoted state support for all shrines and priests, however, politicians were not convinced that Shintō was sufficiently important to justify financial support on such a scale. In 1887 a revision of state support for Imperial and National Shrines was carried out. According to this revision, the money earmarked for support of these shrines was made a trust for a period of ten or fifteen years, with the proviso that state support would end after that time if not formally renewed. The revision was designed to guarantee support for the shrines even in cases where local support failed to provide sufficient funds.[23] A further provision of the revision demoted priests of National and Imperial Shrines from *shinkan* to *shinshoku*, the latter a term for priest lacking any connotation of official appointment or status.[24]

The trust system for Imperial and National Shrines was a move to put those shrines on the same financial footing as the shrines of lower grades as soon as the period of the trust elapsed. If that were allowed to happen, Shintō would become in effect a religious organization dependent upon its followers for support and lacking any governmental significance. This prospect was unpalatable in all quarters of the Shintō world. The priesthood believed that the only way to redress the situation was to assert the non-religious character of Shintō and to reinstitute the Department of Divinity, making it an agency of government that would protect the priesthood's interests.[25]

IS SHINTŌ A RELIGION?

Early in the Meiji period there was much discussion as to whether Shintō was properly called a religion. In fact, both the terms *religion* (*shūkyō*) and *Shintō* were new to vernacular speech, and intellectuals wrote a great deal about religion and its role in a modern nation.[26] For the most part, the Shintō priesthood associated religion with doctrine and such rites as funerals and prayers for this-worldly benefits. The priesthood was generally agreed that Shintō shrines should perform the rites of state, but they were divided on the question of funerals and other rites that were also performed by Buddhist priests and the newly arisen independent religious associations that were gaining ground in this era.[27]

What Shintō priests wanted above all was recognition of a special status for Shintō, based on its performance of state rites. Thus when they argued that Shintō should provide "the nation's rites and creed," they were saying that Shintō was different from Buddhism or other, ordinary religions that did not have a state function, and was uniquely qualified to perform state rites. They understood their claim to entail state responsibility for the shrines—all the shrines; in their view, all shrines should be supported by the state.

By the 1880s, however, it was clear that only Imperial and National Shrines would receive state support. This meant that the vast majority of shrines did not receive funding from the national budget.[28] They had, instead to appeal to their local constituencies. These shrines could only attract the needed revenues from parishioners by taking on a religious character and providing adherents with the pastoral services associated with the Buddhist or Christian clergy.

For Shintō priests, the lack of state support was not simply an economic question, but one of dignity and prestige. Many priests felt it beneath their dignity as state liturgists to stoop to the performance of funerals and other homely rites, and they felt that for them to become involved in such affairs, which they identified with religion, undermined the dignity of both Shintō and the state. Thus they tended increasingly to think of Shintō as a suprareligious entity. Nevertheless, given the reality of severely limited public support, Shintō priests had to take on many of the functions they associated with religion.

To create a pastoral role for the Shintō priesthood was, however, no easy task. To begin with, there was no precedent in all of Japanese religious history for the idea of a ministerial role, to say nothing of the absence of concrete examples in the recent past to which the Meiji priesthood might have looked in order to fashion a new role. Furthermore, the priesthood was deeply divided on the question of whether a pastoral role or the creation of a religious character for Shintō was even desirable.

Since the 1868 founding of the Department of Divinity, there had been a division among administrators in government on the proper character of Shintō. That faction deriving from the National Learning of Hirata Atsutane held that Shintō was principally a matter of the rites of state. Shintō should perform state ritual and manage the people's participation in such rites. It should avoid preaching any particular doctrine. Shintō priests were ritualists; they were not religionists who preached, proselytized, and carried out other pastoral functions.[29]

On the other side were the proponents of Ōkuni Takamasa's National

Learning, for whom Shintō was to be a religion unifying the religious sentiments of the people as well as performing state rites. In the Great Promulgation Campaign, Fukuba Bisei trained the priesthood and appointed them National Evangelists (*kyōdōshoku*) to preach a centrally authored doctrine, to proselytize, and to organize the people into parishes forming a network of branches of the Ise Shrines. According to Fukuba's understanding, it was correct and natural for Shintō priests to adopt a pastoral role, including the performance of funeral rites for their parishioners.[30]

The Hirata faction abhorred the idea of Shintō priests contacting the pollution of death by performing funeral rites.[31] Furthermore, Hirata followers strenuously objected to treating Shintō preaching and proselytizing in the same terms as Shintō conduct of national ritual. This ritualist side was adamant that Shintō, by which they meant Shrine Shintō—kami-worship as carried out in shrines—be distinguished also from the Shintō sects. Their idea was that Shintō's dignity would be undermined by any association with religion.[32]

Thus throughout much of the Meiji period a debate went on about the nature of Shintō: was it or was it not a religion? Because the priesthood itself was unable to resolve its differences on this question, the status of Shintō was unclear both to politicians and to the general populace. Its ambiguous character was reflected in administrative organization. Shintō administrators dealing with liturgy worked in a different ministry from those dealing with doctrine and proselytization. The latter, as well as any questions of a pastoral nature, were increasingly associated with the word religion. Nevertheless, no one was really satisfied with this arrangement, and thus changes in Shintō administration continued into the twentieth century, reflecting Shintō's nebulous character in public life.[33]

THE MOVEMENT TO REESTABLISH
THE DEPARTMENT OF DIVINITY

The priesthood rightly perceived that the revision of the system of public support of the shrines, carried out in 1887, posed a threat to their livelihood and that those in power had ceased to find Shintō politically useful. Hoping to regain Shintō's brief golden hour of the beginning of the Meiji period, the priesthood during the late 1880s and 1890s began a drive to reinstate the Department of Divinity. It was this movement that succeeded for the first time in history in uniting the priesthood and drawing them finally into a single, national organization.[34]

Since 1884 the Shintō priests of Kyushu had been meeting as a group and repeatedly memorializing the government. In 1889 they issued a call for the rest of the priesthood to join them, and with representatives from each prefecture they succeeded in founding a national organization (first called the Shinkan Dōshikai, Fellowship of Shintō Priests, and renamed Zenkoku Shinshokukai, National Association of Shintō Priests, in 1900). Their stated purpose was to clarify the meaning of shrines as providing the nation's rites and creed and to work for the reestablishment of the Department of Divinity. They sent memorials to the government in 1887 and 1890 stating their opinion that all shrines had a public character and stood outside the sphere of religion.[35]

Under this impetus, many regional priests' associations were founded. All priests were called upon to renounce preaching, proselytizing, and especially performing funerals and instead to cleave firmly to their status as ritualists. By 1890 over two hundred petitions advocating the reinstitution of the Department of Divinity and over four hundred calling for the complete and final separation of National Evangelists from Shintō priests had been sent to the Council of Elders (Genrōin).[36]

While the shrine priests were united in their desire to reinstitute the Department of Divinity, they were not hoping for a simple revival of the state of affairs just after the Restoration. Whereas the early Meiji Department of Divinity had combined liturgical functions with proselytization for a centrally authored creed under the Great Promulgation Campaign, shrine priests in the 1880s and 1890s expected to drop preaching and proselytization and to devote themselves instead to the performance of national ritual. The Department of Divinity as they hoped to revive it would carry out national rites, administer all shrines, unite the people through standardized shrine rites, and establish Shintō's hegemony over state rites and creed. These aims were promulgated in a petition to Diet members.[37]

In spite of the hopes of the priesthood for a restoration of the Department of Divinity, in 1900 a Shrine Office (Jinja kyoku) was created within the Home Ministry. This placed shrine administration far from the centers of power, and the Shintō world was very disappointed by this development. The creation of a Shrine Office did have the merit, however, of separating the administration of shrines from that of other religious institutions administered in the Ministry of Education.[38] The shrine question received little attention from powerful politicians or the public until after the Russo-Japanese War.[39]

SHRINE BUILDING AFTER THE RUSSO-JAPANESE WAR

State Shintō became an increasingly prominent element of national life in the twentieth century. Since the Meiji Restoration, new shrines had been constructed to enshrine as national deities emperors or members of the imperial family, military heroes from the civil wars of the fourteenth century, loyalist leaders and the war dead on the imperial side during the struggles surrounding the Restoration, and feudal lords of the Tokugawa period. Particularly after the Russo-Japanese War, these shrines began to perform large-scale rites of state, and these rites of empire were made known more widely than ever before thanks to the increasing circulation of newspapers.[40]

In addition, as Japan acquired new colonies, Shintō shrines were erected there, and colonial subjects were obliged to observe their rites. Shintō priests went abroad with the troops as military chaplains. The hundreds of new shrines built in the colonies were dedicated to Japanese deities. Their rites were used to promote patriotism, and they became symbolic emblems of the subjugation of colonized territories.

Among the new shrines, the Yasukuni Shrine in Tokyo became a great center of State Shintō. Dedicated originally to those who had died during the fighting of the Restoration on the loyalist side, it came to enshrine the dead from the Sino-Japanese and Russo-Japanese Wars, in addition to the dead from World War II. The emperor performed ritual there, and the dead were apotheosized and worshipped as kami of the nation. The idea was promoted that it was a great honor to die in combat in the nation's defense.[41]

A second monument of State Shintō was the Meiji Shrine, dedicated to the deified spirits of the Emperor Meiji (d. 1912) and his empress. Completed in 1920 and situated in Tokyo, it drew upon the widespread and genuine affection of the people for this popular emperor who had led Japan into modern statehood. This shrine was constructed in large part through the volunteer labor of youth groups from all over the country as well as by all Buddhist and Shintō religious groups. This great effort took five years, cost approximately 5,200,000 yen in public funds, and brought Shintō into new, national prominence. The construction of no other Shintō shrine had been a national project of this nature.[42]

The shrines of early Meiji had tended to operate independently of other social groups, and we have seen that the priesthood felt isolated and out of favor, but after the Russo-Japanese War an effort was undertaken to integrate shrines into social life more thoroughly than before. The Boshin Rescript of 1908 proclaimed the charter for this change: "It is now desired . . . that the shrines will be utilized in promoting the unification and administration of the country." In line with the rescript, it became a matter of national policy to integrate the shrines with such bureaucratically inspired movements as national youth groups, women's groups, and army reserve units. Not only were shrine priests called upon to help unite the people, but all religious organizations were called upon to contribute to this cause. It was hoped that shrines would be useful in suppressing such class antagonisms as labor strikes and landlord-tenant disputes. Training Shintō priests became a matter of national importance, and such training institutes as the

Institutes for Study of the Classics (Kōten kōkyūjo), established earlier in the period, received increased support from the Home Ministry as of 1909.[43]

After the Russo-Japanese War, the state took an increasingly active role in managing shrines. In 1906 it launched an ambitious plan to align shrines with village organization by recognizing only one shrine per village as legitimate. This policy necessitated shrine mergers on a large scale. At the time there were 190,265 shrines, and the majority were small Village Shrines or Unranked Shrines lacking a priest. To focus the loyalties of rural people through a single village shrine, the state set out to eliminate the rest. The result was the abolition or merger of thousands of shrines.[44] This dramatic manipulation of shrines by the Home Ministry did not pass without protest but instead became the occasion for renewed debate on whether shrines were religious or not, and whether Shintō was a religion.

FREEDOM OF RELIGION

The Meiji Constitution of 1889 granted Japanese subjects freedom of religion to the extent that religion did not interfere with fulfilling their duties to the state. At the same time, the state increasingly took the position that Shintō was not a religion. On the basis of this view, it was possible to make participation in shrine rites obligatory (for schoolchildren and members of the armed forces, for example). Not being religious observances, it was held, shrine rites could be categorized as obligatory duties of a Japanese subject.[45]

Any religion that objected to shrine rites became suspect. In extreme cases it could be maintained that Japanese subjects were not free to practice such a religion because it infringed on patriotic duties under these circumstances. Many incidents of suppression of Christians in Japan and its colonies arose from this understanding of Shintō's relation to religion and the state. A conspicuous example of the clashes between Christianity and State Shintō was the refusal of the influential Christian leader Uchimura Kanzō to bow his head during a ceremonial reading of the Imperial Rescript on Education (see Chapter 6).

In 1891 a historian of Tokyo Imperial University, Kume Kunitake (1839–1931), published his opinion that Shintō represented the survival of a primitive cult of heaven. The priesthood was enraged and succeeded in having him discharged, an incident also discussed in Chapter 6. With the successful ouster of Kume, academic freedom for Shintō research was increasingly constricted, and Japanese academics were sufficiently intimidated to keep quiet opinions liable to be found insulting by the priesthood until 1945.[46]

The last days of State Shintō were the years of World War II. During this time Shintō provided indispensable ideological support to imperial Japan. The emperor was called a "divine emperor" (*akitsu mi kami*) or "kami in human form" (*arahitogami*). Public school textbooks promoted the idea of the divine origins of the nation and the descent of the emperor and the people from Shintō kami. The idea of the "eight corners of the world under one roof" (*hakkō ichiu*) was interpreted to mean that the Japanese were a superior people with a mission to rule the entire world. By the war's midpoint more than 1,200,000 war dead had been enshrined as national kami in the Yasukuni Shrine and there received imperial rites.[47]

POSTWAR SHINTŌ

After 1945 the relation between Shintō and the state was put on an entirely new footing by the Allied Occupation and postwar constitution. This constitution guarantees religious freedom, mandates a separation of religion and state, and prohibits the state from patronizing any religion. Shintō shrines are now legally religious bodies, and like any Buddhist temple or Christian church, they may incorporate as Religious Juridical Persons (*shūkyō hōjin*) to receive tax-exempt status and other benefits. Thus, in purely official terms, Shintō has been declared a religion. This official designation has not, however, ended debate about whether Shintō is or is not a religion. The postwar decades have seen several important challenges to the postwar constitution's provisions on religion as they affect Shintō, and these are inextricably entangled in conservative politicians' efforts since about 1970 to revive elements of prewar State Shintō symbolism in an attempt to formulate a coherent legitimation of government. The government defends this revival of Shintō symbolism against charges of an unconstitutional alliance of religion and state in part by suggesting that Shintō is not really a religion.

Before 1945 Japanese political culture was so dominated by the state, and opposition so intimidated, that political culture had a monolithic character. The state enjoyed virtual hegemony in articulating the meaning of the symbols of State Shintō such as the Yasukuni Shrine. In those decades no one dared oppose the state's claim that apotheosizing fallen combatants as "glorious war dead" in the Yasukuni Shrine was simply a continuation of tradition from time immemorial, though in fact this practice ran roughshod over the customs of ancestor worship.

In the postwar period, however, political culture has become much more pluralistic, and a voice opposing the state's past and present policies on religion has developed, with the Yasukuni Shrine as a central symbol of contention. The Japanese left, spearheaded by an academic intelligentsia, has consistently opposed moves to reinstate state support for the shrine. Similarly, the Union of New Religions has been consistent in its opposition to state support for the shrine. Both these groups have seen in state efforts to revive the Yasukuni Shrine a resurgence of nationalism and a constriction of personal liberties, especially religious freedom. Another powerful force in the opposition to the shrine is the new religion Sōka Gakkai (founded 1925) and its associated political party Kōmeitō. Opposition to the Yasukuni Shrine by the academic left, the Union of New Religions, and Sōka Gakkai is not systematically coordinated but springs from a common history of persecution in the prewar period. To them the Yasukuni Shrine is a symbol of persecution and the suppression of religious freedom. Far from representing tradition, to these opposition groups the Yasukuni Shrine represents nothing other than the perversion of every laudable element of the national identity.

In the postwar decades the state has lost its hegemony over national symbols, and there is now an active competition to formulate the meaning of the Yasukuni Shrine, the national flag, and the national anthem. The state has vigorously sought to regain its former prerogatives by five times introducing a bill to give the Yasukuni Shrine state support. It has covertly given the shrine administrative support by supplying it, gratis, with information on deceased combatants of World War II, while denying these services to other religious organizations that have requested them. Most recently, the Japanese Supreme Court handed down a ruling involving the actions of the Veterans' Association of the Self-Defense Force that upheld the association's actions in apotheosizing one of its deceased members in one of the former prefectural branch shrines of the Yasukuni Shrine. This case is highly significant because it indicates the state's intention to uphold what it claims as its own prerogatives in manipulating the symbolism of the war dead, even where the violation of religious freedom is involved.

Since 1985 domestic opposition to the state's support for the Yasukuni Shrine has been joined by that of foreign nations, most of them Japan's former colonies. These nations, led by China, have opposed state visits to the shrine by the prime minister and the cabinet. When former Prime Minister Nakasone Yasuhiro and his cabinet tried to reinstate the latter's regular formal tribute at the shrine, violent foreign opposition to their first such visit prevented any further attempt.

Thus the issue of Shintō continues to preoccupy contemporary Japanese domestic and international politics. The issue is increasingly obscure and associated with rightist political sentiments and a resurgence of nationalism. It is debated now, however, in a pluralistic political culture, one in which no single party enjoys hegemony in formulating the content of tradition or the meaning of its symbols.

2. The Great Promulgation Campaign

BETWEEN 1870 and 1884 Shintō leaders experimented with creating a state religion, not initially identified as Shintō, through the Great Promulgation Campaign (*taikyō senpu undō*). The campaign was waged principally by Shintō priests, though for a time the Buddhist clergy was also involved. Some of the Shintō leaders also founded religious groups later counted among the thirteen sects of Shintō.[1] Leaders of the new religions (not all of which derived from Shintō) found religious meaning in state ideology, grafting it onto their individual soteriologies. Through participation in the campaign, many of these leaders came to understand their own creeds as varieties or sects of Shintō and to preach this idea to their followers. They played an important role in creating a popular awareness of Shintō as an independent religion and in the process were able to legitimate themselves in the eyes of the state.

While Shintō entered the religious scene in early Meiji as as a rather confused and incoherent entity, it was in no small part due to the efforts of new religions that it gained social and religious currency. This chapter shows how ambiguous Shintō continued to be well into the Meiji period, how both National Learning figures and leaders of new religions attempted to appropriate it, and how many lay people were drawn into Shintō's orbit without necessarily changing their customary religious orientations fundamentally.

THE CAMPAIGN

The Great Promulgation Campaign was mounted by the government to preach to the people a "Great Teaching," a state-authored doctrine and pantheon. In spite of its mere fourteen years' duration, the campaign was highly influential in creating a popular awareness and understanding of Shintō as independent from Buddhism. While Buddhist and Shintō priests were active in preaching the Great Teaching all over Japan, leaders of such new religions as Kurozumikyō and Konkōkyō were equally zealous and perhaps more effective in proselytizing for this new, state-authored creed.

The Great Promulgation Campaign had three major components: the Three Great Teachings (taikyō, sanjō no kyōsoku), the Great Teaching Institute (Daikyōin), and a corps of National Evangelists (kyōdōshoku). The National Evangelists included Buddhist and Shintō priests, entertainers, actors, storytellers, preachers of National Learning, and ministers of new religions.[2] They were graded into fourteen ranks achieved by examination. The ideal behind the campaign was to create a religious creed, the Great Teaching (taikyō), transcending and subsuming sectarian differences—a state religion. The creed was not yet called Shintō, and neither the National Evangelists nor the Teaching Institute were labeled as Shintō. It was plain, however, that neither the creed itself nor the institute for its promulgation were Buddhist, and certainly they were not Christian. As a diary of one of the officials involved shows, preventing the spread of Christianity was a major goal of the campaign, and its Shintō administrators loathed Buddhism as well.

Although there was no explicit definition of the emerging state religion as Shintō, its liturgical form was in the style of the shrines, utilizing the vestments of shrine priests, mirrors as objects of worship, and Shintō prayers. This unarticulated dimension of ritual and symbol gave Shintō symbolic preeminence in this new invention of creed, rites, and organization. In turn, this meant that Buddhist priests who participated in the campaign had to adopt Shintō vestments and liturgy to do so.

The Great Teaching Institute was responsible for promulgating the Three Great Teachings. Although the institute was a bureaucratic agency, it was also inherently a religious institution. Its building was fitted with an altar and rites were performed for the state pantheon enshrined there: Amaterasu Ōmikami, and the Three Deities of Creation promoted by National Learning figures and seen mainly in early chapters of the classical mythological texts Kojiki and Nihonshoki: Takamimusubi no kami, Amenominakanushi no kami, and Kamimusubi no kami. Of these, only Amaterasu (in the form of Tenshōdaijin) had any popular cult.

The teachings were (1) respect for the gods, love of country; (2) making clear the principles of Heaven and the Way of Man; (3) reverence for the emperor and obedience to the will of the court. The Three Great Teachings were designed in part to draw Buddhist priests into Shintō.[3] Unfortunately, these tenets had no basis in popular thought and were so vague even to the National Evangelists that chapbooks on how to preach about them had to be issued, in sets of eleven, seventeen, and twenty-eight articles. These articles expounded the virtues of paying taxes, and of complying with conscription, compulsory education, and the solar calendar, as well as support for the military buildup (*fukoku kyōhei*, "rich country, strong army") and the importation of Western knowledge and culture (*bunmei kaika*, "civilization and enlightenment"). Thus National Evangelists were actually explaining that the meaning of the Three Great Teachings was paying taxes and sending children to school and sons to the army.

The Great Teaching Institute operated in the manner of a small seminary in that it was principally engaged in training prospective National Evangelists in Shintō doctrine and preaching. Its physical location was shifted several times, with a particularly memorable installation ceremony in 1873 at Zōjōji, the Tokyo temple of the Pure Land sect that had been the patron temple of the Tokugawa family. At this ceremony mirrors and other Shintō ritual gear were set up and Buddhist priests were prevailed upon to participate, wearing wigs and Shintō robes. The head abbots of the Buddhist schools were accorded high ranks within the system and participated in the ceremonies ex officio.

Despite these grand beginnings, however, the institute was plagued with crippling problems. The staff included so many shrine interests, as well as a spectrum of National Learning theories, that personal and ideological differences made concerted action impossible, earning the ridicule of other government bureaucrats, who spoke of the institute as the "Bureau of Indecision" (*injun kan*) and the "Siesta Office" (*hirune shō*).[4] Furthermore, staff were transferred to other government offices with such rapidity and frequency that they had no time in any given post to accomplish anything, even if internal strife had not divided them among themselves.

One of the most fascinating documents from the campaign is a record called the "Shinkyō soshiki monogatari" by a teacher of the National Evangelists, Tokoyo Nagatane. Otherwise unknown, Tokoyo left an intimate account of the campaign and its many problems. Personal, political, and theological antagonisms evidently stymied the operation of the institute almost from the beginning. Followers of Hirata's National Learning were pitted against Ōkuni Takamasa's disciples, and differences in regional origin bred a host of resentments. Tokoyo ends his account in despair, saying, "Looking back over the frequent changes in policy, I cannot help feeling that all was in vain."[5]

Popular opinion seemed to concur. Letters to the editor concerning the campaign were overwhelmingly negative. Scribblers lampooned the campaign mercilessly, opining that the evangelists' internal rivalries were more likely to drive the populace to Christianity than to prevent its advance.[6] No one likes Shintō funerals, they complain; the teachings are not believable; the sermons are boring; the evangelists are ridiculous and unfit to serve the nation; Shintō priests are ritualists—it is absurd to have them teaching a creed; Shintō has nothing to contribute to ethical thought. Satirists made great sport with a Buddhist temple's sudden transformation into the home of the institute, with the transmogrification of Buddhist priests into Shintō priests, and expressed satisfaction when disgruntled former samurai set fire to the building.[7]

Eventually, in 1875, the Ise Grand Shrines asserted their interests and outmaneuvered other contenders for power by combining the headship of the institute's successor, the Office of Shintō Affairs (Shintō Jimukyoku), with the office of the chief priest of the Ise Grand Shrines. This meant that the Great Promulgation Campaign was henceforth administered by Ise, thus extending Ise's control over all the National Evangelists, of whom there were more than ten thousand by 1876.[8] With the de facto merger of the campaign's administration and the Ise Shrines, the campaign and the state religion became for the first time unambiguously Shintō in character.

Buddhist priests became National Evangelists in great numbers. They quickly realized, however, that uprooting their religion was one of the campaign's covert goals. In consequence, the True Pure Land sect of Buddhism withdrew from the campaign in 1875. By then it was clear that the campaign's goal was to establish Shintō as a state religion. Joint Shintō-Buddhist proselytization atrophied after that time, and with its collapse the evangelists carried on without Buddhist priests under the direction of the Office of Shintō Affairs, which inherited the pantheon and rites of the Great Teaching Institute.

The Great Teaching Institute was the apex of a national network of teaching institutes. Each prefecture had a Middle Teaching Institute (*chūkyōin*, usually set up in a prefecture's largest shrine), which administered the National Evangelists' examinations, and the title of Small Teaching Institute (*shōkyōin*) was conferred upon temples and Shintō shrines. As long as joint proselytization was in force, the Buddhist evangelists were supposed to gather their parishioners and preach in the temples. It is estimated that one hundred thousand temples and shrines participated in the system at its height.[9]

Only fragmentary data on the actual operation of the 289 official teaching institutes (62 Middle and 227 Small) exist, but there are enough to gain a sense of the situation in the Northeast and the northern Kantō plain. In these areas the campaign was managed principally by Buddhist and Shintō priests, unlike the case of Okayama, where the preachers of new religions took an active role.

The Middle Teaching Institutes of Yamagata and Aomori Prefectures in northern Japan were established in prominent shrines, and elaborate organizational charts appointing local mayors and ward officials to minor offices were drawn up. In both prefectures, the institutes were headed by Shintō priests, and their main activities were to rank Buddhist and Shintō evangelists and to provide a thirty-day training course for them. In neither case, however, did the Shintō priests have enough standing in their communities ever to get started in earnest.[10]

Like Yamagata and Aomori, Fukushima Prefecture's Middle Teaching Institute had been intended originally to provide a form of primary school in addition to its service to the campaign. Unlike the other two prefectures, however, Fukushima's institute was headed by a Buddhist priest, was housed for a time in a temple, and was the most active in the Northeast, functioning from 1873 to 1875. One hundred ninety-five Shintō priests and 301 Buddhist priests assembled for common vows to inaugurate the institute. Lay people became involved through the creation of several confraternities, and sermons were held at temples (separately for men and women).[11] But the withdrawal of the Buddhist contingent in 1875 apparently ended proselytization in Fukushima, and by 1876 the northeastern teaching institutes were moribund.

In Ibaragi Prefecture, however, proselytization continued through 1876, thanks largely to Tsukahara Naooki, National Evangelist and priest of the Kashima Shrine. Tsukahara recorded in his 1876 diary that in the forty-three days between February 28 and April 10 he preached twenty-two times, on three occasions supervising the practice sermons of novice evangelists. Generally he notified the local mayor by mail in advance, requesting that a suitable number of people be assembled. By this means Tsukahara attracted an average of seventy-seven people, sometimes ranging to more than two hundred. He preached at the houses of Shintō priests or the mayor's home, using the life stories of exemplary persons to illustrate the Three Great Teachings.[12]

Among the campaign's many problems was its inevitable use for purely sectarian ends. While the evangelists were supposed to rise above theological differences and preach on the national creed embodied in the Great Teachings, their sectarian identities could not be entirely suppressed. The Buddhists, because of their longer and richer proselytizing tradition, were simply better preachers, adept at inserting their own doctrines into campaign sermons, and generally their audiences acted much as they would have at any temple sermon. Thus those who came to hear Buddhist preachers of the Pure Land sect commonly recited Buddhist prayers and threw coins as they were lectured on the Great Teachings.[13]

Funding the campaign was a problem of great magnitude as the state offered no financial support. The evangelists were expected to finance their activities independently, and inevitably this meant that the Buddhist side was richer because it could depend upon parishioners of long standing. Large shrines made a practice of sending money to the Great Teaching Institute to support the proselytization of local Shintō priests, but in the absence of government subsidy, resources were severely limited.[14]

Probably in recognition of this fact, the state encouraged the formation of shrine confraternities (*kō, kōsha*) to help support the campaign, and these began to appear in large numbers and to support the Great Teaching Institute.[15] It was those groups that later came to be known as the thirteen sects of Shintō, however, that bore the major financial burden of the campaign, and often their support was offered in return for freedom from official harrassment. A conspicuous example was the Miya-no-mae Church of the new religion Kurozumikyō in Hyōgo Prefecture, which, in 1873, was made a Small Teaching Institute on condition that it give all its revenue to the prefectural Middle Teaching Institute.[16]

The campaign stimulated development of a new type of Shintō organization. A shrine would attach to itself a church (*kyōkai*) that performed such religious functions as preaching and funerals and whose members were organized by territorially based parishes. The church, led by Shintō priests who were also National Evangelists, then became the shrine's proselytizing division and tried to persuade parishioners to allow it to perform funerals and ancestral rites for them, thus cutting their ties with Buddhist temples.

For Shintō clergy, funerals were problematic because of the concept of death pollution, but revenues from funerals and ancestral rites were a considerable incentive to overcome such taboos. Another rationale for overcoming the death taboo was for the shrine priest to adopt a second identity, that of the National Evangelist. He could say that he performed rites in the shrine as a Shintō priest and funerals as a National Evangelist. The churches thus aided priest-evangelists in a subterfuge that allowed them to adopt both ritualist and pastoral roles, but also permitted them to keep the roles separate where a conflation would conflict with traditional pollution notions.[17] Thus it was as an evangelist that a priest performed funerals and other religious functions.

The Ise Grand Shrines created a church called Jingūkyō (later transformed into one of the thirteen Shintō sects), whose branches were attached to the shrines for the purpose of proselytizing for them and to teach followers the ideals of the Great Promulgation Campaign. Organized in 1872 by the chief priest of the Ise Grand Shrines, Tanaka Yoritsune (1836–1897), Jingūkyō's ministers were drawn largely from the former oshi of the Ise Grand Shrines, and in addition to the Jingūkyō ministry they typically became National Evangelists as well. Furthermore, ministers of the new religions and ordinary shrine priests frequently combined their roles with the Jingūkyō ministry and became in addition National Evangelists. Jingūkyō by 1875 claimed 304,704 members, meeting in a nationwide network of sixteen hundred preaching stations, often located in existing shrines. The believers themselves were organized into parish confraternities called Jinpū Kōsha. More precisely, the Jinpū Kōsha were groups of believers attached to local preaching stations of the Jingūkyō. In many cases the pre-Meiji Ise confraternities formerly led by oshi were simply renamed Jinpū Kōsha, and these cult groups continued to exist much as before.

Tanaka mobilized the Ise priesthood to become evangelists and to preach on the Three Great Teachings, and it is reported that they routinely addressed audiences of several thousand.[18] In tracts for believers, Jingūkyō presented Amaterasu as an agricultural deity, recognizing the powerful folk belief that could in this way be harnessed to the goals of the state. Jingūkyō also distributed talismans and almanacs from the Ise Grand Shrines. It is likely that former oshi, simultaneously serving as ministers of Jingūkyō, were the largest single group of National Evangelists. Co-opting pre-Meiji confraternities enabled Jingūkyō to expand rapidly and provided a ready-made bridge between the orientation of popular religion in the Tokugawa period orientation and the new state religion.

Two new religions became independent of campaign control, declaring themselves in 1876 to be independent Shintō organizations: Kurozumikyō (known at the time as Shintō Kurozumi-ha) and Shūseikyō (known then as Shūsei-ha). These were the first two so-called sects of Shintō, and several more were soon to follow as their leaders became dissatisfied with the management of the campaign. Their ministers continued to preach and otherwise act as National Evangelists, but without central supervision. Many were also qualified to serve as shrine priests. Over the next few years, several other groups broke away from the campaign, creating considerable resentment among the campaign leadership, who viewed the sects as schismatics besmirching Shintō's image of a united front. Campaign leaders had no use for voluntary associations within the Shintō fold.[19]

Through participation in the Great Promulgation Campaign, the practice of shrines and some of the new religions came to resemble each other. It was not unusual for someone who began as a minister of a new religion to become a minister of Jingūkyō, a National Evangelist, and a shrine priest as well. It was also common for a shrine priest to become a National Evangelist, a minister of Jingūkyō, and a minister of some new religion. Thus it was possible to maintain several different, overlapping affiliations simultaneously.

The overall result was that Shintō's real identity became increasingly blurred. The extent of Shintō's fluid and permeable boundaries was further called into question by the Pantheon Dispute.

THE PANTHEON DISPUTE

The Pantheon Dispute (*saijin ronsō*) originated in a struggle between the nation's two most powerful shrines, the Ise Grand Shrines and the Izumo Shrine. The Ise Grand Shrines had achieved a preeminent position in 1875 by gaining control of the Great Promulgation Campaign. Senge Takatomi

(1845–1918), chief priest of the Izumo Shrine, challenged Ise's hegemony and declared that the main deity of the Izumo Shrine, Ōkuninushi no Mikoto, should be added to the state pantheon as lord of the underworld. The chief priest of the Ise Grand Shrines, Tanaka Yoritsune, opposed this challenge. The nation's shrine priests were all forced to take sides, and the dispute was so bitterly divisive that the Shintō world was split in half.[20]

The National Evangelists met repeatedly at local, prefectural, and national levels, each branch many times submitting its opinions to the central office, but they could not resolve the argument. The Pantheon Dispute exposed the primitive character of Shintō doctrine and led eventually to the establishment of theological institutes such as Kōgakkan (later Kōgakkan University). Also painfully revealed was the fragility of personal ties in the Shintō fold. The Pantheon Dispute made utterly clear the potential of theological debate to mar the state's ideological self-presentation.

The Pantheon Dispute made Shintō priests very distrustful of doctrinal questions, and it encouraged them to seek a construction of their role as priests and an understanding of Shintō in which doctrinal dispute could be avoided. This drive to avoid doctrinal issues further encouraged the priesthood to think of Shintō as nonreligious in character, because if religion meant doctrine, then the Shintō priesthood wanted none of it. Priests began instead to think of themselves as liturgists and of Shintō as primarily a liturgical practice. This view of Shintō and the nature of its priesthood represented a defeat for that sector of the Shintō world that favored promulgation of Shintō as a national creed and a pastoral role for priests. Thus the Ōkuni line of National Learning thought suffered a major defeat, and the priest-as-liturgist view, represented by the Hirata line of National Learning, gained an important victory.[21]

The Pantheon Dispute was submitted to the imperial house for settlement when it became apparent that the National Evangelists could not settle it themselves, but the emperor gave no resolution. Rather than ruling for or against the inclusion of the Izumo deity in the state pantheon, argument was simply silenced. Instead of a doctrinal decision, Shintō priests above a certain rank were forbidden to become National Evangelists, and thus to minister to parishioners through churches created alongside shrines. This meant that high-ranking priests were forbidden to perform funerals. Once forbidden to perform funerals, priests would have no occasion to pronounce on what deity, if any, ruled the underworld.

Lay membership in the churches, confraternities, and parishes that the shrine priesthood had so painstakingly established and attached to their shrines during the Great Promulgation Campaign revolved around a commitment to having funerals performed by the church. If priests could no longer perform funerals, then they could not effectively minister to their parishioners. The destruction of effective ministry led directly to the almost complete demise of many of these organizations and had a debilitating effect upon the laity's involvement with shrine life. This undermining of priests' efforts to promulgate Shintō as a practice including such distinctively religious elements as funerals made Shintō less and less religious in character and further confined its activities to the sphere of state ritual.

Many evangelists stormed the institute to protest the prohibition on their conduct of funerals.[22] From their point of view, their hard labor in constructing parishes and churches had been brought to nothing. Finding that they could not minister freely to their followers within the campaign, many decided they would act alone. Several evangelists formerly in the campaign themselves founded Shintō sects. Shishino Nakaba (1844–1884) founded Fusōkyō in 1875, Nitta Kuniteru (1829?–1902) founded Shūseikyō in 1873, Yoshimura Masamochi (1839–1915) founded Shinshūkyō in 1880, and Inaba Masakuni (1834–1898) founded Shintō Taikyō between 1884 and 1886. Senge Takatomi founded the sect called Taishakyō in 1870 by renaming all the confraternities formerly attached to the Izumo Shrine.

The Great Promulgation Campaign began with the evident intention of creating a state religion, a composite entity in which the theological differences of Shintō and Buddhism would be subsumed and which would unite the nation. After Buddhism's withdrawal, however, the state religion became Shintō by default, but the shrine priesthood was powerless to make an effective, popular appeal on the basis of the Three Great Teachings. When the Shintō sects began to withdraw, the campaign's fate was sealed. There was no one left who could weld the state-authored creed into a religion with any mass following. Thus it became inevitable that Shintō would become a matter of state rites rather than creed.

The public was understandably confused by the Great Promulgation Campaign. Shintō's public image was definitely tarnished by the campaign's failure and by severe criticism from such leading intellectuals as Fukuzawa Yukichi, who wrote:

There are those who hold that our country is sustained by the doctrines of the Way of Buddhas and Kami, but Shintō has not yet established a body of doctrine. While some identify "restorationism" (*fukko*) with Shintō, Shintō has always been the puppet of Buddhism, and for hundreds of years, it has failed to show its true colors. [Shintō] is only an insignificant movement trying to make headway by taking advantage of the imperial house at a time of political change.[23]

This passage from Fukuzawa's influential *Outline of Civilization* (1875) shows bluntly that he regarded Shintō as derivative, ephemeral, and self-serving.

National Learning figures in the Great Promulgation Campaign never intended to represent or codify the amorphous faith of the people seen in innumerable localized and highly diverse cults of kami. Instead the campaign's purpose was to instruct the populace in a set of novel creeds, issued in the name of deities who, except for Amaterasu-Tenshōdaijin, had no popular following, and (more importantly) simultaneously to inculcate in the people a willingness to follow the state's commands regarding taxation, conscription, and a host of other matters. Meanwhile, aspects of popular religion that did not harmonize with this new creed and its nation-centered ethos were suppressed.

Originally called in an ecumenical way a Great Teaching, the new creed was sufficiently lacking in appeal and popular allegiance that no one seemed to notice when people began calling it Shintō, thus underlining the fact that few people besides shrine priests and National Learning figures had any particular allegiance to that word either. Nevertheless, the ministers of the new religions of the period had their own reasons for participating in the Great Promulgation Campaign.

THE NEW RELIGIONS IN THE GREAT PROMULGATION CAMPAIGN

The new religions of the period offered a new form of religious affiliation, one which came into relationship with Shintō through the Great Promulgation Campaign. New religious associations were founded throughout the nineteenth century. Generally followers were attracted by faith healing or other miraculous events. It was common for a member of one of these groups to remain affiliated with a shrine and a Buddhist temple as well, but the real mark of full commitment to the new religion was the promise to have one's funeral performed by its clergy. That promise meant cutting previous ties to Buddhism. Both the Buddhist and Shintō clergies disliked and feared these new religions because they threatened to steal parishioners and thus undermine the economic base of temples and shrines.

The new religions existed precariously, dependent upon the sufferance of local administrations for their survival. There was in early Meiji no formal, legal framework of incorporation as a religious body or other provisions to guarantee these organizations freedom of operation. They were suspect in the eyes of politicians because of their demonstrated ability to bond people together across traditional boundaries of gender, region, class, and religious affiliation. They were, therefore, frequently persecuted and harrassed. In spite of these insecurities, their supporters were attached to these new religions with a fervor seldom seen among temple and shrine parishioners. They were enthusiastic, first-generation converts, and among their leaders were many powerful preachers and healers. These leaders were desperate for a means to guarantee the survival and freedom from persecution of their organizations. Participation in the Great Promulgation Campaign promised to grant this desire.

The experience of two new religions, Kurozumikyō and Konkōkyō, in the Great Promulgation Campaign illustrates the different ways the new religions responded to Shintō. To participate in the campaign and to reap the benefits of that participation required a new religion to assume a Shintō identity. Accepting the name of Shintō was not problematic for Kurozumikyō, whose founder, though he himself did not describe his Way as Shintō, had been a low-ranking Shintō priest before founding his religion. To the contrary, taking on a Shintō label was not easy for Konkōkyō, whose founder first assumed and then rejected membership in the Shintō priesthood. Disciples forced him to yield, but only with great reluctance. In both cases, assuming a Shintō identity resulted in significant alteration, even falsification, of the founder's creed and practice. To be sure, the benefits of freedom from suppression were high stakes indeed, but both religions were greatly changed.

While the new religions of the nineteenth century vary greatly in their doctrines, there is among them a fundamental unity in perspective upon human relations and upon the relation between the individual and the universe. Their founders participated in the popular religious activities of the Tokugawa period and were especially influenced by Ise pilgrimage. All the founders were familiar with popular preaching, and the conventional morality of rural society became the building blocks of their religious systems. Following prolonged illness or misfortune, all of them had mystical experiences in which they perceived how such values as harmony, sincerity, diligence, modesty, and thrift were connected in the workings of the universe. Though their doctrines were quite different, they came to a common understanding of physical and spiritual well-being. Arising from a disturbance of harmony between self and body, self and family, or self and society, sickness and misfortune were cured by a return to harmony in these disturbed relations, and harmony was restored through cultivating ethical values in all aspects of such interactions.

Kurozumikyō was founded in 1814 after Kurozumi Munetada experienced a miraculous healing by Amaterasu Ōmikami. The sun came down from the sky, entered his mouth, and pervaded his entire body with life force (*yōki*). A group of followers assembled as Kurozumi himself began to perform healings, to expound a Way to achieve unity between humanity and deity symbolized by daily worship of the rising sun and recitation of Shintō prayers, and especially to emphasize the value of sincerity (*makoto*).

Konkōkyō was founded in 1859 after a series of revelations to the founder Konkō Daijin, through which he came to a new understanding of deity. He came to believe that a series of grave misfortunes, including the deaths of his children and cattle, was due to his mistaken beliefs about Konjin, commonly regarded as a malicious directional deity. In fact, Konkō Daijin learned through his religious practice, this deity was the one God of the universe, Tenchi Kane no Kami. The founder's Way enabled humanity to know the nature of deity and to be in accord with God's will by implementing the core values in all human relations, assisted by the mediation (*toritsugi*) of the founder and ministers. Neither Konkō Daijin nor Kurozumi spoke of his Way as Shintō.

The new religions tended to focus on problems defined as applicable to all humankind: sickness, inexplicable misfortune, and poverty brought about by activities deemed folly (drinking, gambling). They adopted a variety of meliorism, the view that all problems were caused by individual shortcomings and were to be solved by collective self-improvement. This perspective entailed the belief that it was wrong to criticize secular authority. It would have been very much out of character, for example, for a new religion to trace the source of rural poverty to fiscal bungling by officials.

Conceptualizing life's problems this way, new religions took the position that people were basically the same, faced the same problems, and could solve them in the same way. This meant that they glossed over society's internal cleavages of class and gender as if these were irrelevant to an understanding of the human condition. Their viewpoint resulted in a principle of equality among believers, weak status distinctions between leaders and followers, and a reduced emphasis on the pollution notions that in the established religious associations barred women from full participation. As believers they defined their situation in terms that would not question the social order but that nevertheless tacitly created an active role for elements kept passive in other religious associations.

During the founder's lifetime, Kurozumikyō established itself in Okayama rural society mainly through the patronage of peasant headmen, but after the 1850s Shintō priests began to become ministers of the group. Kurozumikyō support from Shintō priests was stronger in northern than in southern Okayama. In the South, the venerable Kibitsu and Kibitsuhiko Shrines exercised close supervision over local priests' activities; northern Okayama had no shrine of comparable stature. The Shintō priests of northern Okayama may have hoped to raise their own standing by allying themselves with Kurozumikyō once it had a nucleus of believers in their communities. The area had earlier experienced the vigorous proselytization of Kurozumi's foremost disciple, Akagi Tadaharu (1816–1865).

In numerous areas Kurozumikyō ministers established branch churches and collected followers through faith healing. Many of them achieved recognition for public service, among them Miyake Rikimatsu, minister of the Chayamachi village church, who received a commemorative photo of Emperor Meiji for civic service and commendation from the prefectural governor for filial piety. Yasui Yoshifusa (1855–1912), minister of the Kibi village church and a National Evangelist, became mayor of Koto village in 1891 and later county secretary. Many others were active on local school boards, fire brigades, and town councils, and many ministers were also Shintō priests. The appearance of local civic leaders among the Kurozumikyō ministry enhanced the organization's prestige considerably.[24]

Kurozumikyō grew rapidly in early Meiji. By 1900 there were fifty-two Kurozumikyō churches in Okayama, most established along major roads, with a smaller number along secondary roads. Simultaneously proselytization advanced vigorously in Kyoto, Shikoku, the Oki Islands, and other areas of western Japan.

Becoming National Evangelists, the ministers of these churches preached on the Three Great Teachings, using state-authored chapbooks to expound them. They affirmed the restoration of imperial rule, explaining conscription, taxation, compulsory education, and the establishment of prefectures in terms of divine will, and as sacred goals to be accomplished through a rededication of self to the nation.[25]

From the diaries of one Kurozumikyō minister who was also a Shintō priest and a National Evangelist, Yamano Sadayasu (1833–1905), we can understand the religiosity of the Great Promulgation Campaign as experienced by National Evangelists working in rural society. Born in Kuse village in northern Okayama, Yamano became a disciple of Ōkuni Takamasa as well as of Kurozumi. He spent the early months of 1873 at the Great Teaching Institute and became acquainted with campaign luminaries, meeting with them daily. After several months at the institute, Yamano took to the road on a marathon preaching tour, speaking often in Buddhist temples, sometimes in shrines and primary schools, and most often at village meetings arranged through local officials. He was in constant contact with Kurozumikyō, the Great Teaching Institute, and other National Evangelists by letter. Often he met his fellow evangelists in the countryside, and sometimes they preached together. Frequently returning to Kuse village to tend his own Kurozumikyō church, he was made a minister of Jingūkyō and regularly visited the branch offices of the Ise Grand Shrines in Tokyo, Osaka, and Kyoto, as well as preaching for the organization. Yamano seems to have made little distinction among his various sectarian identities when preaching, and for him, the state ideology and Kurozumi's Way were increasingly melded into a single, seamless message.[26]

During the Great Promulgation Campaign, Kurozumikyō meetings were held in an entirely Shintō form. Shintō prayers were addressed to the national pantheon, as well as to the emperor, and at each assembly believers bowed in reverence during a ceremonial reading of the Three Great Teachings after formal worship of the emperor. In sermons ministers came to use the word *Shintō* as a broader appellation for the founder's Way. Kurozumikyō cooperated with the Jingūkyō, sometimes performing funerals in the manner of that group, and incorporating the name of Kurozumi Munetada into the liturgy.[27]

While such campaign-influenced elements as the above were straight-forwardly incorporated into Kurozumikyō, elements of the founder's teaching that did not harmonize so well, such as Kurozumi's doctrine of immortality and divination by the hexagrams, were abandoned. Mean-while, when Kurozumi's disciple Akagi announced that the "renewal of the world" (*yonaoshi*) was at hand, he was excommunicated, and Kurozumikyō raised no protest when Akagi's follower Honda Onosuke (1825–1872), who took part in a peasant uprising and wrote a satirical pamphlet as a call to revolt, was imprisoned. In these various ways Kurozumikyō tailored it-self to fit the state's conception of religion's role: as its mouthpiece, to promulgate its directives, and to instill a conservative, nation-centered ethic.[28]

By 1883 Kurozumikyō had a total of 1,744 active National Evangelists. As repeated petitions to the home minister show, Kurozumikyō would have had even more evangelists, but for a quota imposed upon it in 1879. It also petitioned repeatedly to be allowed to send evangelists to proselytize overseas.[29]

Konkōkyō was in many ways influenced by its predecessor, and the two were rivals in Okayama. Kurozumikyō found many supporters among peasant headmen and Shintō priests, but Konkōkyō developed in a differ-ent way. It established confraternities and, later, churches (both known as *deyashiro*), as ministers patterned themselves after their founder Konkō Daijin and set up altars where they relayed to followers the words of their deity Tenchi Kane no Kami.[30] Although the first *deyashiro* was recorded in 1863, others probably existed earlier, and it is noteworthy that from the beginning there were numerous women ministers.[31] As in the case of Kurozumikyō, most clients initially came seeking healing. Konkōkyō min-isters prayed on followers' behalf and communicated the deity's pronounce-ments. Through this counsel many believed that they were healed, and counseling of this sort (*toritsugi*) became the core of the ministerial role in Konkōkyō.

Although Konkō Daijin in secular life had held positions of trust in his village, he was a commoner and had no substantive connections with head-men or Shintō priests. While he must be placed with wealthier cultivators, he was not on a par with the cultured rich peasantry (*gōnō*). His followers came mainly from his own stratum of the cultivating class or lower, with a few merchants and artisans.

Probably because of Kurozumikyō's dominant position in northern and eastern Okayama by the 1870s, Konkōkyō tended to spread west of Okayama City, establishing its greatest strength in southern Okayama and in Hiroshima Prefecture. By 1865 there was also a following in Edo, Osaka, Iyo, Sanuki, and Shōdoshima.[32]

The history of Konkōkyō until it achieved independent status in 1885 is the story of how it adopted a number of means to avoid persecution. Inevitably it was forced to compromise with (and be compromised by) state and local authority. Lacking official patrons for the most part, Konkōkyō ministers were in effect outside the law and subject to the sufferance of local authority. Konkōkyō leaders eventually achieved the same type of distinction in local society seen among Kurozumikyō ministers, but not until the mid-1880s and 1890s.

In this precarious situation the founder and his ministers resorted to various strategies to achieve a viable existence. In 1864 the founder petitioned the Shirakawa house for permission to build and officiate at a shrine to be called the Konjin Shrine. Although the Shirakawa disapproved of his practice of reciting a Buddhist scripture, the Heart Sutra, and a Buddhist-influenced prayer called the "Rokkon shōjō harai," permission was granted upon receipt of substantial "contributions." This official permission made the founder a Shintō priest, thus giving him a nominally Shintō identity, but in fact the Konjin Shrine was not built until 1876, and the founder continued his ministry as before, performing none of the usual observances of a Shintō priest. Thus neither he nor his followers subscribed to Shintō except insofar as that identity had to be adopted to ensure the group's safety from suppression.[33]

While the founder's registration with the Shirakawa house supposedly gave his ministers freedom to proselytize as well, they were suppressed and jailed in many areas. After Meiji even the founder's status was called into question, and in 1873 he was forced to stop his ministry for about a month. During that time he reached a new conception of his mission, deciding that he was not meant to be a shrine priest. He also denied his ministers' entreaties to allow them to become National Evangelists, rejecting interviews with local shrine administrators and refusing to worship the national pantheon or to incorporate the Three Great Teachings. Thus, after 1873 Konkō Daijin explicitly denied the Shintō identity he had earlier assumed for reasons of expediency.[34]

From Meiji until 1885 Konkōkyō ministers had to affiliate with some officially approved religious body. During this period many new churches were founded in southern Okayama, but in order to escape persecution they became affiliated with Misogikyō,[35] organizations of mountain ascetics (*yamabushi*), Jingūkyō, and Shinrikyō.[36] The only group with which they rejected affiliation was Kurozumikyō. Though a collection of miracle tales and testimonies called the *Omichi Annai* circulated widely during these years, there was no written creed, and it was extremely difficult for the churches to achieve any unity of belief and practice, especially in the compromising situation of subordination to other religious associations.[37] Strange schisms appeared, such as a Hiroshima group that, while claiming to follow Konkō Daijin, practiced divination with sacred rice and worshiped Amaterasu, Susanoō, and Tsukiyomi-ten (the last evidently an appropriation of the *Kojiki* lunar deity, Tsukiyomi no Mikoto). These three deities were the three pillars of the schism's name, the Shintō Three-Pillar Church.[38]

To Satō Norio (1856–1942), Konkō Daijin's closest disciple, it was obvious that this intolerable situation could not be allowed to continue. He sought the advice of Shintō priests and National Evangelists, and was told that the group must have a written creed. From previous contact with Kurozumikyō, Satō knew the usefulness of a set creed, and he knew also that without one to link all the churches to the headquarters, they faced the danger of disintegrating upon the founder's death. With Konkō Daijin's reluctant permission, Satō composed a "creed" that copied Kurozumikyō's almost to the letter. To prepare himself to become a National Evangelist, Satō began to study National Learning with a disciple of Ōkuni Takamasa.[39]

Over the founder's protests, Satō became an evangelist in 1880 and began preaching throughout Okayama and Hiroshima, using the opportunity to unify the branch churches and to organize them systematically.[40] It was Satō who by these actions pulled Konkōkyō irrevocably into the Shintō fold. Although Konkō Daijin had become a Shintō priest, this was clearly a subterfuge that he later repudiated, and there was nothing inherently Shintō about his religious beliefs or practices; the deity Tenchi Kane no Kami had no connection to the national pantheon. Nevertheless, Satō did his best to present the group as a variety of Shintō. A total of 222 Konkōkyō ministers became evangelists.[41]

When, during the 1880s, the Hiroshima branch of the Office of Shintō Affairs sent evangelists all over western Japan to promote Shintō and castigate Buddhism, speaking of this campaign as "holy war,"[42] Satō traveled with them, preaching on the Three Great Teachings and "national polity spirit" (*kokutai seishin*).[43]

Satō also attacked a Buddhist initiative to reestablish its former status through a movement called "Destroying Iniquity and Establishing Righteousness" (*hajakenshō*).[44] Determined that Buddhism regain no ground, Satō debated the bonzes, championing Shintō as the best "protector of the state."[45] By this time he no longer made any distinction between the ideology of the Great Promulgation Campaign and Konkō Daijin's Way.

Other leaders of new religions also expounded state doctrine and their founders' Ways with equal fervor and little distinction, committing themselves wholeheartedly to the entirety. As they bonded campaign ideology to their founders' Ways, they increasingly expounded their founders' teachings as sectarian versions of Shintō. Followers remained content to leave doctrinal minutiae to specialists.

CONCLUSION

In summarizing the above comparison of Kurozumikyō and Konkōkyō in the Great Promulgation Campaign, the following points emerge. Both hoped to avoid persecution and to legitimate themselves in the eyes of the state by assuming the stance of educator of the populace, and in this they were willing to make significant compromises: to change their deities, to call themselves with greater or lesser justification Shintō, to submit their organizations to government supervision, to derogate Buddhism, to become government mouthpieces to their followers, and to harness their Ways of self-cultivation to such state goals as tax-paying, compulsory education, and a military buildup. Both groups mediated the relation between the state and the rural populace, introducing themselves as extensions of state authority and the state as distant authorizer of their own world view.

These new religions inherited from Tokugawa popular religion an attitude identifying and affirming the social order, as currently constituted, as the locus in which humanity was to cultivate itself and achieve salvation. Before Meiji, however, new religions were largely excluded from that order and had to prove themselves in order to achieve recognition within it. The Great Promulgation Campaign gave them a place in an ideological order, called (after 1875) Shintō, that they accepted. When the state validated the new religions in this way, they reciprocated, committing themselves ever more deeply to Shintō and to the sociopolitical order as a whole. To them this legitimation constituted further validation of the truth granted their founders in revelation. They did not seek to become helmsmen of the political order but instead saw their mission as providing pathways to salvation within society. They came increasingly to identify a merger of their founders' teachings and Shintō as the pathway to salvation.

The Great Promulgation Campaign illustrates the several ways in which different kinds of people became involved in Shintō during the early Meiji period. The idea of Shintō as a collective entity representing all the shrines and their priests and lay followers was new, a product of the separation of Buddhist elements from the shrines and the establishment of shrines as independent from Buddhist temples. Although the worship of kami was ancient, the concept of Shintō as a name for all the cults of kami was unfamiliar to priest and lay person alike.

The idea of Shintō was also subject to a number of different interpretations among priests, National Learning figures, lay people, and politicians. Each of these groups had distinctive interests in spreading their particular understanding of what Shintō was, and each could see in Shintō distinctive ways in which it could be used to personal advantage.

Early Meiji politicians saw in Shintō a tool useful in the legitimation of the political regime. State sponsorship of the Great Promulgation Campaign indicates that politicians believed that Shintō would be useful in uniting the populace in a common creed that would transcend regional loyalties and differences of class, in bonding the people together in the service of national goals, and in overcoming resistance to such novelties as conscription, a national taxation system, and compulsory education.

Lay people were granted the status of parishioner of shrines on an egalitarian basis for the first time in history in early Meiji, and this offered a host of new opportunities. The status of parishioner had formerly indicated a position of prestige, and its extension to the masses motivated some to become active supporters of shrines. Because Shintō priests were associated with government, parish membership offered informal channels to the political arena, a mode of access formerly available only to social elites. No doubt there was a certain quid pro quo involved between wealthy parishioners and the priesthood, so that help in gaining access to the political realm was repaid with support of local shrines and their priests. Other lay people, unable to take advantage of these channels for lack of resources, probably continued to venerate the local kami much as they always had, maintaining the localized cults of the past, pleased by priests' assurances of the importance of kami-worship in the eyes of the state.

3. The Shintō Priesthood

THE SHINTŌ priesthood entered the Meiji period as a highly diverse group, and it has retained a high degree of internal variety to the present. Priests associated with shrine administration, the priests of traditional sacerdotal lineages, and the priests of local tutelary shrines shared a ranking system and common vestments after the Meiji Restoration, but they differed among themselves in many important respects. Their reasons for entering the priesthood varied greatly, as did their interpretations of what Shintō was, and how it was related to the idea of religion. They interacted with local and national political administrations in a variety of ways, and their dealings with their parishioners took many different forms. Emphasizing the Meiji period, this chapter discusses the priesthood in terms of these factors and in relation to the ideas about religion that were entering Japan at this time.

THE INTERNAL DIVERSITY OF THE SHINTŌ PRIESTHOOD

The Meiji shrine priesthood was composed of several distinct clusters. First, the Tokyo administrators of Shintō affairs were dominated by adherents of one or another branch of National Learning thought, the followers of Hirata Atsutane[1] and Ōkuni Takamasa[2] being the most influential. Second, high-ranking figures of the Yoshida and Shirakawa houses maintained important roles in imperial ritual. Third, sacerdotal lineages of the National and Imperial Shrines continued to control those shrines and sometimes to play important roles in local administration of shrine affairs, because the offices for administering the examinations for the priesthood were typically housed in their shrines. Often they also served in the central administration of shrine affairs. Fourth, appointees to the priesthood were chosen on the basis of local administrative needs, or they chose the priesthood as a secondary or postretirement occupation. Fifth, a number of "recycled religionists" entered the priesthood, persons whose religious allegiances, beliefs, and practices originated elsewhere—in Buddhism, the cult of sacred mountains, pilgrimage associations, and the new religions. These people became priests either because they were forced out of their former religious associations (yamabushi, oshi, and some Buddhist priests) or because certification as a shrine priest enabled them to practice their original religion without fear of persecution (ministers of the new religions). Among all five groups there were distinctive individuals who, for other purposes, might well be classed with the *shishi*, "righteous men," of the Meiji Restoration, fierce loyalists clinging to such Restoration slogans as "Revere the emperor and expel the barbarian" long after the rest of society had turned to other objectives.[3]

These five clusters were not internally homogeneous, nor were they entirely distinct from each other, and their activities were not necessarily coordinated. They were linked to central and local governments in a variety of ways. Their relationships with lay persons showed great variety, and they competed with each other for the power and influence symbolized by appointment to high-ranking shrines. They had very different ideas about what Shintō might be, and how it was related to religion. The nature of their religious experience and commitment varied widely.

While all of these groups might have accepted the label "Shintōist," few would have thought of it themselves. They were an uneasy coalition united more by negative than positive aims: they disliked Buddhism, Christianity, and the Tokugawa administration of shrines. The forces drawing them together were counterbalanced by divisive local loyalties to specific shrines, to the territory and people of their birthplaces, and to different lines of National Learning thought.

After the Restoration, the Department of Divinity (later called the Ministry of Divinity) was established and controlled by National Learning ideologues and shrine priests. The department succeeded in wresting authority over the shrine priests from the Shirakawa and Yoshida, and attempted to take over such national rites as New Year's, the harvest rite called Niinamesai, and the commemoration of imperial ancestors (Kōreisai). It was able to gain recognition of its own performance of these rites, but Yoshida and Shirakawa officials continued to perform them in the palace, so the department was unable to draw all national rites into a single ritual complex under its exclusive control.[4]

The Yoshida and Shirakawa retained their cults of the tutelary deities of the imperial house and also their hereditary court ranks and the title of Jingihaku, Councillor of Divinities. Imperial rites continued to be performed by the Shirakawa, at a newly built shrine in the palace called the *kashikodokoro*.[5] Control of imperial ritual was a matter of intense competition in early Meiji, and no party achieved a clear hegemony. Since, however, the Yoshida and Shirakawa exercised little influence over popular shrine life after the Restoration, they are not treated in detail here, except as an example of the conflict and diversity among the priesthood.

The Yoshida and Shirakawa had controlled the priesthood before the Meiji Restoration by issuing licenses and ranks, the equivalent of ordination. After the Restoration, however, these licenses were invalidated, and their holders had either to be recertified by national examination or be laicized. Hereditary succession to the priesthood (the general rule before the Restoration) was prohibited in 1871.

Sacerdotal lineages were common in the many larger, more powerful shrines discussed in the Introduction as the second level of Shintō. The shrines served by such lineages were mostly ranked as Imperial or National Shrine (*kanpeisha*, *kokuheisha*) after 1868, the two highest ranks. Their actual operation seems to have continued more or less as before.[6] They were directly administered by central offices of shrine administration in Tokyo and were partially supported from public funds. Their priests found ways of circumventing the prohibition on hereditary succession and most maintained, in fact, sacerdotal lineages.

Besides the shrines existing before the Meiji Restoration, a number of new shrines were constructed at the rank of National or Imperial Shrine. These included the Yasukuni Shrine, which later became a national shrine for the war dead, several branches of the Ise Grand Shrines, called Kōtai Jingū, and shrines for such famous loyalists as Kusunoki Masashige, enshrined at the Minatogawa Shrine in Kobe.[7] Their priests were drawn mainly from the nobility and prominent National Learning figures and tended to have close and substantial ties to the government offices handling the administration of shrines.

Smaller, less prominent shrines, discussed in the Introduction as level three, were generally ranked Prefectural Shrine (*kensha*), District Shrine (*gōsha*), or below. These shrines constituted the vast majority of the total, and most Shintō priests served a shrine of this kind. Both shrines and priests of these lower ranks were placed under the supervision of local civil administrations. Tokyo exercised less direct control over these shrines and gave no substantial financial support.[8] Consequently, their priests had much more tenuous ties to the national government, but they were often quite influential in prefectural politics.

Local and prefectural governments exercised great autonomy in shrine administration. In many areas local administrations allowed priests themselves to take the lead in carrying out such edicts as that separating Buddhism from Shintō. They were able to do so without central supervision from Tokyo. In this way local shrine priests were able, in some places, to give full vent to the anger they felt against Buddhism and to destroy much Buddhist property.[9]

There was considerable variety in the treatment of shrine priests after the Restoration in different areas of the country. Shrine priests formerly licensed by the Yoshida and Shirakawa were turned out of office in some places and replaced by persons formerly uninvolved in shrine affairs. In other cases some former licensees of the Yoshida and Shirakawa were recertified by local governments and remained in their posts. A central edict dismissed many women who had formerly been employed at shrines as mediums and performers of sacred dance; women were denied the option of recertification. In a separate development, many former oshi from the Ise Grand Shrines, yamabushi, and even Buddhist priests entered the shrine priesthood in early Meiji, as did ministers of new religious movements such as Misogikyō,[10] Kurozumikyō[11] and Konkōkyō[12]. These persons were concentrated in those shrines controlled by local governments.[13]

Having surveyed the major groups within the Shintō priesthood, we must now ask what their views on Shintō were, and how they understood Shintō's relation to Buddhism and to the state. In order to do so, however, it will be necessary to discuss the terminology involved and to place the views of Shintō priests in the context of the opinions of secular and Buddhist intellectuals of the early Meiji period.

THE EVOLUTION OF A CONCEPT OF RELIGION

When ideas about religion originating in Europe and America came to Japan, they entered a society that had no equivalent concept or term, no idea of a distinct sphere of life that could be called religious, and no idea of a generic religion of which there might be local variants like Christianity, Buddhism, and so on. Nevertheless, if only for the purposes of translating treaties with foreign powers, the Japanese found it necessary to develop their own term for the various Western-language words for religion, and a period of experimentation ended with the adoption of a Buddhist technical term, *shūkyō*, as the official translation.[14] This term took some time to enter the national vernacular vocabulary. Meanwhile, a number of terms were used indiscriminately until some consistency in usage developed.[15]

Soon Japanese thinkers began to examine religion critically. For them Christianity was prototypical. It posed a formidable intellectual challenge to those who had been abroad and seen its power in European and American life and thought. The best philosophical minds understood Christianity as a system of thought, in relation to the state, and as a moral philosophy.

The thinkers who spoke out soonest and loudest did not base their remarks, for the most part, on religious experience. Instead, theirs was the standpoint of the would-be social engineer. They assumed that after distinguishing the good from the bad in religion, they would have the new Japan adopt only the former.[16] As individuals they generally were not strongly attached to any religious tradition, and they freely criticized both Shintō and Buddhism.

In the face of the philosophers' critiques, Buddhist thinkers quickly came to the defense of the faith. And since many of their elite had also studied abroad, they could argue Kant and Hegel with the best. Several influential Buddhist thinkers, such as Kiyozawa Manji,[17] Shimaji Mokurai,[18] Ouchi Seiran,[19] and Inoue Enryō,[20] carved out important positions in Japanese intellectual life.[21]

By contrast with the lively exchanges between the Buddhists and the philosophers, Shintō adopted an ostrich-like approach. Few priests had been abroad, and many would have found the prospect abhorrent, an experience that could only cover them in moral and spiritual pollution. Though many shrine priests were tremendously learned, they had not often studied Western philosophy and could not reply in the terms of the original challenge. Instead, their Tokyo intellectuals tended to form a closed world, isolated from the stronger currents in Meiji thought on the one hand, and from their own provincial constituency on the other.

To the great minds of the period, Shintō posed neither intellectual threat nor challenge.[22] The more Shintō priests withdrew from the exciting debates on religion, the less often did anyone beckon. This meant that their input into evolving definitions of religion had a negative, absentee quality. Their withdrawal guaranteed that they would be consigned by the stronger players to a residual category.

The Shintō priesthood did not like the associations of the term *shūkyō*, for the several reasons explained in detail in earlier chapters. And, as we have seen, they did not uniformly use the term *Shintō* to describe all the cults of kami. Instead, early Meiji Shintō figures frequently used the terms *honkyō* or *hongaku*, rather than *Shintō*, as their most inclusive terms for their enterprise. These were National Learning terms, particularly associated with Ōkuni Takamasa, which referred principally to doctrine about the three creator deities, the Japanese system of government, and notions of Japan's superiority.[23]

They also used other terms for aspects of their belief and practice that did not necessarily carry exclusivist or purely Shintō connotations. The term *kyōhō* ("doctrine," "creed") was widely used by early Meiji Shintō writers to refer to the ideas and attitudes they sought to promulgate among the masses, but since it was also a technical Buddhist term meaning "the teaching of the Buddha," it invoked a variety of associations militating against an exclusively Shintō appropriation. It was also used to mean "a way of teaching" or "pedagogy." By comparison, *kyōri* and *kyōgi* were fairly straightforward terms for "doctrine."[24]

Since Shintō discussions of both Shintō and religion were for the most part carried out in isolation from those of secular or Buddhist intellectuals, Shintō did not contribute much to the evolving concepts of religion and its role in a modern nation. Nevertheless, as the ideas outside Shintō's world gained currency among the general populace, Shintō was inevitably influenced by them and could not ignore them. These ideas were heavily influenced by nineteenth-century Protestantism of the rather theologically simple, evangelical style of those missionaries who came to Japan. The evolution of a Japanese concept of religion thus tended to devalue ritual and customary observances such as festivals, which, as we have seen, were at the heart of shrine life. Thus, a clash between Shintō and the evolving concept of *shūkyō* was inevitable.

Among Japanese thinkers, Western ideas about religion eventually superseded Japan's heritage, in which liturgical-communal praxis was central. The best books on religion reproduced Western notions of the privileged position of doctrine-faith-religious experience and tacitly or openly characterized rite and festival as superstitious. To these writers Shintō's doctrinal component was nil, and a comparable judgment was made about ethics. Except for groups later known as sects of Shintō, the Shintō priesthood exhibited a deep mistrust of the transforming experience of the sacred. Thus to the best philosophical minds, Shintō did not look much like religion.

Among all Shintō priests, it was the Tokyo administrators who were in closest contact with secular and Buddhist intellectuals. They were the most influential in formulating an understanding of Shintō and a Shintō understanding of religion, and their views were widely accepted among the provincial priesthood. Let us preface an examination of their conception of Shintō with general remarks on their attitude to the rest of the priesthood and to popular shrine life.

SHRINE ADMINISTRATORS

Administrators of Shintō affairs in the capital universally assumed that their mission was to shape and direct shrine life, to uphold the dignity of shrines, and to promote closer ties to the state. That is, they had no desire to advocate existing shrine practice, but to transform it, to prune away undesirable elements and implant the desirable, by fiat if necessary. They insulated themselves from local circumstances, and the religious sentiments of the populace appalled them. That is, they believed that the prayers for health, wealth, and safety, the baby blessings, prayer healings, and occasional shamanistic communications with spirits and ancestors had no real place in true Shintō. Since the offending popular quest for this-worldly benefits was pervasively manifested at shrines, however, priests' elitist disdain for the people was compromised from the outset. They understood themselves to be bureaucrats, not religious leaders.

Shrine administrators were united more by common enemies than by a shared vision. They found the zeal of the new sects and their association with the lower orders vulgar and an affront to the dignity of the enterprise of registering, ranking, and standardizing shrines. If they could have ejected the ministers of the Shintō sects without endangering their own financial support, they probably would have. They had an extreme dislike of Christianity, which they believed capable of converting the entire populace if given a chance. Their opposition to Christianity's advance was their strongest bond.

Shrine administrators tended to identify religion first and foremost with Christianity, and then with Buddhism. They sought an understanding of Shintō that would distinguish it from both Christianity and Buddhism and preserve its exclusive prerogative to perform state rites.

THE IDEA OF A NATIONAL TEACHING

Shintō administrators developed the notion that Shintō was superior to religion. Not all priests were aware of the view, and not all accepted it, but a virtual party line was forged and presented to the state in a memorial of 1874, calling for the restoration of the Department of Divinity, and signed by an impressive array of Shintō leaders. This text will serve to introduce administrators' proposed alternative to religion: a National Teaching.[25]

National Teaching (*kokkyō*) is teaching the codes of national government to the people without error. Japan is called the divine land because it is ruled by the heavenly deities' descendants, who consolidate the work of the deities. The Way of such consolidation and rule by divine descendants is called *Shintō*. . . . The Way of humanity in the age of the gods is nothing other than Shintō in the world of humanity. Ultimately, Shintō means a unity of government and teaching. . . . [The Department of Divinity should be restored in order to make it clear that] the National Teaching of the imperial house is not a religion, because religions are the theories of their founders. The National Teaching consists of the traditions of the imperial house, beginning in the age of the gods and continuing throughout history. Teaching and consolidating these traditions for the masses are inseparable from government, related as the two wheels of a cart or the wings of a bird. The National Teaching is Shintō . . . and Shintō is nothing other than the National Teaching.

This passage establishes a string of equations: National Teaching equals Shintō equals the Way of humanity in the age of the gods equals traditions of the imperial house equals codes of government. The whole sequence differs from religion because religion is based on human theories that, not originating in sacred time, are subject to human error. Shintō originates in sacred time and is perpetuated by a line of imperial scions. The descent line constitutes a perpetual link to divine ancestors and hence guarantees the sacred status of the lineage's traditions as embodied in law and government. The Department of Divinity should be restored to prevent confusion on these points.

The term *kokkyō* invokes a number of associations. The first element, *koku* (*kokk-* when elided with a following consonant), means "nation" or "country." The *kyō* element means "teaching," as in *bukkyō*, "the teaching of Buddha," i.e., Buddhism, or *kirisutokyō*, "the teaching of Christ," i.e., Christianity. A late twentieth-century translation of *kokkyō* would be "state religion." But the signatories of the memorial under investigation here were not invoking a preexisting concept of state religion in their use of *kokkyō*, so that translation is not appropriate, though, as we will see below, their vision of Shintō might well, by some definitions, be called a state religion.

The authors of this memorial sought to remind the government of its commitment to sponsor a doctrinal orthodoxy, first proclaimed in the Great Promulgation Campaign. What distinction the memorial's signatories intended to make between the Three Great Teachings and National Teaching is unclear, except that National Teaching seems to be employed as a comprehensive term that could include the Three Great Teachings as well as codes of law and imperial pronouncements.[26]

In order to understand fully the significance of this memorial, we should set it beside contemporary influential writings on religion that were also under consideration early in the Meiji period. No doubt shrine administrators intended their memorial as a strong statement, but theirs were not the only opinions being voiced on these matters, even though the memorial made no reference to the theories on religion being developed around the same time.

Mori Arinori (1847–1889), the future minister of education, had published an influential essay, "Religious Freedom in Japan," in 1872, and the famous intellectual journal *Meiroku zasshi* featured lively debate on religion over many issues. These writings generally favored a guarantee of religious freedom. Thus they were opposed in principle to the idea of any compulsory national creed or teaching. Similarly, they tended on the whole to favor a separation of religion and state. While a variety of views were expressed, the philosopher Nishi Amane championed the principle of separation between state and religion starting with the first of his many articles on religion.[27]

Gradually the state was inclining in the direction of affirming a separation between any doctrinal orthodoxy and government. In that climate a reassertion that National Teaching was inseparable from government failed to challenge the opposition and seemed anachronistic. The response of Shintō administrators was too slight and came too late to influence the state.

The 1874 memorial examined here tells a great deal about the views of Shintō administrators on Shintō, religion, and on the relation of both to the state. Their opinions were not, however, accepted or implemented. Nevertheless, the memorial was signed by some of the most powerful figures among them. A brief discussion of six will serve to illustrate their diversity and the nature of their attachment to the idea of a National Teaching. A discussion of their activities after the state's dismissal, in effect, of their memorial will show how shrine administrators influenced other sectors of the Shintō world, such as the Shintō sects.

SHRINE ADMINISTRATORS' DIVERSITY AND INFLUENCE

Tanaka Yoritsune (1836–1897), chief priest of the Ise Grand Shrines, held office in the Ministry of Divinity (Jingishō) in 1871 and later held office in each of its successors. As we have seen, he led the opposition to the Izumo Shrine in the Pantheon Dispute. After the Pantheon Dispute, Tanaka became head of Jingūkyō, which was recognized as one of the thirteen sects of Shintō at that time.

Motoori Toyokai (1834–1913), fifth-generation successor to the great National Learning figure Motoori Norinaga, represented the latter's philological and literary approach to nativist thought in the early Meiji administration. Just after the Restoration, he was dispatched to deal with the Urakami Christians,[28] and soon thereafter he was appointed to head one of the great shrines of Tokyo, the Kanda Shrine. Toyokai attempted to eliminate the shrine's popular cult and replace it with one more in keeping with National Learning, with the result that the shrine's popularity rapidly declined. Besides being instrumental in standardizing the rites of the imperial palace, Toyokai was appointed head of all National Evangelists in Tokyo in 1875. He held high office in the Shintō sect Taishakyō, which acted as the proselytizing arm of the Izumo Shrine.[29] After the debacle of the Pantheon Dispute, in which he supported the Izumo position, Toyokai resigned his official posts and devoted himself full time to Taishakyō.[30]

Hirayama Seisai (1815–1890) served the shogunate as foreign minister (*gaikoku bugyō*), in which post he gained experience of diplomatic affairs.[31] In holding an extremely positive view of the West, he was very unusual among shrine administrators. In 1876 he was appointed head priest of the Hikawa Shrine in Omiya City, Saitama Prefecture, important as the site of the imperial proclamation of the Charter Oath[32] and intended to serve as the tutelary shrine of all Tokyo. In 1879 Hirayama united formerly unrelated confraternities of mountain ascetics under two umbrella organizations, Ontakekyō and Taiseikyō, both later recognized as sects of Shintō. In Saitama Hirayama exercised great influence over such provincial priests as Yamada Morii and Tanaka Sen'ya, treated in a later section of this chapter. In the Pantheon Dispute, Hirayama opposed the Izumo side.[33] After the dispute ended, however, he resigned his shrine post and devoted himself entirely to Taishakyō.[34]

Inaba Masakuni (1834–1898) served the Tokugawa shogunate as domain ruler (*daimyō*) of the Yodo domain, as a member of the Council of Elders, and as Kyoto Inspector.[35] Inaba adhered to the Hirata line of National Learning. He wielded great influence in the Office of Shintō Affairs—in fact, he was largely responsible for its creation. Resigning from government in disgust with both sides in the Pantheon Dispute, he became the first head of the sect Shintō Honkyoku, later known as Shintō Taikyō. This organization represented Inaba's effort to perpetuate National Teaching after the Pantheon Dispute; it had no creed independent of its bureaucratic inspiration, nor any discernible basis in religious experience.[36]

Otori Sesso (1814–1904) belongs to the category of recycled religionist, though he was closely associated with Shintō administrators. He began as a Buddhist priest and headed several temples before renouncing Buddhism and entering the Shintō priesthood in 1871. Otori served in the Council of State (Dajōkan) after facilitating the establishment of relations between the nobility and former domain rulers after the Restoration. He became a priest of the Tokyo Kotohira Shrine, which, as an important shrine located in central Tokyo, was an ideal base from which to play an active role in the Office of Shintō Affairs. Otori's stance on the Pantheon Dispute was consistently vague, but tended to oppose the Izumo position.[37] Withdrawing from government after the dispute, Otori served as the second head of Ontakekyō from 1885 to 1904. Ontakekyō served to unite former mountain ascetics dedicated to pilgrimage to Mt. Ontake and as a forum to promulgate to them former administrators' understandings of National Teaching.[38]

Maruyama Sakura (1840–1899) was one of the most interesting personalities of the early Meiji priesthood. Jailed before the Restoration for his vehement advocacy of overthrowing the shogunate, Maruyama was deeply influenced by the National Learning thought of Hirata Atsutane. He was appointed briefly to high office in the Department of Divinity and later to diplomatic service. He was dispatched to Karafuto, where he negotiated border disputes with Russia and become known as a hard-liner in foreign relations. Returning to Japan in 1870, he was jailed for advocating an invasion of Korea. It was in jail that he signed the 1874 memorial apparently, as he was not released until 1880. Thereafter he founded Chūaisha, a group dedicated to suppressing the popular rights movement of the 1870s and 1880s. This stance found favor with Prime Minister Itō Hirobumi,[39] who appointed Maruyama to the Imperial Household Ministry, where he helped codify the regulations of the imperial house. Under the direction of Inoue Kowashi,[40] he was sent to study constitutional law in Austria. Becoming a member of the House of Peers in 1898, he worked to reestablish the Department of Divinity.[41] In the early 1880s Maruyama regularly hosted a well-attended salon for discussion of shrine affairs. His position on the Pantheon Dispute shifted, but eventually he came to oppose Izumo.[42]

The signatories of this memorial were the luminaries of the early Meiji Shintō world. Contemporary diaries show that they set the policies of the Office of Shintō Affairs, and that lesser priests looked to them for guidance on all official matters. Their shared views on National Teaching would surely have been highly influential among the priesthood, though they could only have been perceived as anachronistic by secular politicians.

The devotion of these administrators to the notion of a doctrinal orthodoxy was so strong that all but Maruyama founded or led one of the bureaucratically inspired Shintō sects in order to oppose the spread of Christianity and to promote National Teaching. They sought to organize such preexisting clienteles as the mountain ascetics, confraternities of the Ise and Izumo Shrines, and oshi and to make of them the embodiment of National Teaching.[43]

NATIONAL TEACHING IN PRACTICE

The signatories of this memorial were promoting closer ties between Shintō and the state, offering their services as teachers of law, local-level agents of social control. The services that Shintō figures in fact provided, however, were not quite so straightforward.

How the ideals of this memorial were implemented can be known from the memoirs of Tokoyo Nagatane. Among other things, Tokoyo was charged with establishing a Teaching Institute in Nagasaki during the Great Promulgation Campaign,[44] but his regular post was in Tokyo. His diary reveals aspects of National Teaching that were aired only when administrators were speaking among themselves.[45] Tokoyo's memoirs show that while most administrators assented to the idea that Shintō was the National Teaching and the basis of a Way of government, they were also committed to a variety of ideas that can only be called theological. They did not perceive any necessity to distinguish these theological stances from the "merely human" ideas identified with religion in the 1874 memorial. Their reluctance to address such a glaring inconsistency directly can only have been perceived by politicians and intellectuals as proof of Shintō's lack of sophistication. They fought to defend various positions on such questions as the following: the significance of the three creator deities,[46] how deities implant the soul in the human body, the location of the world of the dead, and the identity of deities ruling it.[47]

Shintō administrators called upon the priesthood to engage in proselytization (*fukyō*) by giving sermons on national law and policy. These sermons were performed in priestly vestments before altars of the kami, prayers were conducted, and audiences were led in making obeisance to deities and to the imperial house. Thus while Shintō administrators announced their intent to assume the job of making law and policy known, the settings created for the civics lessons closely resembled such acknowledged religious institutions as Buddhist temples, the churches of new religious movements like Tenrikyō,[48] and Christian churches. As for content, a parallel point exists in reference to deities and ritual. It may be that while Shintō administrators did not consciously intend to produce a state religion, in the sense that they possessed no such concept, they ended up with something that closely resembled one, or would have, had they succeeded in spreading it across the country.

Administrators did not perceive much inconsistency in saying in a memorial that they would promulgate law, and then doing so against a theological backdrop. For them, more serious problems arose in the establishment of sects of Shintō based on a historical founder's revelations. The religious agenda of such organizations as the rapidly growing Konkōkyō, Kurozumikyō, and Tenrikyō, all deeply involved in faith healing and the promotion of a very enthusiastic, evangelical spirituality, was not fully consonant with administrators' notions of what Shintō should be.[49] Although shrine administrators generally disliked these sects founded by revelation, they nevertheless depended heavily upon the revenue the sects contributed.

The idea of National Teaching was clearly incompatible with organizations founded by revelation, and administrators clearly perceived the incompatibility. Tokoyo Nagatane's own definition of Shintō was "a great Way of government, the basis and wellspring of *kokutai* (national polity); it is not a creed (*kyōhō*)."[50] He recognized that granting permission for sect ministers to preach as National Evangelists would allow them to promulgate their own, independent creeds alongside law and policy, and permit them to perform their own rituals of healing, blessing, and so on in combination with rites created by the state. The inevitable mixture of official and sectarian phenomena in the popular mind could only mar Shintō's appearance of a united front. There were sects of religions, but not of "great Ways of government." This was an inconsistency that Shintō administrators could not ignore, but they were powerless to prevent it.

However, once sects began to operate independently, the Shintō administrators lost revenue and initiative. After the Pantheon Dispute, they also lost state sponsorship for promulgation of any doctrinal orthodoxy.

The only way they could perpetuate any semblance of a unified Shintō identity was through sects they founded themselves. Thus Tanaka, Motoori, Otori, Hirayama, and Inaba became responsible for the creation or leadership of five of the thirteen Shintō sects: Jingūkyō, Taishakyō, Taiseikyō, Ontakekyō, and Shintō Taikyō.

Once involved in sects, shrine administrators could not avoid preaching and proselytizing. We have seen in Chapter 2 how the preaching of the Great Promulgation Campaign emphasized obedience to secular government. Nevertheless, in the context of sectarian preaching, the priesthood had to develop a consistent doctrine.

QUESTIONS OF DOCTRINE AND RITES

Shrine priests had no heritage of learning or of preaching a common doctrine. There was a tendency in the early Meiji period to assume that doctrine would emerge from National Learning, but there were several schools of National Learning, and since each was conducted as a private academy,[51] there was little opportunity for open discussion or a broad exchange of opinion. In practice, then, National Learning was a divisive force among the priesthood. The same was true of the Three Great Teachings of the Great Promulgation Campaign, because they could not command the same popular loyalty as the message of groups like Tenrikyō, Konkōkyō, and Kurozumikyō. The only way to avoid the intricacies of doctrinal conundrums was to lecture on the core values of the Tokugawa era: loyalty, filial piety, sincerity, diligence, humility, and thrift.

Taking refuge in the conventional morality was a safe strategy for the short run, but fraught with unforeseen consequences. On the one hand, no one denied the validity of these values, and they were so well known and universally proclaimed by other ideological agencies (the school, the military) that priests were in all cases preaching to the converted, and they could be sure of encountering no opposition. On the other hand, there was nothing distinctively Shintō about these values and, as some priests were eager to point out, it would be more accurate to identify them with Confucianism.[52] Conventional morality could be called Shintō only by equating Shintō with all that was traditional and hence could be called, if no one examined the historical grounds for the claim very carefully, "the ancient Way of the Japanese."[53]

Ultimately, in any discussion of Shintō's content beyond a recitation of law and policy, the word *Shintō* was only vaguely distinguished from conventional morality or National Learning in popular preaching. The field of shrine rites was, by comparison with doctrine, more unified and less problematic.

There was broad agreement among shrine priests on one point of ritual: people should be taught to participate in the cult of local tutelary deities.[54] Later National Learning figures of the Tokugawa era wrote widely on this theme. Priests' diaries reveal that the priesthood believed that worship of the tutelary gods would inculcate attitudes of reverence for all kami, not just the tutelary deities.[55]

Advocating worship of local tutelary deities included an element of self-service, because it was in shrines staffed by these same priests that the tutelary gods were to be worshiped. To worship them entailed the offerings and ritual fees that provided priests' livelihoods,[56] making support of the shrines equivalent to supporting priests. In general, then, priestly promotion of cults of tutelary deities translated into an advocacy of strong links between local people and their shrines, expressed as a parishioner (*ujiko*) relation, entailing obligations of material support for shrines and priests in return for the blessings of tutelary deities.

Shrine priests thus preached on loyalty, filial piety, and the cult of tutelary deities and linked these to the attitude of respect for the kami. This complex of ideas, cults, and attitudes was justified as a continuation of tradition. "We should revere the kami, be filial and loyal because this is the Japanese Way," because these are the attitudes that bind communities together and ultimately guarantee Japan's strength. This is to say that priests' advocacy of conventional morality and shrine patronage originated in a certain understanding of history and ethnic-racial identity; it did not well up out of religious experience or the faith and zeal that characterized those sects originating in a founder's revelations.[57]

Shintō administrators were not able to hold the line and impose unity within the Shintō world in such a way that their public pronouncements on doctrine, rites, and religion were entirely compatible with their actual conduct of religious activity. That new religious movements should have been beyond their control is perhaps inevitable, but what about Shintō priests outside the capital?

THE PROVINCIAL PRIESTHOOD

We have seen that in several respects there existed much variety and many contradictions in the views of Shintō administrators on Shintō and shrine life. Even more variety existed among lower-ranking priests in the provinces. We can sample this variety by comparing the experience of two priests from the same prefecture, serving shrines of the same rank. The diaries of Tanaka Sen'ya and Yamada Morii offer a valuable opportunity to learn of the actual implementation of state policy and the interpretations given Shintō in rural society.

The diary of a local priest like Tanaka Sen'ya (1826–1898) of Chichibu (present-day Saitama Prefecture), who had little contact with (and less interest in) Tokyo administrators of Shintō, reads much like that of a village mayor. Tanaka entered the priesthood in the spirit of public service and sacrifice so prominent in Meiji Japan's ethos.[58]

Tanaka was a local appointee to the shrine priesthood. His village mayor urged him to seek certification as a priest after prefectural policy ousted former Yoshida-Shirakawa licensees. Tanaka had been active in local government and served as the village accountant, and he had a long-standing interest in religious matters, actually conducting funeral rites years before his formal entry to the priesthood. Every page of his 617-page diary testifies to his deep concern for all aspects of social life and his sense of responsibility to contribute to it. He took on the job of priest with no expectation that he could make a living at it. In fact, all concerned were aware that to be a priest of a small, rural shrine was *not* a living. Hence it only made sense to appoint a man of sufficient substance to support himself from other resources, and old enough to devote time and energy to it without worrying about financial remuneration (Tanaka was in his late forties and could entrust cultivation of his land to his son).[59]

Unlike central administrators, Tanaka was not removed from local religious life; he was a dedicated participant. Before the Meiji Restoration, he had been involved in temple affairs and attended a wide variety of Buddhist rites[60] as well as shrine rites and such communal observances as *hi-machi*[61] and various confraternities.[62]

His case provides a useful reminder that just as the religious consciousness of the people did not immediately bifurcate in recognition of the 1868 fiat separating Buddhism and Shintō, neither did that of priests. Tanaka composed calligraphic scrolls for his parishioners invoking such Buddhist deities as Jizō with no apparent sense of contradiction. While Tokyo administrators sought to restrict the shrine pantheon to deities mentioned in the *Kojiki*, Tanaka increased popular support for his shrine by incorporating a local cult of a dog spirit.[63] Tokyo administrators urged the priesthood to limit their performance of healing and prayers for this-worldly benefits strictly, but Tanaka performed *kitō* (a catchall term for prayers for healing, well-being, prosperity, and other this-worldly benefits) regularly and was also available to exorcise fox spirits.[64] Thus he frequently chose to ignore the directives he received from Tokyo shrine administrators.

So little research has been carried out on the Meiji priesthood that it is impossible to say with any confidence that Tanaka Sen'ya was typical. Comparing him with another provincial priest of the same prefecture, Yamada Morii (1849–1907) of the Kawagoe Hikawa Shrine of Kawagoe City shows how much variety could coexist among priests of the same prefecture.[65]

Whereas Tanaka was a local appointee, Yamada had married into a Yoshida-licensed priestly family that passed over its first son in his favor.

Apparently he was chosen to allow the family to preserve its position in the shrine and simultaneously to purge itself of the stigma of Yoshida associations. Furthermore, Yamada Morii proved to possess formidable artistic and administrative skills.

The Muku Shrine in which Tanaka Sen'ya served had become a Prefectural Shrine by his death, but during his most active years it was small and rural, and while it had a laity-sponsored festival antedating the Meiji state's reform of shrine rites, Tanaka was one of only two priests.[66] The Kawagoe Hikawa Shrine, on the other hand, was also a Prefectural Shrine, but there the similarity ended. Located in a satellite city of Tokyo, it had a huge festival, numerous subordinate priests, and a powerful parishioners' group over which Yamada Morii had little control.

Tanaka Sen'ya had studied National Learning with a local figure of no distinction, but he continued his studies independently, researching the classics, reading widely, and taking on disciples of his own.[67] Yamada Morii had studied National Learning in Tokyo in his teens with Hirata Nobutane, successor to Atsutane and a figure of national prominence, and he quickly forgot the experience, if his silence in the diary is an accurate gauge of his interest.[68]

Tanaka Sen'ya maintained close, daily, direct, and sustained contact with his parishioners, whereas Yamada Morii left these matters to subordinate priests. Tanaka performed many funerals and preached vigorously in addition to the smorgasbord of rites for which he was available to his flock.[69] Yamada Morii performed rites only for his wealthiest parishioners, apparently, though he was a conscientious fund-raiser and maintained close contact with members of the city and prefectural government through such shared artistic pursuits as painting and poetry, losing no opportunity to promote closer ties between the shrine and government. To appear as a star at a poetry gathering was a traditional method of attracting the attention of local gentry.[70]

Tanaka Sen'ya was committed to the priesthood as a way to improve local solidarity and morality; he had a genuine reverence for the kami and little interest in theology. He had hardly any contact with Tokyo administrators except for receiving their directives and carefully discussing these with other local priests. Yamada Morii, on the other hand, was personally acquainted with the Tokyo elite, meeting often with Hirayama Seisai, Maruyama Sakura, and Motoori Toyokai, and frequently travelling to Tokyo on shrine business. Yamada was a bon vivant who loved to drink, and who achieved some fame as a painter of shrine scenes and of the 1868 imperial progress to the Hikawa Shrine. In this he contributed to a broader trend in the 1870s to paint *fukko yamato-e*, paintings in a traditional style (*yamato-e*) on the theme of "returning to the ancient way" (*fukko*). He received hundreds of commissions for calligraphy and painting; one of the subjects he returned to most frequently was portraits of Emperor Jinmu.[71] He also painted Buddhist subjects such as the Ten Worlds upon request.[72]

Neither man used the words National Teaching or *Shintō*. Tanaka Sen'ya preferred the term *honkyō*. He writes (p. 470) quite explicitly that shrines should not be confused with religion (*shūkyō*). In Yamada Morii's diary, except in the formal names of organizations, the term *Shintō* appears only once, in an entry of 1886 (p. 303), in which he says merely that he discussed various matters relating to Shintō. When the 1882 order prohibiting priests of National and Imperial Shrines from performing funerals was promulgated, Yamada was relieved and claimed always to have believed it a mistake for priests to get involved in funerals. Tanaka, however, signed a memorial deploring the decision (p. 250). Both men tended to leave philosophical debate on religion, Shintō, and doctrine to Tokyo administrators.

Tanaka Sen'ya and Yamada Morii were shrine priests of vastly different experience and personality, and even a brief contrast of the two suggests how different they were from Tokyo administrators of shrine affairs and from each other, though they were both priests of Prefectural Shrines of the same prefecture. It suggests further how mistaken it is to think of the Meiji priesthood as monolithic. Moreover, the shrine priests—vast as their internal variety was—were yet different from the ministers of those so-called Shintō sects that had originated in a founder's revelations.

CONCLUDING REMARKS

In early Meiji the cultural space for religion was in process of demarcation, both by rhetorical attempts at definition and by actual occupation of sectors of the field. The Shintō priesthood did not play an active role in straightforward efforts to define religion, but they occupied a turf broadly continuous with phenomena coming to be understood as religious. They rejected the label of religion. While administrators championed the alternative notion of a National Teaching, this idea seems to have failed to take hold among the provincial priesthood. Administrators could distinguish National Teaching from religion only on the quasi-theological grounds seen in the memorial of 1874, in terms of an ideology about the divine origins of the imperial house and its connection with Shintō. They propagated National Teaching/Shintō in a liturgical context and filled in the gaps with National Learning ideas. Making no bridge to popular shrine practice, priests were unable to create any popular enthusiasm for National Teaching. Tanaka Sen'ya fell back on local cults to sustain a following for his shrine, while Yamada Morii cultivated ties with Tokyo administrators and local city government and more or less ignored the real basis of popular attraction to his shrine, which probably lay in its large annual festival.

The priesthood tended to identify religion as a whole with Christianity; their dislike for Christianity hastened their conclusion that Shintō should not be regarded as a religion. At the same time, intellectuals were drawing the same conclusion, but for different reasons: they discerned in Shintō neither doctrine nor ethics. The result was a limited consensus that Shintō was not a religion.[73]

In spite of consensus on a distinction between Shintō and religion, however, the task of articulating a positive characterization of Shintō remained uncompleted. Shintō came to occupy an ill-defined, residual cultural space lacking positive identification. The priesthood created several neologisms in the effort to achieve an authoritative definition: National Teaching (*kokkyō*), Great Teaching (*taikyō*), and National Rites (*kokka no sōshi*).[74] None of them really gained currency. So long as these ideas lacked any connection with the cult life of shrines, not even the provincial priesthood could assimilate these terms except in a superficial way. Inevitably they remained empty verbiage, and the popular religious life of shrines went on, more or less unaffected by this unsuccessful attempt to produce a compelling ideology of Shintō's importance in political culture.

Rejecting the idea that Shintō was a religion, priests had no incentive to develop a standardized doctrine that would unite the priesthood, unify shrine practice, and help priests gain influence among the laity. Furthermore, priests' distrust of religious experience closed off revelation as a means of generating doctrine, and lack of philosophical training hindered the production of theology/ideology as a branch of learning.

In the realm of ethics, most priests seemed to assume that they could adopt the core values of the Tokugawa era as the ethics of Shintō. No one was prepared to answer the accusation that these values originated not in Shintō but in Confucianism. Similarly, the fact that these values were also the standard fare of sermons by Buddhist priests passed without serious effort at justification by shrine priests. Nor did shrine priests draw a connection between these values and the ritual life of particular shrines.

Abandoning ethics and doctrine left to shrine priests only the field of ritual, and that is where the priesthood came to concentrate its energies. Having no pre-Meiji heritage of common doctrine and ethics, priests did, however, share the assumption that, if nothing else, the role of the shrine priest called for the performance of rites for the kami. The history of Shintō after 1890 is largely a story of how the priesthood enlarged and codified shrine rites and promoted the notion that shrine rites were essential to the conduct of personal and political life.

The most obvious conclusion one must draw from these preliminary investigations into the character of the Shintō priesthood concerns its internal diversity. That it was not a monolithic body speaking with a single voice on the basis of a comprehensive, shared vision of a common enterprise is quite evident. And that conclusion is inescapable even if one leaves out of account those ministers of revelation-based sects like Kurozumikyō and Konkōkyō who were also certified as shrine priests. A more complete picture of the Meiji priesthood would have to include them, and the resulting image of diversity in the priesthood would be even stronger.

Nowhere is the internal diversity of the priesthood more evident than in the nature of their calling. Shrine administrators thought of themselves as bureaucrats and educators of the populace, not as religious leaders. The examples of Inaba Masakuni, Otori Sesso, Hirayama Seisai, and Maruyama Sakura suggest that the priesthood could provide a titled sinecure for politicians and loyalists left unemployed by the Meiji Restoration, a holding pool where they could make themselves useful until (in some cases) they could be drawn into more important areas of government. Tanaka Yoritsune promoted the interests of the Ise Grand Shrines by stressing their imperial connections, while Hirayama Seisai did the same for the Hikawa Shrine. Motoori Toyokai continually asserted the relevance of National Learning to the conduct of politics.

It was quite possible for provincial priests also to take up the priesthood without direct reference to the spiritual life—either of the laity or their own. Nevertheless, that concern was not entirely absent, as the example of Tanaka Sen'ya suggests. Provincial priests seem to have been more concerned, however, to promote the image of shrines as the node of an area's connection to government. Tanaka Sen'ya tried to build village solidarity through shrine activity, while Yamada Morii used his artistic pursuits to promote strong ties to local, prefectural, and national government. Both spent much time distributing talismans and almanacs from the Ise Shrines, symbolically asserting that their shrines were branches or representatives of Ise, entitled to represent an imperial presence in the village or town, and simultaneously suggesting that their shrines had imperial authorization. Neither shrine administrators nor provincial priests based their activities on religious experience such as revelation or conversion.

Another conclusion concerns the relation of the priesthood to the state. We saw in the memorial of 1874 that shrine administrators had to assume the attitude of supplicant, and that their views did not prevail. In the early Meiji period it is inaccurate to identify the priesthood with the national bureaucracy as if they shared a blueprint for what Shintō should be, or as if Shintō at this time were a state religion (except in the wilder dreams of some shrine administrators). Similarly, if one examines the relation of provincial priests to local and prefectural governments, it is apparent that the character of relations varied widely even within a single prefecture.

4. Shrines and the Rites of Empire

Part I: Shintō Shrines

FOR THE PURPOSE of gaining an understanding of the relations between Shintō and the state, it is important to study shrines and their rites in tandem. There is an intimate and obvious connection between them, yet shrines and rites are also separate and independent in the sense that they have distinct histories, each of which must be understood in order to see how the two together functioned in the context of Shintō's relation to the state. This chapter and the next, on the rites of Shintō shrines, then, are two parts of a single whole. The significance of the issues set out in the early sections of this chapter will become clear through the next, and the conclusions one can draw from both will be set out at the end of Chapter 5.

Shrine rites of the Meiji and subsequent periods have taken place in an institutional context different from any previous era of Japanese religious history. Shintō was created as an independent body by a state policy separating it from Buddhism. For the first time all the shrines were organized in a single hierarchy, and each member of the populace was systematically affiliated with a shrine. The highest-ranking shrines received state support, and their priests had the status of national civil servants. The state played an important role in determining the deities worshiped in shrines, and all shrines were encouraged to worship deities with a national, patriotic significance. In particular, the state attempted to universalize the cult of the Ise deities and to promote a cult of the war dead. Both cults were enacted at central cult places, and local areas staged coordinated rites in village, town, and prefectural shrines.

Construction of the Meiji Shrine marked the first time a shrine had ever been constructed with labor and monetary donations from all over the country, a project inconceivable without active state support. For the first time in history shrines were constructed outside of Japan, in the colonies of the Japanese empire. An entirely new ritual calendar was established by state initiative, and many customary observances—domestic rites, kin-group rites, rites of territorial and occupational groups—came to be performed by Shintō priests at shrines where previously they had been performed informally. An elaborate program to involve schoolchildren in shrine rites was universalized. These changes, coming as they did after centuries of Shintō's subordination to Buddhism and a long history of a purely local focus in shrine life, were truly revolutionary and succeeded in radically changing the character of Japanese religiosity.

Even as these revolutionary changes were taking place, however, most shrines continued to perform rites and festivals of a purely local scope, so that shrines assumed a double character of national and local significance. Popular consciousness of shrines changed. Since shrines constituted one important link between local society and the state, local elites generally welcomed the chance to capitalize on this new opportunity. People began to perceive in shrines a vehicle for the promotion of themselves and their local areas.

Japan held many state rites between 1868 and 1945, and some of the country's most important ceremonials, such as those festivities surrounding the promulgation of the constitution and the funeral for Emperor Meiji, took place in public spaces, some of them newly created, not in shrines. It is undeniable that such ceremonies were essential to the state's image and presentation of itself to its subjects; in a broad sense these rites of the state that did not take place at shrines were part of the rites of the empire. In any study of the modern Japanese state's public presentation, they would have to occupy center stage. Nevertheless, I have not included them here because, while they sometimes included a role for a shrine priest, they were not dominantly or exclusively Shintō in character.

One could argue that such state rites did, however, sometimes borrow the symbols, paraphernalia, and liturgical structure of shrine rites. One could also point out that the state went to some lengths to instill in the populace attitudes of reverence for the state, focused upon the person of the emperor, and that such attitudes were directly continuous with the attitudes approved for worshipers at shrines. In their symbolism and emotional patterning, then, state rites such as those for the promulgation of the constitution owed much to Shintō.

While such rites were dependent upon Shintō in the ways just mentioned, however, they were not Shintō in an institutional sense. They were not planned or executed primarily by the Shintō priesthood; they did not take place in the prototypical Shintō institution, the shrine. At most they had a vaguely Shintō ambience. To call such rites Shintō, and to think of them as properly a part of State Shintō, is to open the floodgates to muddy notions of Shintō as encompassing anything Japanese, and hence to lose all precision in investigating the topic of State Shintō. That result being intolerable, this chapter limits itself to shrine rites invented, controlled, or performed by members of the priesthood at shrines, and school ritual.

THE SEPARATION OF BUDDHISM FROM SHINTŌ

After centuries during which shrines had generally operated as part of a temple-shrine complex controlled by the Buddhist priesthood, the idea of separating the two was highly novel, and it stemmed in no small part from the pent-up resentment of the shrine priests at their enforced subordination to Buddhism.

The subject of the separation of Shintō and Buddhism (*Shinbutsu bunri*) has been extensively explored from the standpoint of Buddhism's losses, and it has often been pointed out that there was much resistance to the policy: but what did the policy mean for shrine life?[1] The research on the significance of this policy for Buddhism rests on painstaking research on each prefecture; no comparable body of documentation for shrines has yet been assembled, and thus it is impossible to generalize with confidence. Nevertheless, an examination of some relevant documents and case studies will help to clarify the situation.

The policy to separate Buddhism from Shintō was implemented at the local level in a variety of ways, and local administrations enjoyed considerable autonomy. A document of 1867 cautioned officials of Taishidō Village near Tokyo that separation of the two was on no account to be equated with the abolition of Buddhism, suggesting that here as elsewhere the government's policy was implemented with a vengeance.[2] In many areas, Buddhism came under severe attack and lost many of its assets and much of its prestige. Combined with loss of land, the situation was grave indeed.

Let us examine two examples of the implementation of the separation: the Miwa Shrine and the experience of those shrine-temple complexes formerly operated by mountain ascetics. The Miwa Shrine in Nara Prefecture had been linked with several temples during its long history, giving rise to a lineage theology known as Miwa Shintō, heavily influenced by Shingon doctrine and emphasizing a series of esoteric initiations (*kanjō*). The shrine was traditionally served by both male and female priests, and eighteenth-century texts describe a tradition of healing priestesses who performed vigils, sun worship, prayers, and sacred dance at the shrine. The shrine was distinctive in having no object of worship but the mountain of the site.

After severing all ties with Buddhism, in 1871 the shrine was declared a

Major Imperial Shrine, the highest rank except for the Ise Grand Shrines. The eighteen hereditary priestly positions were abolished and the priests dispersed. Leadership of the shrine was apparently assumed by men appointed by central administrators in Tokyo. An official history of the shrine completed in 1873 managed to omit all reference to Buddhism.

Previously the shrine had had attached to it a number of subsidiary shrines for the worship of such popular deities as Inari (the rice god) and Konpira Daigongen (a sea god principally associated with a pilgrimage site in Shikoku). Since these deities had no connection to the patriotic deities whose cult central administrators were eager to promote, their shrines were of no interest. Accordingly, these subsidiary shrines were severed from all connection with the Miwa Shrine.

During the Great Promulgation Campaign, a Small Teaching Institute was established in the Miwa Shrine, and its priests became National Evangelists. In 1882 this institute was converted to a church for preaching Shintō, called the Miwa Kyōkai. Among other activities, the church and shrine performed rites for victory in war and in 1924 established a confraternity to "protect the imperial house."[3]

The experience of the Miwa Shrine suggests that during the separation of Buddhism and Shintō long-standing sacerdotal lineages could be summarily dismissed in an effort to purify an institution of Buddhist influence, that a shrine's history could be rewritten so as to suppress the reality of Buddhism's dominant influence, and that a shrine could be transformed in alignment with state policy without meeting effective resistance from priests or lay adherents. It suggests further that a shrine could quickly become a place for the propagation of state-approved doctrine, ritual, and communal activity of a religious nature.

It seems likely that local people may have tolerated the change in the shrine's character because they saw an opportunity to create closer links to the state that would enhance their own prestige and that of the area. It may also be possible that much popular worship and festival at the shrine were actually unaffected by these changes. If that was indeed the case, there would have been little incentive to challenge the designation of the shrine as Major Imperial Shrine, a title that called attention to the whole area and entailed support for the shrine from the national government. In exchange for all this attention, tolerating state manipulation of the shrine may have seemed a small price to pay, jettisoning the hereditary priests, their esoteric rites and doctrines a small sacrifice.

Different dynamics were involved in separating Buddhism from Shintō at temple-shrine complexes where mountain ascetics were powerful. The mountain ascetics were outlawed in 1871, after which they had to join either the Shintō or Buddhist priesthood or return to lay life. Many former yamabushi joined the Shintō priesthood, thus "converting" overnight from their former religious identities. The former yamabushi of the temple-shrine complexes at Mitsumine-zan in Saitama Prefecture apparently went over to Shintō en masse and transformed this pilgrimage site into a shrine. It seems highly likely, however, that fundamental change in religious consciousness took much longer, and that the Shintō-ization of the yamabushi remained fragmentary and incomplete for some time, if indeed it was ever fully accomplished.

Whereas pre-Meiji yamabushi temples frequently worshiped deities called *gongen*, usually closely associated with the mountain to which the ascetics were devoted, after the Restoration there was a systematic effort to relabel these deities with Shintō-sounding names. This renaming was a way to reassign the *gongen* to Shintō, although they had not been regarded as necessarily either Buddhist or Shintō before 1868. These campaigns enjoyed success in some areas, such as the Dewa Sanzan in northern Japan, while pilgrimage sites in the Yoshino area had reverted to Buddhist rites by 1888.[4]

Separating Buddhism from Shintō was the first step in linking the whole populace to shrines as their parishioners. That linkage was accomplished through a policy of shrine registration.

SHRINE REGISTRATION

In the Meiji period, for the first time in Japanese religious history, shrine affiliations became universal, obligatory, and defined as nonreligious in character. Compared to the pre-Meiji shrine guilds (*miyaza* and other terms), which restricted parishioner status to local elites, the new system was highly egalitarian in extending shrine affiliation to all Japanese.

A short-lived plan for using shrine registration as the basis for a national census contributed to a fundamental change in the relation among shrine priests, parishioners, and the nation. Known as the *ujiko shirabe*, this plan lasted only from 1871 to 1873. It closely resembled the use of Buddhist temple registration for census data in the Tokugawa period. In the Meiji analogue, parents reported the birth of a child to the ward head, who gave them a certificate assigning the child to the parents' shrine of registration. Upon presenting this certificate to the priest of the shrine, the priest registered the child as a parishioner (*ujiko*) of that shrine and presented the parents with a protective talisman. The parents paid tribute to the shrine in the child's name.[5]

Although the census function of shrine registration soon ended, shrine affiliation remained an essential part of local government. The status of parishioner and the notion that everyone was obligated to support a local shrine endured even when in the mid-Meiji period parishioners' associations again assumed a hierarchical character. Everyone became a parishioner automatically, regardless of personal religious beliefs. As early as 1879 government directives maintained that this status did not have a religious character, in response to Buddhists of the True Pure Land school who resisted shrine registration on religious grounds.[6]

SHRINE RANKINGS

One of the earliest Meiji shrine policies was to assign a rank to each shrine in the nation, placing the Ise Grand Shrines at the head of them all. The underlying idea of the Ise Grand Shrines as the ancestral and protective shrine of the whole nation can be traced to the eighth century, but it was not a prominent element of popular consciousness until the late nineteenth century at the earliest.[7] In the medieval period, when a new overlord took power, the people in his bailiwick adopted worship of his clan deity as a mark of their submission to his authority. The Meiji expression of this pattern is to be seen in the placement of Ise as highest shrine in the nation, to which all Japanese were putatively connected by a tie of common descent from the imperial house and a concomitant obligation of obeisance.[8]

To the extent that popular society perceived these changes, the reaction was favorable. It is doubtful that most people even noticed the change that took place when all the shrines were linked in a single hierarchy. Where people were aware of change, however, they were generally pleased to have the gods they worshiped locally recognized by the new government.[9] For one thing, they were encouraged to incorporate deities having some patriotic significance into their pantheon, and if that change were successfully accomplished, their shrine could assume the title of *jinja*. This term for shrine first came to be widely used in Meiji, superseding a number of less august-sounding terms. To most people, the new title for the local shrine sounded like a promotion, suggesting an elevation of the status of the area and its people.[10] That the incorporation of new deities could fundamentally change the character of shrine life was not immediately apparent.

There were two major divisions in the shrine ranking system and a number of subcategories. The two principal categories were "government shrine" (*kansha*) and "civic shrine" (*minsha*); government shrines received financial support from public funds of the central government, and the civic shrines did not. In addition, the category of Special Shrine (*bekkakusha*) was created to include newly founded shrines dedicated to national heroes and the war dead. The Special Shrines are discussed later in this chapter. In the category of government shrines were those shrines ranked as Imperial Shrine (*kanpeisha*) and National Shrine (*kokuheisha*). There were Major, Middle, and Minor grades of both Imperial and National Shrines. The Imperial Shrines as a class received significantly more financial support from the government than the National Shrines. In the category of civic shrines were Prefectural, District, Town/Village, and Unranked Shrines (*kensha, gōsha, chōsha, sonsha, mukakusha*). These shrines received support from the level of government to which they were pegged (prefecture, county, town, or village) and from parishioners' groups consisting as a matter of course of those persons residing within the territory of the shrine's customary jurisdiction. The shrine rankings may be schematized as follows:

ISE GRAND SHRINES

Government Shrines	Civic Shrines	Special Shrines
Imperial Shrine (Major, Middle, Minor Grades)	Prefectural Shrine	
	District Shrine	
National Shrine (Major, Middle, Minor Grades)	Town Shrine	
	Village Shrine	
	Unranked Shrine	

Table 5 gives a summary of the change in the number of shrines from 1879 to 1929. Part A shows that the number of government shrines roughly doubled during that period, and Part B demonstrates that the number of civic shrines rose until 1889, then decreased steadily until 1929. The most significant factor in the decrease was the shrine merger policy of 1906 to 1911. This policy, discussed below, mandated a single shrine per village or town administrative unit, seeking to align shrine territories with the boundaries of civil administration. To achieve this goal it was necessary to merge or abolish thousands of shrines.

Throughout the period it was a matter of great frustration for the priests of civic shrines that they and their shrines received no support from the national government. There was extreme local variation in the level of

5. Government and Civic Shrines, 1879–1929

	A. Government Shrines				B. Civic Shrines
	Major Imperial Shrine	Middle Imperial Shrine	Minor Imperial Shrine	Special Shrine	
1879	30	12	2	10	176,722
1889	33	22	6	20	193,133
1899	41	28	3	21	191,709
1906	43	26	3	23	190,365
1909	43	26	3	23	147,270
1919	53	22	4	23	115,016
1929	55	24	5	24	111,699

SOURCE: Naimushō jinja kyoku, *Jinja ni kansuru tōkei sho* (Tokyo: Naimushō, 1933), chart 1, p.1.

support accorded civic shrines, and in any single area the priesthood had no guarantee that the level of support it received in a given year would be continued dependably. In public opinion the prestige of priests of civic shrines was considerably lower than that of priests of the government shrines. Whereas priests of government shrines had the status of national civil servants, priests of civic shrines had no such prestige or security. It appears that the great majority of priests of civic shrines had to take by-employment to support themselves, and many had charge of many more shrines than they could serve adequately. They had to depend on the changing whims of local constituencies in a way that priests of government shrines did not. Priests of civic shrines were obliged to defer to parishioners and to bend to prevailing sentiments about the conduct of local rites and festivals, while the priests of government shrines had much greater autonomy and could represent themselves as members of the national bureaucracy, and hence entitled to respect on that basis, quite apart from the loyalty of traditional adherents of the shrines they served.

This, then, was the hierarchy within which all shrines functioned from the 1870s until 1945. Not surprisingly, all shrines were significantly affected by the nation's head shrine, the Ise Grand Shrines. The nature of their concrete connection to the apex of the hierarchy is discussed in the next section.

DISTRIBUTION OF ISE TALISMANS AND ALMANACS

From 1871 the support of the Ise Shrines was entirely underwritten by the state. An administrative reform abolished hereditary succession to the Ise priesthood, the former division between Inner and Outer Shrines was abandoned, and a single priestly hierarchy put in charge of the whole. The oshi, who formerly managed popular pilgrimage to Ise, were abolished, and the newly unified Ise priesthood took charge of conveying commoners' offerings to the shrines. It had traditionally been the practice to bestow a talisman of the shrine upon pilgrims, and almanacs published by the shrine had been widely distributed by oshi before the Meiji Restoration.[11]

In one sense the chief business of the Ise Shrines between 1868 and 1945 was the promotion of Ise as an institution to which all Japanese were connected; it was a main focal point of the myth of the unification of the populace. The distribution of talismans was an important aspect of this presentation. In a variety of local patterns, Ise talismans were distributed by local shrine priests and ward heads, or by shrine priests and officers of local government working together. Diaries of shrine priests show that annual distribution of talismans was the occasion for considerable interaction between priests and local politicians and between priests and parishioners.[12]

The distribution of Ise talismans and almanacs became a major activity of Shintō priests of all areas and ranks. It was this pervasive participation of virtually all shrine priests in distributing Ise talismans to their parishioners that constituted the palpable basis for the claim that all shrines in the nation were in some vague sense branches of Ise, and that the Ise Grand Shrines were the principal shrine center of the nation.

Talismans were distributed annually throughout Japan. Recipients paid a fee for them, and while it varied locally, it was generally quite a negligible sum.[13] Priests were instructed to give them to the indigent gratis. Talismans were to be enshrined in the domestic altar to the kami, and it was expected that every household had such an altar, a *kamidana*. Priests encouraged people to acquire and maintain domestic altars, to place Ise talismans in them as an object of worship, and to perform obeisance before the altar daily.

Nevertheless, it sometimes happened that people refused the Ise talisman. In the records of Taishidō Village, a document of 1874 instructs priests not to use coercion in talisman distribution; receiving talismans is to be left to the faith of the individual.[14] We find in the periodicals of the national association of the priesthood even in the twentieth century many queries to the editors on this point. In fact, however, a government order of 1878 had established the principle that people were free to refuse the talisman.[15]

That the queries should have continued suggests that the priesthood was not fully aware of government policy. Further, it suggests that pressure was sometimes exerted to universalize the acceptance of Ise talismans. While this sort of thing is difficult to document, it seems likely that members of the True Pure Land school of Buddhism,[16] left-leaning liberals, and Christians would have been in the vanguard of those refusing the talismans.

THE ISE SHRINES AND THEIR OUTPOSTS

A priest of the Ise Shrines in the early Meiji period, Urata Nagatami (1840–1893), conceived of a plan to spread the cult of the Ise deities by establishing outposts of the shrine in every prefecture. A total of some seventy shrines for this purpose, called Daijingū or Kōtai Jingū, were established. Most of these were existing shrines, but others were newly constructed, and some were "places for worship from afar" (*yōhaisho*), buildings too small to be called a shrine or be served by a resident priest.[17] Urata intended these outposts to receive official worship and tribute from prefectural governors, thus becoming local-level centers for state rites. These provincial branches of the Ise Shrines would both popularize worship of the Ise deities and lend a patriotic, state-authorized air to their cult. In this way shrines would provide a focus of awareness of national identity, symbolically integrating the local level into the nation, reminding local people of their obligations to the state through the medium of rites stressing the state's connection to a sacred realm.[18]

The connection of the provincial Daijingū or Kōtai Jingū to the Ise Shrines was more symbolic than real. A rite of "dividing the spirit" (*bunreishiki*) was performed so that a portion of the supernatural substance of the Ise deities was transferred to the object of worship in the new shrine (generally a round, polished, metal mirror). Thereafter the new shrine might collect money for Ise or provide housing for the proselytizing arm of the Ise Shrines, called Jingūkyō, but the new shrine had complete autonomy from the Ise priesthood and was responsible for its own upkeep.[19]

Besides the function of spreading the Ise cult, the provincial Daijingū and Kōtai Jingū also seem to have been designed symbolically to protect the nation by stationing supernatural aid at strategic points of entry by foreign elements. Four of the most significant of these local-level Kōtai Jingū were located at the port cities of Nagasaki, Yokohama, Kōbe, and Niigata.

The Niigata priesthood petitioned for a branch of the Ise Shrines to be built in order to counter the area's longstanding allegiance to Buddhism.[20] The founder of the Niigata Daijingū, Kanda Yukitane, was an adherent of National Learning who preached in the Niigata area during the Great Promulgation Campaign. He founded some thirty-six Shintō confraternities and was largely responsible for collecting the funds for constructing the shrine, completed in 1889. Even in 1879 he claimed some two hundred thousand followers in the area, suggesting that he enjoyed some success in promulgating the Ise cult.[21]

The founding documents of the Niigata Daijingū explain that the shrine would promulgate all matters of state, demonstrate to the people the unity of government and rites, lead the people to a correct teaching, and ward off foreign religions.[22] This last point is of interest in illustrating the notion attributing to shrines and their deities a magical power to protect against influences that might be evil, foreign, and impure.

According to its founding documents, the Yokohama Ise Yama Kōtai Jingū, which was located on a great promontory overlooking the harbor and was declared the city's protective shrine in 1870, echoed the Niigata shrine's supposed apotropaic efficacy:

This port is the site of mixed residence [referring to foreigners residing in Yokohama] and commerce of peoples and thus is a place where it is most necessary to unify the hearts of the [Japanese] people (*sadame jinshin o kōketsu suru*). If this [unification] is not accomplished, there will come a day of great calamity. . . . [The shrine must] proclaim the unity of rites and government to the people and be a witness to the divine authority of the imperial nation to the outside world.[23]

Later documents speak repeatedly of the shrine's function in unifying the hearts and minds of the populace. This Yokohama shrine was in fact conceived of as a measure to prevent the spread of Christianity.[24]

Some of the local-level Daijingū originated not in the plans of the priesthood but through popular initiative based on a variety of motives. The Kōbe Daijingū began with a request from local merchants and innkeepers to build a shrine to exhibit to foreigners the power of the kami. They volunteered land after having regularly participated in "worship from afar" (*yōhai*) of the Ise deities and because they wanted to express their devotion on a larger scale. They paid all costs of the shrine.[25] In another case of popular initiative, a commoner named Nakanishi Genpachi requested and was granted permission to build a Daijingū on private land in Tokyo. Permission was revoked, however, when it was discovered that he was merely pocketing all contributions offered by local people who came to pay tribute there.[26]

Some Daijingū originated in the resettlement of people after the Restoration. A Daijingū was founded in Kyoto Prefecture when some three hundred former itinerant merchants were resettled in the area. They petitioned for permission to build a Daijingū because there was no shrine in the area, and they agreed to bear all costs. They enshrined a god of wealth and the mountain deity as well as Amaterasu, apical ancestress of the imperial house, sun goddess, and chief among the Ise deities. In early Meiji the government resettled numerous former samurai and had them take up agriculture in Fukushima. In 1875 a group of ten of them petitioned for the building of a Daijingū to serve them. Similarly, some 163 shrines were established in Hokkaidō as lesser branches of the Ise Grand Shrines.[27] An important Tokyo shrine known as the Tokyo Daijingū originated in a "worship from afar" site built in early Meiji.[28]

In addition to prefectural Daijingū and Kōtai Jingū, *yōhaisho* and *yōhaiden* (the terms are interchangeable) began to be built around the country in the early 1870s as part of the effort to universalize the Ise cult. These abbreviated cult centers were apparently most used by areas not having easy access to a shrine served by a full-time priest. All provincial officials were to perform worship from afar on the annual festival for Emperor Jinmu, April 3. They were to face the direction of the Ise Grand Shrines and offer up a sprig of *sakaki*.[29] Area residents also assembled for brief worship of the Ise deities on other festival days of the national calendar. As in the case of the Tokyo Daijingū, some of the yōhaisho later became shrines.

THE STATE-SPONSORED CULT OF THE WAR DEAD AND LOYALISTS

In earlier sections of this chapter, we traced the evolution of policies that linked all shrines in a single hierarchy, linked the entire populace to shrines as parishioners, installed deities with national or patriotic significance in virtually all the shrines of the nation, and attempted to universalize the worship of the Ise deities. Another important area of state initiative in shrine life was a concerted and sustained effort to promote a cult of the war dead and historic loyalists. Though not entirely separate from the phenomena discussed earlier, the cult depended upon the creation of the Special Shrines (chief among them the Yasukuni Shrine), local-level shrines for the war dead (*shōkonsha*), so-called Nation-Protecting Shrines (*gokoku jinja*), and hundreds of lesser war memorials (*chūkonhi* and other terms).

The Special Shrines eventually numbered twenty-seven. In principle they enshrined persons who had loyally served the emperor. For example, the Minatogawa Shrine, established in 1872, enshrined Kusunoki Masashige, a fourteenth-century loyalist who served the ill-fated Emperor Daigo. The Takeisao Shrine, established in 1875, enshrined the strongman and would-be shogun Oda Nobunaga, while his fellow "unifiers" of the sixteenth century, Toyotomi Hideyoshi and Tokugawa Ieyasu, were enshrined at the Hōkoku Shrine (established 1873) and the Nikkō Tōshōgū (made a Special Shrine in 1873). Unlike those Special Shrines having only a single deity, the Yasukuni Shrine enshrined all those who died on the loyalist side in the Meiji Restoration or in national wars after that time.[30]

The Yasukuni Shrine received respect exceeded only by that accorded the Ise Grand Shrines. The special status of this shrine derived from the fact that the emperor himself paid tribute there to the souls of the war dead. The significance of enshrining the soul of a human being in Yasukuni is that the rite of enshrining is an apotheosis symbolically changing the soul's status to that of a national deity. Accordingly, it ceases to be a mere ancestor of some household and instead attaches to the nation. When the emperor paid tribute at Yasukuni, the head priest handed him a sprig of the sakaki plant, which he held for some time, eventually returning it to the priest to place upon the altar. In no other case did the emperor so honor the enshrined souls of commoners. For this reason it was believed to be a great honor to be enshrined there. Enshrinement was a privilege bestowed by the emperor; it was not a right.[31]

Until 1895 only those who actually died in battle were enshrined there; those who died of wounds later were excluded and thought disgraced. The following example illustrates, however, how this exclusionary clause could sometimes be modified. A soldier named Kuga Noboru was believed to have died in the fighting in China in 1931, and he was scheduled to be enshrined as a deity in the Yasukuni Shrine. In fact, however, he had been captured by the Chinese. When he recovered from his wounds, he escaped and made his way back to the Japanese forces, where he committed suicide to atone for the shame of being captured. He was removed from the list of people to be enshrined in Yasukuni, but there was so much public interest in his case that he was enshrined by special dispensation.[32] Thus a figure whose manner of death technically disqualified him could become a deity at Yasukuni if in some other way he exemplified the appropriate spirit of loyalty and self-sacrifice.

The Yasukuni Shrine was a powerful vehicle for the glorification of war in general and of death in battle in particular. Emperor Meiji announced the beginning of the Russo-Japanese War with a visit to the shrine, and after the victory a tremendous celebration took place there, in which all troops in Tokyo and a representative from every military unit in the country paid tribute. In all, Emperor Meiji paid tribute at Yasukuni seven times. The Taishō emperor went twice, and up through the defeat in 1945 Emperor Hirohito paid twenty visits, always as supreme commander, in military uniform.[33]

National awareness of the Yasukuni Shrine of course did not arise spontaneously, concurrent with its founding. But that it did come to play a central role in popular thought is indisputable. During the 1870s and 1880s, the shrine's annual festival was a rather quiet affair, but in the 1890s, and especially after the Russo-Japanese War, Yasukuni was increasingly prominent in popular consciousness. In its early days, Yasukuni's annual festival featured horse racing and sumō wrestling, as well as a fireworks display. An especially large-scale festival following the Sino-Japanese War featured a visit by the emperor and empress, and after this time more and more military weapons and equipment were placed on permanent display. In the festival of 1898 the whole area was decorated with national flags and sacred rope (*shimenawa*), and free cigarette coupons were given away during the fireworks (unfortunately, at least one person was killed in the scramble for these coupons). A newspaper editorial took the occasion to say that whereas the shrine had previously been regarded as the preserve of military people, now that "every subject is a soldier," everyone should regard the shrine with personal concern and see in its rites a form of spiritual education. The latter point was especially directed to schoolchildren, who should realize that one day they might have the honor of dying for the nation.[34]

Around 1893 a board game became highly popular with schoolchildren, in which the quickest way to win was to land on a certain square by a role of the dice. "Death" in that position took the player to instant enshrinement at Yasukuni. This game, reinforced by the custom of school trips to Yasukuni, carried a powerful message.[35] The notion that death in battle followed by enshrinement at Yasukuni was in fact a victory was voiced even by bereaved survivors, as in this statement by one widow:

The Fukugawa household (*ie*), which up to now has been mere poor peasants, has now become the fine house of a hero, the house of the military nation, upon which the honor of the Japanese people shines. That's what the Mayor said. I also heard that the emperor himself pays tribute at the Yasukuni Shrine, where my husband is enshrined. I must never allow such an honored household to die out.[36]

This testimony shows how directly Yasukuni was linked in popular thought to ancestor worship and to the high priority given to perpetuation of the family line.

By 1906 the annual festival of Yasukuni had been expanded to a three-day event in which all manner of amusements (including all those previously mentioned plus *nō* drama and geisha dancing) were available. The emperor and empress attended enshrinement rites for the new war dead, and survivors came in such great numbers (making use of specially issued discount train tickets) that they could not all be accommodated. These large-scale annual festivities grew throughout the period.

PROVINCIAL CENTERS OF THE CULT OF THE WAR DEAD

As Ise had its provincial branches in the Kōtai Jingū, so Yasukuni found a symbolic echo in the hundreds of war memorials and local-level shrines for the war dead, the shōkonsha. Some of these shrines originated as burial grounds for the war dead. Even by 1876 some 105 shrines for loyalists of the Restoration were receiving state support. In 1901 all these shrines were made shōkonsha. In addition, another thirty-three were recognized as private memorials, and in 1939, all of them were renamed Nation-Protecting Shrines (*gokoku jinja*).[37]

After the Russo-Japanese War, there were large-scale moves to erect war memorials in every prefecture. The writer Lafcadio Hearn, who lived for many years in Japan, recorded this testimony by a father upon seeing his son's name inscribed upon a memorial, showing clearly that local-level war memorials could inspire much the same sentiments as Yasukuni.

I married very young and for a long time had no children. My wife finally bore a son and died. My son grew up fine and healthy. Then he joined the emperor's forces in the Seinan War and died a manly death in southern Kyushu in a great battle. I loved my son. When I heard that he had died for the emperor, I cried with joy, because for my warrior son there could be no finer death. My son was buried on a mountaintop near Kumamoto. I went there to care for the grave. My son's name was carved on a war memorial for those from Izumo who had fallen for the emperor's sake. I felt glad when I saw my son's name there. I talked with him and felt that he was again walking by my side beneath a great pine tree.[38]

The growth in building war memorials was sponsored by towns, private individuals, and reservists (Teikoku zaigō gunjin kai, founded in 1910). Once a monument was completed, annual services were held at the site to commemorate local men who had died in battle. Such services commonly included both Shintō and Buddhist rites.[39] It is important to note, however, that most war memorials were erected not in shrines or temples, but in such places as schoolyards.[40]

The modern period has seen an unprecedented involvement of the state with shrine affairs, entailing the separation of Buddhism from Shintō, a universal system of shrine ranking, universal affiliation of the populace with shrines, state support for shrines, and state promotion of cults of the Ise deities and of the war dead. In addition to these phenomena, the period saw two further developments that lacked any parallel in previous religious history: the construction of a shrine using contributions of money and labor from all areas of the nation in the establishment of the Meiji Shrine, and state promotion of shrine construction outside Japan, in the colonies of the empire. We turn next to examine these two developments.

THE MEIJI SHRINE

The Emperor Meiji ruled for forty-five years, from 1867 to 1912. He presided over a period of truly revolutionary change in Japanese history, and when he died the sense of an ending was widespread. More visible to the populace than any previous (and perhaps subsequent) emperor, he was genuinely beloved. Tens of thousands came to kneel in the palace grounds when it was reported that the end was near, and shrines and temples all over the country prayed continuously for his recovery. When all these hopes failed, it was inevitable that he would be deified and worshiped in a great shrine.

Construction began at the site in the Yoyogi area of Tokyo in 1915, but because of a great rise in construction costs after World War I and a severe labor shortage, the project lost momentum and seemed doomed. Then in an unprecedented mobilization of youth groups and other civic associations from all over the country, the shrine was completed in 1920. Thousands of people had contributed their labor and money to the project.[41]

Shintō's long history before the Meiji Restoration consisted mainly of the relatively autonomous activities of shrines, supported by local people putatively under the protection of shrine deities. Exceptions to this generalization include the Tokugawa-period practice of Ise pilgrimage and other transregional pilgrimage shrines, as well as the opportunity to see shrine treasures of such shrines when these were displayed in exhibitions (*kaichō*) in Edo or Osaka. Never before had people from every area and social station been invited to think of themselves as having a rightful connection to a national cult center. Never before had a shrine become the recipient of labor and donations. In that sense, the construction of the Meiji Shrine was a truly significant event in Shintō history. This event undoubtedly could not have come about without the state's active promotion.[42]

As in the case of provincial Kōtai Jingū, provincial cult centers of the Meiji Shrine offered irresistible opportunities for self-aggrandizement. The following example will illustrate one side of the new popular consciousness of shrines. Beginning in 1912, this incident has to do with a yōhaisho of the Meiji Shrine, i.e., a provincial place from which to perform obeisance to the shrine. Since it is highly suggestive in several ways, we will discuss it at length.[43]

In Akita Prefecture a local mayor named Shindō Shigekichi was tremendously moved by Emperor Meiji's death and determined to commemorate him by opening a yōhaisho at which to worship him. Through the good offices of an Akita man in the Home Ministry, Shindō secured an item of Emperor Meiji's clothing that he planned to make the official object of worship of the yōhaisho. He had local school pupils attend the yōhaisho's opening ceremonies. In all this Shindō's stated desire was to increase awareness of and a sense of gratitude to the departed emperor among local people. A success in this field would also increase his own political capital.

Unfortunately, a law of 1886 had made it illegal to establish new shrines by private initiative, and furthermore Shindō had not employed a qualified Shintō priest at the opening ceremonies. To make matters worse, yōhaisho were not supposed to have objects of worship enshrined within them, so the facility lacked official standing entirely. That being the case, the attendance of school pupils became illegal, since they could not be asked to pay tribute at unrecognized shrines of any kind.

Shindō was not to be so easily defeated, however. His position was that even if there had been errors in the registration process, the yōhaisho was fully consonant with national morality. He hoped to appeal to the prefectural governor for a resolution of the affair, but the two were on opposite sides of the political fence and had clashed before. Shindō was rudely rebuffed.

The newspapers and the Prefectural Youth Group stood beside Shindō and branded the governor a mean-spirited pettifogger who would sacrifice public spirit for the letter of shrine law. Finally, Shindō and his supporters submitted the matter to the shrine administrators of the Home Ministry. Eventually the governor was recalled, and the yōhaisho was approved and in 1940 upgraded to the status of a shrine.

In the course of this incident Shindō and his supporters won a political victory by using a Shintō facility, the yōhaisho, as a focus for local loyalties. By sponsoring the yōhaisho and assuming the stance of proponent of devotion to a departed emperor and of an approved ethic of loyalty and patriotism, Shindō found it possible to evade the more picayune details of shrine administration and to enhance his own prestige in the process.

SHRINES IN THE COLONIES

Just as the Ise cult was extended over the main islands to symbolize the hegemony of the new Meiji regime, colonial subjects of the empire were expected to pay obeisance to Japanese deities as a mark of their submission to imperial authority. The last Manchū emperor was forced to adopt worship of Amaterasu as an expression of his "desire for good relations" with Japan.[44] The great majority of colonial shrines were dedicated to Amaterasu, other Japanese deities, and a collective designation for founding deities of the colony, Kunitama Daijin. Colonial shrines were directly controlled by the Japanese military forces.[45]

Many colonial shrines originated in the desire of subjects from the home islands to have a shrine in their new homes. Thus the statistics on the rites of these shrines show that they were overwhelmingly used by immigrants from the home islands. The colonials never developed deep religious attachments to these symbols of Japanese domination.

By 1940 there were 137 shrines in Manchuria. In Korea by 1937 there were a total of 368 large and small shrines.[46] On Taiwan as of 1941 there were 18 shrines. Of these, only one major shrine was dedicated to a Chinese deity.[47] Following the annexation of Korea in 1910, the influential journal of the Shintō priesthood, *Zenkoku shinshoku kaikaihō*, instructed its readership that they must now become missionaries to this benighted land that had for so long been under the sway of Buddhism and Confucianism.[48] By 1935 there were sixty-one Shintō priests in Korea[49] and sixty-six in Taiwan by 1941.[50]

It is quite evident that colonials and their shrines were to occupy a distinctly inferior position in Shintō. Problems arose several times in Korea, while Taiwan and mainland China were more quiescent. At its 1906 annual meeting the national association of the priesthood took up the question of enshrining in Yasukuni Koreans who had died in the Russo-Japanese War. Only a few priests favored enshrining colonials who had died in battle; the majority favored restricting this privilege to "real" Japanese, by whom they meant those born in the home islands of Japanese parents.[51]

When Korean teachers and Christian missionaries in Korea resisted orders that they worship at the Korea Shrine, they were stripped of their teaching credentials.[52] Another dispute developed when Koreans asked to have their national founders enshrined at the Korea Shrine and the military governor dismissed this request, saying there was no reason why colonials should not worship the imperial deities. In 1894 Konishi Senkichi, a Shintō missionary active in Korea, was attacked by Koreans with stones and tiles.[53] With this history of strife over the shrines in Korea, the Japanese military government knew full well that the shrines would be destroyed immediately at the end of the war, so they made arrangements to have the symbols of deity airlifted out when news of the final defeat came.[54]

STATE SHRINE SUPPORT

The 1870s was a decade of considerable state support for Shintō, evidenced in the policy of *shinbutsu bunri*, shrine registration, and construction of new shrines. During this period the state began to make official offerings to the Imperial Shrines on certain of their festivals.[55] From the 1880s until the Russo-Japanese War, however, state interest in and support of shrines was at an ebb. As explained in an earlier chapter, Shintō lost considerable prestige in the eyes of politicians as a result of the failure of the Great Promulgation Campaign.

Part of government support of shrines came in the form of official tribute (*shinsen heihaku ryō kyōshin*). Basing its calculations on ancient models found in the tenth-century classic of shrine lore, *Engishiki*, the Home Ministry determined amounts of cash to be presented as offerings on (usually) three annual festivals: the shrine's annual festival, the Kinensai, and the Niinamesai.[56] These offerings were tokens of the state's committment to shrine rites; they were not intended to provide comprehensive support for the shrine as a whole. This renewed state support for shrines was instituted over the first two decades of this century and eventually extended to all but the Unranked Shrines.[57]

While all the government shrines received official tribute from public funds under this policy, not all civic shrines did. This policy did not, that is, automatically allot public funds to all shrines. Instead, it made all shrines but the unranked *eligible* for public support. It was then up to the governing body corresponding to a shrine's territorial jurisdiction (prefecture, town, etc.) to designate *one* shrine at that level for official support. While standard amounts were stipulated, no large sums were required of the prefectures.[58]

In principle the prefectural governor or his proxy were to journey to the shrines of prefectural rank and higher to present the offering. Tribute offered at shrines below that rank was to be offered by the governing official corresponding to the territory/rank of the shrine.[59] As of 1940, it was understood that authority over shrine rites was a major element of imperial authority and that provincial officials would present offerings at local shrines as direct representatives of the imperial institution.[60] Thus in the final years of State Shintō, shrines played an important role in enacting the symbolic presentation of the nation, and the system of official shrine tribute constituted one aspect of the sacral dimension of imperial rule. In the presentation of official tribute to local shrines by prefectural governors the ideals of the unity of rites and government (*saisei itchi*), and of shrines as offering the rites of nation (*kokka no sōshi*) were finally embodied in public life.

From this brief outline of the changing tides of state support for Shintō as measured by fiscal outlay, we can see several broad trends. First, state support was not constant but shifted according to politicians' perceptions of the social utility of shrines and, perhaps, according to their estimate of the political astuteness of the priesthood. Second, state support was stimulated by military victory and thus expanded considerably in the twentieth century. Third, support from the national budget was limited to the government shrines, thus markedly dividing them from the civic shrines. Fourth, public support for civic shrines was left to provincial administrations, and the state had little direct investment in them. Finally, shrine rites were the occasion for the state's display of its connection and commitment to a sacred realm.

As yet we have no comprehensive studies of shrine finances before 1945, but the few data available suggest that government support even at its height covered only a small portion of the expenses even of Imperial and National Shrines, those funded at the highest level (except for the Ise Grand Shrines).[61] One study shows that in 1932 the government contributed only 18 percent of the actual expenses of Imperial and National Shrines.[62]

Shrines at the prefectural level and below had attached to them parishioners' groups from which they derived some large portion of their income. Parishioners were those persons living within the customary territory of the shrine and registered with it as ujiko. Local administrations levied a charge on parishioners for the upkeep of civic shrines as a matter of administration, quite apart from the religious persuasion of the individual. Local priests' associations met considerable opposition to these levies in many areas.[63] Many shrines had rice land allotted to them by local governments and were partially supported by the income from these fields.

Imperial and National Shrines did not have parishioners' groups; that is to say, they had no ujiko attached to them. They did, however, have lists of devotees (*sūkeisha*) of the shrine, persons who felt some attraction to the shrine in question, quite apart from the question of residence in the shrine's customary territory. Funds could be solicited from the devotees.

SHRINE MERGERS

By far the most controversial policy affecting the economic history of shrines during the modern period was shrine mergers. The implementation of shrine mergers was spotty and uneven, but the cumulative effect was considerable. Most mergers took place between 1906 and 1912, but the policy remained in effect long afterwards. It was principally the civic shrines that were subject to merger, mainly District, Town, Village, and Unranked Shrines. Between 1903 and 1920 no less than 52 percent of the Unranked Shrines were merged. However, great regional variation is concealed in that figure; only 4 percent of Aomori Village and Unranked Shrines were merged, but 89 percent of those shrines in Mie Prefecture were closed by mergers.[64]

Shrine mergers were carried out in a policy atmosphere dominated by the state's desire to raise the status and social prominence of shrines in the train of heightened patriotism after the Russo-Japanese War. Heightened prestige was linked to greater financial support, but it would have been fiscally impossible to make even a token gesture of support to all the shrines in the nation. Therefore the state embarked upon a campaign to have not more than one shrine per village (*isson issha*), thereby aligning civil administrative districts with shrine territories, creating a parallel ritual and administrative hierarchy. Only in this way would it be possible to establish a unified policy of state support for all shrines.[65]

Between 1905 and 1929, over 83,000 civic shrines were abolished by merger. After a merger, the remaining shrine appropriated the land and other property of the merged shrine, thus acquiring significant assets. Land freed by merger was awarded at no cost to the remaining shrine.[66]

Shrine mergers drastically changed the character of local shrine life. A shrine that was merged was essentially abolished as an independent institution. In some cases the building was razed. The only thing that remained of it was its object of worship (*shintai*), or some symbol thereof, which was moved to the shrine with which the merger had been carried out. The parishioners of the merged shrine had to change their affiliation and become ujiko of the remaining shrine, where, no doubt, they had a distinctly subordinate status. They had to adapt themselves to the customs and rites of their new shrine and to give up everything connected with their old shrine.

The journals of the priesthood are full of testimony that priests and local administrations were thoroughly confused and divided among themselves about shrine mergers. Without a doubt the major subject of readers' queries to priests' journals was shrine mergers: how to carry them out, on what rationale, how to explain the situation to parishioners, how to integrate newly merged groups of parishioners, etc. One priest developed elaborate arguments against mergers, declaring that the very idea showed foreign (and hence undesirable) influence, that reducing the number of shrines would make it impossible to respond to inevitable increases in the population and would weaken Shintō as a whole, and that instead of reducing the number of shrines, the government should increase the number of priests, so that they could fully staff existing shrines.[67] In 1912 a Hiroshima shrine priest wrote to protest shrine mergers, saying that they confused the people and lessened popular respect for Shintō.[68] There was a case in which the men who carried the object of worship of a small shrine to the larger shrine with which its original home was to be merged all died sudden deaths. This incident so provoked local residents that they succeeded in reinstating the former shrine.[69]

If shrine mergers received only partial support from the priesthood, their support in civil society was even more in doubt. The policy met with considerable opposition because it overrode previous boundaries of economic cooperation and other kinds of local associations, quite apart from questions of changes made in local religious life.[70] Furthermore, there were areas where people refused to give up the rites of the original shrine, and far from realizing a saving on shrine rites as a result of mergers, local administrations had to provide funds for both.[71] Yanagita Kunio, government official-cum-social pundit and folklorist, criticized the policy as one tending to attenuate the relation between ordinary people and the shrines, and to weaken faith in the kami.[72]

This brief survey of the economic situation of shrines completes an overview of institutional developments necessary to an understanding of shrine rites during the period. Appendix 1 provides data comparing the Japanese state's expenditures on Shintō with national expenditures for the Eastern Orthodox Church in imperial Russia. In the following chapter we turn to an examination of changes in ritual.

5. Shrines and the Rites of Empire

Part II: Shrine Rites

IN THE LAST chapter we saw how state patronage greatly strengthened Shintō institutions, and how greatly the post-Meiji character of shrines differed from what had come before. In this chapter we will see that similarly vast changes came about in shrine rites as well, greatly changing the character of popular religious life and bringing much of it within the purview of state supervision.

SHRINE RITES: TYPES AND STANDARDIZATION

In ritual as in so many other areas, shrines before 1868 conducted their observances on a local scale with little connection to cult centers and hardly any coordination among individual shrines. Shrine rites comprised only a part of the annual observances in popular society.

In addition to Buddhist rites, rites of passage, and the annual calendar of local shrine rites, there were five annual observances (*gosekku*), not necessarily carried out in shrines, that constituted an important core of Tokugawa-period popular religious life. Originally derived from Chinese calendrical lore, rites of the seventh day of the first month, the third day of the third month, the fifth day of the fifth month, the seventh day of the seventh month, and the ninth day of the ninth month were marked with seasonal rites. These five days plus rites for the New Year and *obon* (traditionally observed in the eighth month, the occasion when ancestral spirits are believed to return to their families in this world), formed the core of popular annual rites.[1] Added to these were rites of the rice cycle, typically directed to local tutelary deities, the *ujigami*. Some, but by no means all, of these rites of the rice cycle were conducted in shrines by persons in a priestly role. It goes without saying that each aspect of popular ritual life was subject to enormous regional variation, but the rites outlined here were widespread and typical. It can be readily appreciated that while shrine rites occupied an important position in ritual life, they did not predominate.

In the Meiji period a national calendar of rites centering on the nation and the imperial house was introduced that dramatically altered the character of ritual life. While the emperor had always had a sacerdotal role, the people previously had been little aware of it. Now his rites were to be their rites. The new calendar of rites gave him a high-profile, center-stage role as head priest of the nation.

The national ritual calendar meant the end of the *gosekku*, and some areas tried to abolish rites for *obon*, a move that failed virtually everywhere it was tried.[2] The new calendar was comprised of the following rites:

Shihōhai	January 1	Worship of the deities of the four directions to welcome the New Year
Genshisai	January 3	Rites for the New Year; emperor performs rites at the palace for imperial ancestors
Shinnen enkai	January 5	Rites for the New Year; palace rites feature a banquet for members of the imperial house and foreign emissaries
Kōmei Tennōsai	January 30	Commemorating the emperor preceding Meiji
Tenchōsetsu	February 3	Emperor Meiji's birthday
Kigensetsu	February 11	Commemorating the founding of the Yamato dynasty by Emperor Jinmu
Kinensai	February 17	To pray for the year's harvest and the peace of the emperor
Shunki Kōreisai	Spring Equinox	Spring rites for the imperial ancestors
Jinmu Tennōsai	April 3	Commemorating the day of Emperor Jinmu's death
Shūki Kōreisai	Autumn Equinox	Autumn rites for the imperial ancestors
Kannamesai	October 17	An offering of firstfruits of the harvest to the Ise deities by the emperor
Niinamesai	November 23	The emperor both offers and partakes of firstfruits of the harvest

Some of these rites had ancient precedents in the *Kojiki* and *Nihonshoki* or other ancient sources: the Genshisai, Kigensetsu, Jinmu Tennōsai, Niinamesai, Kannamesai, and the equinoctial rites for the imperial ancestors. These rites were concatenated as a unified national calendar of rites for the whole nation during the 1870s. Thus they were observed simultaneously in the imperial palace, at the Ise Shrines, and at the Imperial and National Shrines. Gradually the civic shrines came to observe them also, so that in theory, at least, the liturgy of all the shrines of the nation was orchestrated according to a single plan, penetrating all areas and all levels of society. After millennia of local autonomy and uncoordinated shrine rites, the change was revolutionary.[3]

While the outline of a new national ritual calendar was established in the 1870s, it was not until much later that it really began to be observed. Diaries of the 1880s indicate that the police had to force people to fly the national flag on the new holidays, and that for the most part the populace continued to be attuned to the old customs. A famous diary of a village mayor of the period, the *Aizawa nikki*, does not even mention the new holidays until 1900. Like so many aspects of State Shintō, things really began to change after the wars with China and Russia. These rites began to be incorporated in the schools as of the first decade of this century, and it was also about this time that local authorities began to promote the new holidays in many areas.[4]

THE LITURGICAL STRUCTURE OF SHRINE RITES

While it goes without saying that each of these rites embodied different symbols and conveyed a different meaning, the liturgies shared a common framework derived from traditional shrine rites. Beginning with prayers to invoke the relevant deities' presence, virtually all shrine rites included as a first step the presentation of offerings and making obeisance. Then, in the gods' presence, priests read a prayer (*norito*) prepared for the occasion to announce the rite's purpose, to request the deities' aid in its accomplishment, and to invoke the deities' blessings in a general way. Lay persons assumed an attitude of obeisance during the reading of the prayer, and, depending on the character of the rite, they might afterwards make an offering of a sakaki twig festooned with paper streamers symbolizing an offering of cloth. In some cases priests purified congregants by waving over them a large wand of paper streamers. The rite itself concluded, the food and drink offerings were removed, and these might be consumed by the priests and lay people at a concluding meal (*naorai*).

Before the Meiji Restoration, the imperial house was attached to the Shingon school of Buddhism and had as its patron temple a Kyoto temple called Sennyūji. In the palace itself the imperial ancestors were enshrined in Buddhist style, using memorial tablets.[5] After the Restoration, Buddhist memorial rites and ancestral tablets were eliminated from palace rites, Buddhist statues and other articles were removed, and Buddhist titles ceased being applied to members of the imperial house. The relationship with Sennyūji was abolished.[6] The emperor then began to make personal visits to shrines, whereas previously a proxy messenger had been dispatched. When Emperor Meiji visited the Ise Grand Shrines in 1869, his was the first imperial visit since that of Emperor Jitō (645–702).

In 1889 three palace shrines, collectively called the *kyūchū sanden* were completed. Here the emperor personally performed rites for the imperial ancestors, as well as the other rites of the new liturgical calendar discussed above. One of the shrines, the *kashikodokoro*, had the character of a miniature version of the Ise Shrines, but combined with it the element of the emperor's direct attendance, thus transferring to him headship over Ise and hence over all shrines in the land.[7]

Palace rites formed the basis for the emperor's liturgical function. Most numerous were the rites for imperial ancestors which upheld the idea of the unbroken line of emperors descended from the sun goddess, Amaterasu. The Genshisai rite celebrated the inception of the imperial line. The nation was presented as beginning with the accession of Emperor Jinmu, an occasion commemorated in the annual Kigensetsu rite. The accession was thought to have occurred 2,530 years earlier, and in 1870 a system of counting historical time based on it was begun. Similarly, in the Jinmu Tennōsai, a rite commemorating the anniversary of this first "historical" emperor's death, all provincial officials were to face the region of the dynasty's beginning, Yamato, and offer a sprig of sakaki in parallel with a homologous rite conducted simultaneously in the palace. Members of the imperial family participated with the emperor in spring and autumn equinoctial rites for the imperial ancestors. The rite for Emperor Kōmei was a special sort of ancestral rite, directed to the immediately preceding emperor, and Tenchōsetsu, the living emperor's birthday, completed the sequence of rites for living and dead imperial scions.[8]

In a slightly different category, but still retaining the character of ancestral ritual, were those imperial rites focusing upon the harvest and the Ise Shrines. Here we bear in mind that along with Ise's significance as the main shrine of imperial ancestors, its deities were popularly perceived as harvest deities. This idea had a mythic expression in the story of Amaterasu giving her grandchild Ninigi rice grains when he descended from the High Plain of Heaven to the earthly realm. In this category of rites were the Kinensai, a rite praying for a good harvest, conducted simultaneously in the palace and at important provincial shrines, and the Kannamesai and Niinamesai. These latter two rites were both, in essence, harvest rites offering firstfruits of the harvest. In the Niinamesai, the emperor himself partook of the offerings, and in the Kannamesai firstfruits were offered to Amaterasu at the Ise Grand Shrines and in the palace.

Through these various rites, the emperor's religious authority was based on the unity of his person with Amaterasu, the apical ancestress of the imperial house. The idea that all other deities were putatively descended from her had a parallel in the notion that all the Japanese people were ultimately descended from the imperial house. Similarly, all deities being ultimately linked to Amaterasu, all shrines were ultimately subordinate to Ise. Thus Ise was the apex of a pyramidal hierarchy of shrines; their rites should conform to imperial rites conducted both at Ise and in the palace. In the person of the emperor was bound up the unity of the nation and its people and myriad deities. This unity was symbolized in local society by shrines and shrine rites.[9]

LARGE-SCALE STATE RITES

Besides the calendar of annual liturgy carried out at the palace, at Ise, and mirrored by local shrines, there were important rites of state that reveal notable aspects of State Shintō. In general, the more important the rite, the less important the roles allotted to Shintō priests. The priesthood seems to have had an unfortunate knack for bungling any festivities on a scale exceeding their own shrine precincts. This is hardly surprising, for the priests had a long history of purely local focus and until 1900 lacked any national organization. While not completely disastrous, the memorial services on the thirtieth anniversary of Emperor Kōmei's death were but one example of the Shintō priesthood's general ineptitude for conducting large-scale rites outside their customary shrine settings. The following account is taken from the *Asahi* newspaper and precedes a discussion of the more limited role priests usually assumed in state rites, exemplified in the 1895 ceremonies commemorating the one thousandth anniversary of moving the national capital to Kyoto (Kyoto Sentōsai).

First announced as planned for 30 January 1897, the ceremonies for Emperor Kōmei were to be held on the plaza before the museum in Tokyo's Ueno Park, in conjunction with imperial rites at his tomb in Kyoto and at the imperial palace in Tokyo. Early advertisements noted that permission to use this space was still pending. Permission was, in the final event, never granted, which ultimately prevented the rites from being held.

Fukuba Bisei, named honorary head of the committee staging the ceremonies, praised Kōmei for uniting the people in a time of unrest when foreign intrusion impended and the shogunate was about to fall.[10] Kōmei had met the foreign threat by offering prayers personally at the Kamo Hachiman Shrine, and in Fukuba's view it was these prayers that brought the country through the crisis and paved the way for the Meiji Restoration.

A six-foot-high altar was constructed at Ueno for the rites, installed by a grounds purifications rite (*jichinsai*) presided over by Fukuba, assisted by sixty other priests. Sacred dance, horse racing, liberation of captive birds and beasts (*hōjō-e*), *nō* drama, a parade of floats, sumō wrestling, and geisha dancing were to accompany the more solemn memorial rites.[11] A special song to be sung by schoolchildren at the ceremonies was published in the paper. Subjects were invited to present rice, art objects, calligraphy, books, fruit, and other fresh foods as offerings.

The Imperial Household Ministry halted the selling of tickets to the ceremonies when a suspicious situation came to light. Several people were found selling the twenty-sen tickets and giving the buyers a receipt rather than the ticket itself. The receipt was in the name of one Naitō Seihachi, and when the police investigated his residence, they found 3,500 yen there. It also came out that 500 yen had gone to the kabuki actor Ichikawa Danjurō for promoting the ceremonies.

To make matters worse, the committee tried to hush up the story, which reporters then related as part of the tale. The prestigious Mitsui family, who were to have donated a thousand yen, canceled this commitment because of the scandal. The new religious association Renmonkyō had bought two hundred tickets to sell to its members, and when the scandal was discovered it asked for its money back.

The police raided more residences of ticket canvassers and found that the practice of issuing invalid receipts was widespread. One of Fukuba's subordinates published a public apology, resigned from the committee and took to his bed, refusing to meet with Fukuba, who was left solely responsible for the debacle.

On 3 March 1897, Fukuba was denied permission to use the Ueno Plaza, and public ceremonies on a large scale had to be canceled. Only with difficulty and embarrassment did Fukuba locate a place on private land for the ceremonies. On 19 March he performed a small-scale rite attended by only a few people.

The Shintō priesthood's image was badly sullied by this affair. It was well-publicized bunglings of this kind that, coming so soon after the failure of the Great Promulgation Campaign, made politicians highly sceptical of Shintō. As we have seen, there were concrete consequences in the form of reduced government support for shrines. Nevertheless, the priesthood's attempts at public ceremonial did not always go so badly. The commemoration of Kyoto's designation as the nation's capital was a success and instituted one of Kyoto's most important annual festivals, the Festival of the Ages (*Jidai Matsuri*), still performed today.

The Kyoto Sentōsai was a three-day festival celebrating the nation's history in several ways. First, a building was constructed in the precincts of Kyoto's largest shrine, the Heian Shrine, which itself was considerably enlarged for this occasion. The building housed a room illustrating the styles and fashions of each era and also included a miniature version of the Ise Grand Shrines. The festival itself reenacted the tributary missions of provincial officials to the capital, featuring separate parades characteristic of each era down to Meiji. These grand parades of the ages wound through the city to the Heian Shrine. Local shrines on the route of march held special rites and staged exhibitions of their treasures for the occasion. Each prefecture made large monetary contributions as well as lending costumes, musical instruments, and other equipment.[12]

On this occasion the Shintō priesthood was evidently able to avoid the multiple disasters of the Kōmei memorial affair. The Sentōsai was a remarkable historical pageant that drew on the resources of the entire nation to celebrate the idea of a unified history of the whole. Regional, class, and gender differentials in access to resources and opportunity, political estrangements, and warfare loom large in the perspectives of academic views of Japanese history, but in the Sentōsai all was harmony. All differences were submerged in the symbolism of shared submission to the imperial seat of authority. Hence, it was possible to bring shrines in on the sidelines of the pageant to provide the event with an aura of sacrality. It is noteworthy, however, that after the Kōmei disaster no one trusted shrine personnel to function too close to center stage, too far from their customary jurisdictions, the shrine precinct.

CIVIC RITES IN PROVINCIAL SOCIETY

If shrine priests tended to play minor roles in large-scale state rites of national significance, how can we best characterize shrine rites in provincial society? How were they viewed by local lay people? Was the character of customary rites at the local level altered by the state's pervasive intervention in Shintō affairs during the modern period?

In spite of the state's dominant role, there was much popular initiative in ritual. Examination of popular cults by Saigō Takamori (1827–1877), for example, shows that the public often sought different things from ritual than did the priesthood and the Tokyo administrators of shrine affairs. As a leader of the Seinan Rebellion of 1877 against the modernizing reforms of the Meiji government, Saigō was persona non grata for some years in early Meiji, but he was also an immensely popular hero. There were many private circles dedicated to his memory, and in 1888 one Urakabe Masaka announced a plan to build an amusement park by popular subscription that would house a shrine to Saigō. Urakabe found his initiative halted by state pressure, only to have the state take the lead in building a famous statue to Saigō in the Ueno Park in Tokyo in 1898.[13] Similarly, the grave of Mori Arinori's assassin, Nishino Buntarō, received so much unofficial prayer and memorial that the state dug it up to prevent the formation of a martyr cult of this killer of a minister of education thought to be guilty of a slip in etiquette during an official visit to the Ise Shrines.[14]

Besides grass-roots cults of popular heroes, the Meiji reorganization of religious life created ample opportunity for religious entrepreneurs. Take for example, the Japan Ena Company (Nihon Ena Kaisha), providing to citizens of Tokyo the service of disposal of afterbirth. This company was created by taking over rites formerly performed by six Tokyo temples and shrines. The company created six Shintō churches (*kyōkai*) where ministers of the Shintō sect Taiseikyō performed rites to dispose of effluvia and to pray for the happiness of the newborn child. Consumers of these services could receive the navel string packed in boxes of various grades of ornamentation, depending on the price. The company issued stock and listed its total assets in 1893 as 120,000 yen; three years later these had increased many times.[15]

A brief survey of popularly initiated shrine activity reported in the *Asahi* newspaper shows that the state by no means controlled all groups claiming to be Shintō or all religious activity at shrines.[16] A group called the Confraternity of Wondrous Tenshōdaijin (Tenshō Daijin Myōkyō) held lectures in June 1892 calling for Japan to give up Buddhism and Christianity (25 June 1892). A Tochigi Prefecture shrine called the Kanshi Shrine created a Tokyo outpost and attracted a following by successful prayers for rain (3 September 1893). Four months later the Tokyo outpost was renamed Shintō Kijima Kanshi Church and started selling medicinal panaceas for smelly armpits, hip pain, eye disease, etc. It also offered individual consultations on changing one's luck; these could be had in person or by correspondence (30 January 1894). A minister of the Shintō sect Shinshūkyō, Arimitsu Sakae, was arrested after it was discovered that, in an effort to bring about the speedy demise of an old couple, he had made paper dolls of them and had driven nails into the dolls' head, hands, and feet (25 April 1894). Tokyo rice dealers established a shrine called the Sakigake Shrine inside their warehouse and created an annual festival for it; the festival then became the occasion for lavish annual displays of dancing girls, comic storytelling, and lion dancing. Each dealer paid ten yen (a handsome sum in 1893) in order to sample the best that the red-light districts had to offer (1 October 1893). A Kamakura Shintō prayer healer had an establishment in a local Nichiren Buddhist temple, but it was abolished when he was found to be promoting immoral associations among his followers (24 May 1896). A group called the Ancient Way Church (Kannagara Kyōkai), led by a man treated as a living god by his followers, was investigated when the leader was turned in by one of the followers for fraudulent healings by holy water (12 April 1899). These examples should make it clear that shrines and Shintō churches continued to provide ample scope for entrepreneurs, and that there was a widespread public interest in the ideas, images, and services available.

These activities continued unabated and relatively unaffected by the state's various policies on Shintō. They serve to remind us that the state by no means overwhelmed popular religious life or achieved an instant revolution in popular religious thought. Finally, it goes without saying that there was surely much more activity than reached the press, and that much of it undoubtedly was devoid of the potential for titillating scandal.

Local projects to build a shrine or raise an existing shrine's rank provided a powerful vehicle for increasing the prestige and prominence of provincial elites. There were countless cases of such initiatives, but here let one account illustrate the phenomenon. In 1892 local notables of Suma planned to construct a shrine to be called the Ichi no Tani Shrine, commemorating the infant Emperor Antoku (1178–1185), who was lost at sea near the site. In order to establish a shrine at the rank of Imperial Shrine of the Middle Grade, local elites from the area journeyed to Tokyo and made contact with administrators of shrine affairs and members of the nobility. They were assured of a favorable hearing by their offer to contribute 25,000 yen to the project.[17] Paying money to public administrators for a shrine could give provincials valuable contacts useful, no doubt, in a variety of contexts outside the original shrine-centered negotiation.[18]

SHRINE OBSERVANCES INVOLVING SCHOOLCHILDREN

The incorporation of liturgy into educational institutions during the Meiji period had important precedents in the customary rites for Tenjin, the god of learning, at pre-Meiji temple schools (*terakoya*) and in the rites for Confucius typically held at domain schools. As early as 1875 schoolchildren in Nagasaki attended shrine rites, and such days were school holidays, but practices of this kind became truly widespread only after 1900.[19]

An important precursor of the involvement of pupils in shrine rites was the distribution of a photograph of the emperor to virtually all the nation's schools. This distribution began around 1882 and was virtually complete by 1888. The imperial photo eventually became part of a liturgical set, the other element of which was the school's copy of the Imperial Rescript on Education (1890), a text that came to be revered as holy writ. The scroll on which the rescript was written and the photograph had to be housed in some portion of the school not used for any other purpose. Sometimes a special room was constructed and a special night guard hired to protect them in case of fire or other emergency. They were placed in a shrine-like box, and offerings were set before them. When opening the box one had to bow low enough to place the hands on the knees, an obvious borrowing from shrine etiquette.[20]

Several texts on how to carry out the ceremonial reading of the Imperial Rescript on Education were produced. Ceremonial readings were held on Tenchōsetsu, Kigensetsu, and Jinmu Tennōsai. For a school's first reading of the rescript, the scroll had to be paraded to the school by teachers, pupils, local notables, the mayor, the post office chief, local people in government, and the area's eldest residents. A sacred space was prepared for the reading with fresh gravel and hung with red, white, and blue curtains. An offering of rice cakes was presented to the scroll as if it were a deity. The school principal assumed the priestly role, donning white gloves to intone the text.[21] There were even cases of principals committing suicide to atone for mispronouncing a syllable.

At first schools found it difficult to motivate pupils to attend the ceremonial readings on national holidays; why should a pupil appear in uniform on one of his/her few days off? One solution was to distribute sweets, and another was to link the holidays to exhibitions, music festivals, or athletic meets. With the wars against China and Russia, more rites to welcome returning soldiers were added. In spite of a general increase in patriotic expressions, however, local schools consistently complained to the Ministry of Education that the populace continued to be quite unaware of the significance of these holidays.[22]

It might be objected that these observances, not being held in shrines, nor presided over by an ordained Shintō priest, do not properly belong in a discussion of State Shintō. There is an important connection between the priesthood and school rites, however, because priests who held the rank of *kundō* (second from the lowest) and higher were automatically qualified as primary school teachers.[23] In fact, most priests of civic shrines had to take by-employment of some kind, and school teaching provided a ready-made opportunity. Furthermore, it was the shrine priesthood that was largely responsible for distributing the texts teaching principals how to make ceremonial readings of the Imperial Rescript on Education.[24]

From about 1912 onward, school rites such as those described above were greatly intensified, and schoolchildren were taken to shrines to participate in ritual with increasing frequency. Over 70 percent of schools had kamidana, shrines for the kami, in addition to the shrines for the imperial photo and the Imperial Rescript on Education, and many also enshrined a talisman from Ise. Local principals had the authority to decide how many holidays to declare for shrine festivals; one Tokushima Prefecture school had as many as seven such holidays per year. A Tochigi Prefecture document of 1928 called for schoolchildren to visit the local shrine on Kinensai, Niinamesai, yearly school opening day, and graduation, all for the purpose of increasing their reverence for the kami. The document also called for monthly shrine visits and monthly shrine cleaning by pupils. The role of shrine priests in these observances is not specified, but as pupils made formal offerings at the altar, priests must have been involved. From the mid-1920s the custom of holding morning reverence of the imperial palace became widespread.[25]

6. School Trips and Pupil Visits to
the Ise Shrines, 1934–1942

	Schools	Pupils
1934	13,098	1,062,127
1936	16,232	1,456,348
1938	20,238	1,923,414
1939	24,902	2,200,173
1942	19,530	1,969,823

SOURCE: Gomazuru Hiroyuki, "Jingū hyakunen no ayumi," in *Meiji ishin Shintō hyakunenshi*, ed. Shintō bunkakai (Tokyo: Shintō bunkakai, 1966), 1: 495.

Besides excursions to local shrines, school trips by whole classes to prominent shrines, especially the Meiji Shrine, Yasukuni, and Ise, became an important part of school life. The increasing number of such trips to Ise is shown in Table 6. These visits were encouraged as part of the local movement to improve the moral quality of village life that occurred in the Taishō period (1912–1926).[26] Some years later, in 1938, the annual festival at Yasukuni was declared a national holiday, and all schools, including kindergartens, had to worship the shrine from afar on that occasion.[27]

The priesthood assumed an active role in encouraging the participation of schoolchildren in shrine rites. In Okayama priests instituted rites to "encourage learning" (*kangakusai*), in which new first graders were taken to shrines. They also supported regular worship at shrines by schoolchildren, the custom of schoolchildren cleaning shrines, and services for local youth groups at shrines.[28] A number of Shintō-influenced songs appeared in primary school textbooks. Priests were highly enthusiastic about shrine visits by schoolchildren, but their queries to their professional journals show that they encountered a good deal of trouble from obstreperous youngsters, and some incidents verged on lèse majesté.[29]

CUSTOMARY OBSERVANCES AND SHINTŌ

Before the Meiji Restoration, many of the rites of the life cycle, communal rites, rites of kin groups, and rites of occupational groups were customarily performed informally, in private homes, without the attendance of a Shintō priest. A major, though subtle, change in Japanese religious life came about after the Restoration with the increasing tendency to hold such rites in shrines and to have them conducted by a Shintō priest. While it is very difficult to document this change precisely, contemporary Shintō scholars attest to it uniformly.[30]

Examples of rites of passage that have come increasingly under the aegis of shrines since the Meiji period include the following: *hatsumiya mairi*, *shichi-go-san*, rites of coming of age, rites of marriage, and, to a lesser extent, funerals. *Hatsumiya mairi* is a ceremony in which a newborn child is taken to the shrine at which its parents are parishioners and presented to the deity, whose protection is invoked by a priest. This rite establishes the child as a shrine parishioner. *Shichi-go-san* means "seven-five-three," referring to the custom of taking five-year-old boys and three- and seven-year-old girls to the tutelary shrine to pray for their protection. Rites of coming of age marked the time at which young people were considered adult.[31]

Before the Meiji period, weddings were hardly ever celebrated at shrines, and priests did not routinely learn how to perform them. It was largely in imitation of the Christian wedding ceremony and on the basis of the Taishō emperor's shrine wedding that the custom spread widely, actively encouraged by the priesthood.[32] Similarly, pre-Meiji shrine priests seldom performed funerals, and it was only after Meiji that the ritual spread at all. Diaries of priests show that there was a brisk circulation of funeral manuals to teach priests how to perform the rite.

Besides rites of passage, communal and kin-group rites increasingly came under the supervision of shrine priests. Prior to the Meiji period, the annual festival for the tutelary deity (*ujigamisai*) had not necessarily been presided over by a priest. Frequently the responsibility for this rite passed in rotation among elite village men of a shrine guild, who underwent abstinences and purification to prepare for the year-long tenure of duty. In this way local tutelary shrines could be managed without an ordained priest. The takeover of these rites by Shintō priests coincided with the decline of traditional shrine guilds. Similarly, rites of the extended joint-stem family (*dōzoku* and other terms) were frequently held privately before Meiji but thereafter came to be held increasingly in shrines and to be conducted by a Shintō priest.

It is mainly after Meiji that industries and occupational cooperatives such as fishermen's unions and brewers' associations began to hold rites to pray for their success and safety by calling in a Shintō priest. Companies began to establish shrines on their premises or in their headquarters. Particular occupations tended to become associated with certain types of shrines, for example, brewers with the Matsuo Imperial Shrine in Kyoto. In addition, the deity Inari had a generalized connection to success in business, regardless of the nature of the enterprise.

Finally, a number of occasional and miscellaneous rites came under Shintō influence after the Meiji Restoration. The custom of maintaining a domestic altar for the kami, a kamidana, increased markedly. Many areas had the custom of all-night vigils ending with communal worship of the sun, known as *hi-machi*, "waiting for the sun." Whereas these had been performed without priests before Meiji, after that time priests were routinely called upon to officiate.

Priests were pervasively involved in rites sending soldiers off to war and in rites invoking divine aid in achieving victory. The diary of Tanaka Sen'ya shows clearly that his involvement in rites related to the armed forces came to occupy a major portion of his time after the war with China in 1895. He and other priests were at the center of village send-offs for the soldiers and officiated at their funerals. In this way the priesthood acquired a close association with the military and with war in the popular mind. The growing strength of patriotic sentiments and the high tide of emotions involved when whole villages attended funeral rites for young men killed in battle gave the priesthood a social prominence and prestige it had not necessarily enjoyed universally before Meiji.

In most cases, in the rites and customs just reviewed there was no intrinsic relation of the ritual in question to shrines or to Shintō "theology." That such a broad range of religious observances should in the modern period be assigned a Shintō meaning, and that they should come within the scope of the priesthood's supervision, represents an important change in Japanese religious life. Whereas much pre-Meiji religious life was conducted independently by kin, territorial, or occupational groups, the priesthood's bailiwick has widened greatly and rapidly in the last century. The change is probably to be accounted for in large part by the greater professionalization and prestige of the priesthood after Meiji, which on the one hand enabled priests to assert their claim to such traditional rites and, on the other, made priestly attendance more attractive to potential consumers of these ritual services.

CONCLUSION

Shrines and their rituals were completely transformed by 1945 as a result of massive state manipulation of shrine affairs dating from the time of the Meiji Restoration. Chapter 4 showed how all the shrines were hierarchically ranked and the populace universally made their parishioners. The state underwrote the construction of new shrines and systematically promoted the universalization of a cult of the Ise deities as the nation's highest ancestors and a cult of the war dead as prototypical ancestors and heroes. A strong association between Shintō and war was the inevitable result, and the priesthood voiced no reservations about the use of shrines to glorify death in battle. Under the aegis of the state, the Meiji Shrine became the nation's first and only shrine to be constructed by nationwide contributions of money and labor, and hundreds of shrines were built in the colonies. Furthermore, this chapter has shown how unified ritual placed the emperor unambiguously in the role of head priest of the nation and symbolically coordinated the rites of all the shrines with palace and imperial rites.

All this was accomplished not according to a single blueprint agreed upon from the beginning, but by fits, starts, advances, and retreats. Political support from public funds was erratic, unpredictable, and subject to significant regional variation. The priesthood was so distrusted by politicians that priests were virtually powerless to influence state funding consistently.

The cumulative effect upon popular religious life of this massive state intervention was very great, producing a unified symbolic and institutional system where localized cult life and extreme diversity had been the norm for centuries. We have seen that shrines could link local and national communities, and that shrine life and affiliation could provide an organizational vehicle for the promotion of individual and communal interests and a means of access to the prestige of the state. Whereas shrines had functioned in this way before Meiji only for a limited elite, these possibilities expanded greatly in the modern period.

Thus we can see that there were tangible incentives for the populace to support shrines and to participate in their rites. These incentives probably compensated considerably for the alteration of religious life as it had been before Meiji and sugarcoated the pill of shrine mergers and other locally disruptive policies. Undoubtedly State Shintō operated through a great deal of central direction, but it was much more than the unidirectional imposition of state policy from above. It depended equally upon the popular perception of the interest, value, and utility of shrines and shrine rites.

6. Religious Freedom under State Shintō

A DISTINCTIVELY modern concept, the right to freedom of religious belief was not recognized in Japanese law before the enactment of the Meiji Constitution in 1889. Prior to the Meiji Restoration, religious freedom had become an issue most notably with respect to the treatment of Japanese Christians, but it had appeared also in the history of Japanese Buddhism and Shintō.[1] The concept of religious freedom embodied in Article 28 of the Meiji Constitution was framed in a context of considerable foreign influence, exerted both by foreign governments and German constitutional scholars called upon to give assistance by the drafters of the constitution. Drafting a constitutional provision for freedom of religion was not, however, a purely academic exercise. The constitution's provision for religious freedom, as interpreted at various levels of government and by various religious leaders, had important consequences for the character of Japanese religious life, especially for Shintō.

We explained in the introduction that before the Meiji Restoration the Japanese populace was required to become affiliated with a recognized school of Buddhism in order to ensure that no one practiced Christianity, which was proscribed by the state. Early Meiji Japan was thus greatly shocked when it was discovered in 1867 that in the village of Urakami near Nagasaki there were many "hidden Christians" (*kakure kirishitan*), and that villagers had been practicing Christianity in secret for well over two centuries. These hidden Christians revealed themselves in 1865 to French missionaries, who built chapels in Urakami and encouraged these Catholics to defy the ban on Christianity. On 10 July 1867 the governor of Nakasaki

114

arrested sixty-eight leaders of the hidden Christians and had them tortured to force them to deny their faith.[2]

The discovery of the Urakami Christians became a cause célèbre among Western diplomats, and French and American officials protested strongly against their treatment. For Shintō figures in government, the Urakami Christians represented a crisis of the first magnitude. As we have seen, they believed that Christianity was an evil religion that should never have been allowed to enter Japan and certainly not to take root there. Fukuba Bisei encouraged the emperor to have the Christians removed from Urakami. All 4,010 Christians were dispersed, to a total of thirty-four domains. In Tsuwano and other domains that received these Christians, Shintō and National Learning figures were entrusted with their "reeducation." To no one's surprise, many died in exile, victims of Shintō zeal.

The deportation of the Urakami Christians provoked an immediate, sharp reaction from Western diplomats. Widely reported in the Western press, the incident had grave consequences for Japanese diplomacy. The diplomatic mission charged with negotiating the revision of unequal treaties signed by the shogunate in the 1850s heard charges everywhere it went that because Japan did not provide for freedom of religious belief, it could only be considered an uncivilized nation. Citing this reason, Western nations refused to revise the treaties. Thus, the issue of religious freedom was a tremendous stumbling block in achieving the main goal of Japanese diplomacy at that time. It was this diplomatic frustration that motivated the Meiji government most strongly to include a provision for religious freedom when it came to the drafting of the Meiji Constitution.[3]

THE MEIJI CONSTITUTION

In 1872 Aoki Shūzō (1844–1914), Japanese chargé d'affaires in Berlin, was directed to draft a constitution for Japan.[4] In this endeavor he was much aided by the German constitutional scholar Rudolf von Gneist. Gneist warned Aoki against permitting the free operation of foreign religions and suggested that Catholicism be specifically proscribed. Further, he advised that Buddhism be established as the state religion. The document Aoki submitted in 1873, *Governmental Principles of Great Japan* (*Dainihon seiki*), incorporated Gneist's advice and thus rejected the principle of religious freedom. A second Aoki draft, *Governmental Code for the Japanese Empire* (*Teigo dainihon seiten*), composed between 1873 and 1874, did, however, stipulate that Japanese subjects' rights were not to be affected by their religious affiliation, thus seeming to permit the practice of Christianity and other religions besides Buddhism.[5]

Between 1876 and 1880, the Council of Elders (Genrōin) produced three draft constitutions. Fukuba Bisei was one of four committee members appointed to draft these documents. The three drafts of 1876, 1878, and 1880 all included a provisional guarantee of religious freedom, on condition that the practice of religion did not hinder the conduct of government or challenge established social customs. The drafters wrote in a commentary to the constitutional drafts that in composing their provision for religious freedom they were guided by the constitutions of Prussia, Austria, and Denmark.[6] Thus the Council of Elders understood that a constitutional provision for freedom of religion conformed to the common practice of modern nations, but they qualified the provision and implicitly established the conduct of government and the undisturbed perpetuation of social custom as higher goods.[7]

When the Emperor Meiji asked his Confucian tutor Motoda Eifu (1818–1891) to critique the Council of Elders' 1878 draft, Motoda attacked the provision for religious freedom. His preferred version stipulated that subjects could believe in any religion so long as it did not contravene civil and governmental conduct, and so long as it did not run counter to the religion of the state. He proposed that Confucianism be established as the state's religion, and that the emperor rule over the religion and morality of the people. Thus Motoda's draft constitution, submitted to the emperor in 1880 and titled *Essentials of the National Constitution* (*Kokken taikō*), gave the emperor theocratic powers, advocated the unity of state and religion, and hence precluded the principle of religious freedom.[8]

In an earlier chapter we examined the views on religion of Nishi Amane, who had studied law in the Netherlands under the shogunate's sponsorship. His draft constitution, submitted in 1882 under the title *A Draft Constitution* (*Kenpō sōan*), included a provision for religious freedom, with several highly influential riders.

Citizens shall enjoy the freedom of religious belief, provided that building chapels, performing religious practices, organizing religious congregations, and propagating religious doctrines shall be prohibited for those who open or import a religion not extant as of the present unless they are granted the toleration of the government and conform to . . . regulations stipulated by the law.

Note: Toleration means for the government to permit the religion's entry only and does not mean for the authority to support it. . . .

Worship at indigenous Shintō shrines is the symbolic expression of acknowledging civic obligations and human virtues, and shall not be understood as a matter of religious belief. Shintō worship shall be based upon the popular will and the donation at such occasions shall be decided by citizens in accordance with the local customs and individual resources.[9]

This constitutional draft established a principle of religious freedom for those religions already operating in Japan at the time of the drafting, but it reserved to the government the authority to regulate those entering

Japan thereafter. Further, it specified that Shintō was not to be considered a religion. Significantly, the view that advocated separation of Shintō from religion was in accord with the position being reached among the Shintō priesthood, as discussed in Chapter 3, though based on different reasoning.

These constitutional drafts commissioned by government figures tried simultaneously to achieve two contradictory aims. On the one hand, all except Aoki's first draft and Motoda's guaranteed religious freedom, but on the other, they sought to limit that freedom by appeals to established custom and the priority placed on continued governance. Support for the idea of a state religion, seen in the first Aoki version and in the Motoda version, received no support in government, probably because the magnificent failure of the Great Promulgation Campaign was fresh in the oligarchs' minds. That the oligarchs were prepared to guarantee religious freedom in any form was due more to the pressure exerted from abroad than to their own convictions about fundamental human rights. In the circumscribed provisions for religious freedom they countenanced, the emphasis was more upon the limitations and qualifications than upon the right itself. We can see from Nishi's version that the position of Shintō continued to be somewhat ambiguous in the early 1880s.

Members of the People's Rights Movement (*jiyūminken undō*) also composed drafts for a constitution.[10] Their perspective differed greatly from that of the government figures who produced drafts. They made popular rights the standard to which government must conform, rather than the reverse. An 1881 draft written by one Chiba Takasaburō, while not a sophisticated document, nevertheless illustrates well this crucial difference.

If the government transgresses the constitutional principles of religion, morality, freedom of belief, and individual freedom, or if it does not respect the principle of the equality of all people and the right to property as written in the Constitution, or if it impairs the defenses of the country, the national assembly shall have the power to argue resolutely against, remand, and prohibit the promulgation of such acts.[11]

Chiba's version reserved extraordinary powers for protecting civil rights. In general, however, the constitutional drafts of the People's Rights Movement treated religious freedom as an inherent right, requiring only that religious practice conform to law and custom. The 1880 draft composed by the Association of Mutual Brotherhood stipulated that religious practices not in accord with the law should be liable to punishment under the law. A draft of 1881 composed by a group of merchants and landowners in Kyoto specified that funerals and festivals should be supervised by state authority.[12]

We can see in this survey of major draft constitutions that a clear division separated those who emphasized the limitations to be placed upon religious freedom and those who emphasized the liberty granted subjects and the undesirablilty of further qualifications. In both cases, however, there was a tendency to adopt Protestantism's concept of religion, which privatized religious belief and behavior and tended to regard social action associated with that belief as subordinate to subjects' discharge of civic responsibility.

Feeling the need for further deliberation on the framing of a constitution, the government sent one of the reigning oligarchs, Itō Hirobumi, to study European constitutional thought. In Germany Itō studied principally with Rudolf von Gneist[13] and Lorenz von Stein.[14] Again Gneist advocated the establishment of a state religion as a means to promote the spiritual unification of the people, and hence the strength of the nation. Opposing the separation of religion and the state, Gneist proposed that while Buddhism as the state religion could receive special patronage, other religions might be tolerated.[15]

Itō was not persuaded by Gneist's proposition. He believed that Buddhism could not unify the populace, and he held further that if there were in Japan an analogue to Christianity's role in Europe, it was loyalty to the emperor. For Itō, none of the existing religions in Japan precisely fit the bill.

Itō was apparently more impressed with the views of Lorenz von Stein, who held that although the people must be granted religious freedom, the state must reserve the authority to "guide" religious organizations. Only in this way could untrammeled competition among religions be checked and thus make possible that true religious freedom that would advance the self-fulfillment of individuals. Stein seemed to regard religion as having its core in private mental acts, and he saw religious associations as peripheral by comparison.[16]

In 1886 Itō commissioned his principal assistant Inoue Kowashi to draft a constitution, and it was the Itō-Inoue draft that was eventually enacted.[17] Inoue was aided by Herman Roesler (1834–1894), a German political scientist who had been a member of the Tokyo Imperial University since 1878 and who had served the government as a legal advisor. Roesler prepared notes on the question of religious freedom that closely informed the corresponding provision in Inoue's draft. Roesler wrote:

The freedom of religious belief implies the following rights: (1) everyone is free to adopt a certain religious faith, or change the same according to his own internal conviction, but in some countries a certain age, as conditional of the maturity of judgement, is required therefore; (2) upon no one can a certain religious faith be enforced by the government; (3) no one can be persecuted or punished, or deprived of the full enjoyment of his civil and public rights on account of his religious faith; (4) no one can be obliged to confess a religious faith at all; (5) no religious faith can be forbidden in the country except for reasons of peace and order. . . .

The freedom of religious belief does not include the right of public exercise of any faith, as mainly by public worship and public teaching or preaching. Such public exercise of religion is intimately connected with the formation of religious communities, the institution of religious authorities and ministers with powers of administration, jurisdiction and discipline in religious matters, of erecting churches and chapels, of levying contributions and the like. Religious communities may be either corporations, public or private, or mere associations without the privileges of corporate bodies. The formation of such communities requires generally the sanction of the State, and their organization is subject to the approbation of the State authorities according to the existing laws and ordinances.

By the Japanese Constitution the public exercise of religion is not freely permitted, but remains entirely under the existing laws and ordinances; and further settlement of these grave matters belongs to the future policy of the government. Religion is not altogether a private affair, nor can all the different religious denominations enjoy the same equality of rights. A state religion may be established upon the basis of national faith, and privileges may be accorded to such religion or to others related therewith.[18]

Roesler's remarks included an important distinction between the exercise of freedom of belief in private and in public. For him, freedom of belief included private and domestic worship, the right to express religious opinions privately, and the right to live in accordance with one's religious beliefs. These matters were to be left to individual discretion so long as the exercise of freedom of belief so understood did not conflict with law and public morals. Thus if bigamy were enjoined by a religion but forbidden by law, bigamy would not be a legitimate exercise of religious freedom. Except for such collisions with law and custom, however, freedom of religious belief was to be guaranteed. The freedom of religious belief did not, however, imply absolute freedom of public exercise of that faith. For example, public worship, teaching, and preaching could be regulated by the state.

In drafts of 1887, Inoue included this provision: "Every Japanese [subject] shall be protected in the enjoyment of the following rights. . . . (9) Freedom of religious belief within limits not prejudicial to peace and order and not antagonistic to the duties as citizens." He provided an alternative article, as follows: "Religious freedom shall be inviolate. Enjoyment of public and civil rights shall not differ due to the difference of religions. However, the duties of citizens shall not be exempted because of religious convictions."[19]

In 1887 Itō incorporated Roesler's views as well as his own in the final version of the Meiji Constitution's twenty-eighth article, which read, "Japanese subjects shall, within limits not prejudicial to peace and order, and not antagonistic to their duties as subjects, enjoy freedom of religious belief." Itō presented a fuller version of his views in his *Commentaries on the Constitution of the Empire of Japan* (*Kenpō gikai*). In this work, which was also drafted by Inoue Kowashi, Itō incorporated Roesler's distinction between freedom of religious belief and the public exercise of that faith.

To force upon a nation a particular form of belief by the establishment of a state religion is very injurious to the natural intellectual development of the people, and is prejudicial to the progress of science by free competition. No country, therefore, possesses by reason of its political authority, the right or the capacity to an oppressive measure touching abstract questions of religious faith. By the present Article, a great path of progress has been opened up for the individual rights of conscience, consistent with the direction in which the Government has steered its course since the Restoration.

Belief and conviction are operations of the mind. As to forms of worship, to religious discourses, to the mode of propagating a religion and to the formation of religious associations and meetings, some general legal or police restrictions must be observed for the maintenance of public peace and order. No believer in this or that religion has the right to place himself outside the pale of the law of the Empire, on the ground of his serving his god and to free himself from his duties to the State, which, as a subject, he is bound to discharge. Thus, although freedom of religious belief is complete and is exempt from all restrictions, so long as manifestations of it are confined to the mind; yet with regard to external matters such as forms of worship and the mode of propagandism, certain necessary restrictions of law or regulations must be provided for, and [in addition], the general duties of subjects must be observed. This is what the Constitution decrees, and it shows the relation in which political and religious rights stand toward each other.[20]

In Privy Council discussion of the Meiji Constitution, only one question was raised with regard to the provision for religious freedom. That concerned the traditional observance by government officials of Shintō ceremonies. Would this custom be threatened if an official who followed some religion that prohibited participation in rites of other religions refused to participate in the Shintō rites of the state? No one objected that failure to observe such rites constituted a breach of the duties of a subject. In the end, Article 28 was passed by a vote of eighteen to two.[21]

We can summarize the accomplishments of the deliberations surrounding the drafting of the Meiji Constitution's provision for religious freedom as follows. The idea of establishing a state religion was rejected. A limited provision for religious freedom was enacted. This both guaranteed subjects' right to private exercise of their faith and gave the state the authority to limit that right by appeal to civic duty and law. A crucial distinction between private and public exercise of religious faith was introduced, and the status of Shintō remained ambiguous, with a growing tendency to separate it from the sphere of religion and to align it instead with custom and patriotism.

This distinction between the private and public exercise of religious faith was clear-cut in law, but it did not conform well to the reality of Japanese religious practice. The distinction was based on Protestant-derived notions according to which religion was fundamentally a matter of private mentation, the private, spiritual relation between God and an individual human person. Action based on that relation or devotion was regarded as secondary to the privatized faith of the individual. We have seen in the Introduction that much of Japanese religiosity, especially shrine life, was in essence liturgical and communal in character. This was true of Buddhist life as well. Thus it was inevitable that the private implementation of religious belief in prayer, domestic ceremonies, and the general conduct of the personal life would extend into public settings. The state's desire to retain control over all public religious expression motivated some spectacular instances of suppression, examined later in this chapter.

THE IMPERIAL RESCRIPT ON EDUCATION

The 1890 promulgation of the Imperial Rescript on Education (Kyōiku chokugo) profoundly affected the exercise of religious freedom although its content did not refer to the question at all. Throughout society the rescript was treated in its content and as an artifact as a holy thing, symbolic of the spiritual unification of the Japanese people. As such it was used to identify and stigmatize as traitorous and unpatriotic anyone failing to uphold it as sacred. Shintō figures were active in promoting public reverence for it.

The rescript originated in the reaction against the importation of many Western ideas and material goods. Such traditionalists as Yamagata Aritomo[22] and Motoda Eifu led the move to secure an imperial statement that could serve as the basis of public morality. Again leaders turned to Inoue Kowashi, but he cautioned his sponsors that the government should not initiate instruction in matters of ethics and religion because of the conflict with the constitutional provision for religious freedom. Eventually he accepted the assignment to draft the rescript on the following conditions. It should have no legal function; it should advocate no particular religion or political philosophy; it should adopt neither Confucian nor Western terminology; and it should not restrict subjects' constitutional rights. These conditions were accepted, and the rescript was completed as follows.

Know ye, Our subjects,
Our imperial ancestors have founded Our Empire on a basis broad and everlasting, and subjects ever united in loyalty and filial piety have from generation to generation illustrated the beauty thereof. This is the glory of the fundamental character of Our Empire, and therein also lies the source of Our education. Ye, Our subjects, be filial to your parents, affectionate to your brothers and sisters;

as husbands and wives be harmonious, as friends true; bear yourselves in modesty and moderation; extend your benevolence to all; pursue learning and cultivate arts, and thereby develop intellectual faculties and perfect moral powers; furthermore, advance public good and promote common interests; always respect the Constitution and observe the laws; should emergency arise, offer yourselves courageously to the State; and thus guard and maintain the prosperity of Our Imperial Throne coeval with heaven and earth. So shall be not only ye Our good and faithful subjects, but render illustrious the best traditions of your forefathers.

The Way here set forth is indeed the teaching bequeathed by Our Imperial Ancestors, to be observed alike by Their Descendants and the subjects, infallible for all ages and true in all places. It is Our wish to lay it to heart in all reverence, in common with you, Our subjects, that we may all attain to the same virtue.[23]

The Imperial Rescript on Education became the pillar of prewar Japan's ethics and morality. Its supercharged symbolic value exceeded by far the prestige and authority of anything but the emperor himself. It provided an identifiable focus of unity for the populace as a whole and for the Shintō priesthood in particular. It made loyalty and filial piety into absolute, universal values that could not be questioned or subordinated to anything else.[24]

The Imperial Rescript on Education received great attention from the press, but its most influential interpretation was Inoue Tetsujirō's *Commentary on the Imperial Rescript on Education* (*Chokugo engi*), published in 1891. This work used such figures from Western history as George Washington, Joan of Arc, and Socrates to prove the universal truth and superiority of loyalty and filial piety as ethical values. Loyalty and filial piety were made the foundation of the state, thus laying the groundwork for the family-state ideal that so completely pervaded imperial Japan. Some four million copies of this work were printed.[25]

The rescript was far more consequential as a result of its use than because of its content. Copies were distributed to all public elementary and middle schools, and all schoolchildren were required to memorize it from the second grade. The minister of education enjoined prefectural governors to treat the scroll respectfully and to hold monthly assemblies of school pupils for its ceremonial reading.[26] These ceremonies soon developed into elaborate school rituals of paying homage to the rescript and the imperial photo. These rites were examined in detail in Chapter 5, where we saw how Shintō priests were mobilized in the distribution of the rescript and in the standardization of rites.

The role of Shintō priests in the promulgation of the Imperial Rescript on Education and in accompanying rites gave the document itself as well as the rites a Shintō character in the popular mind. Supercharging the document and its rites in this way helped to promote the idea that observance of these rites and of Shintō rites in general was a part of each subject's obligation to the state, giving these ceremonies an obligatory character in popular perception. Needless to say the priesthood was quick to capitalize on that perception. The opportunity to do so arose almost immediately, when a Christian schoolteacher named Uchimura Kanzō (1861–1930) refused to pay obeisance to the rescript.

Uchimura was a graduate of Sapporo Agricultural School and Amherst College. He had converted to Christianity by forsaking worship of the kami as a form of idolatry. Also a strong nationalist, he had no quarrel with the content of the Imperial Rescript on Education, but he deeply resented the deification of the document itself. Thus he faced an ethical crisis when on 9 January 1891 the principal of the First Higher Preparatory School in Tokyo directed Uchimura and all the other faculty of the school to make obeisance to the scroll of the rescript after he, the principal, had given it a ceremonial reading. Uchimura describes what happened next as follows:

After the address of the [principal] and reading of the [Imperial Rescript on Education], the professors and students were asked to go up to the platform one by one, and bow to the Imperial signature affixed to the [rescript], in the manner as we used to bow before our ancestral relics prescribed in Buddhist and Shintō ceremonies. I was not at all prepared [for] such a strange ceremony, for [it] was the new invention of the [principal] of the school. . . . Hesitating in doubt, I took a safer course for my Christian conscience, and in the august presence of sixty professors (all non-Christians, the two other Christian professors beside myself having absented themselves) and over one thousand students, I took my stand and did not bow. . . . For a week after the ceremony, I received several students and [professors] who came to me, and with all the meekness I could muster . . . I told them also that the good Emperor must have given the [rescript] to his subjects not to be bowed unto, but to be obeyed in our daily walks in life.[27]

This celebrated incident became the occasion for renewed invective against Christianity as an unpatriotic, foreign religion, incompatible with "the Japanese Way." Uchimura was pilloried in the press and removed from his position by the minister of education. Blind to the challenge to the principle of religious freedom and the potential implications for themselves later on, Buddhist writers enthusiastically leaped to the attack. It goes without saying that Shintō figures were unanimous in their condemnation of Uchimura. Perhaps the most compelling attack came from Inoue Tetsujirō (1855–1944), then professor of philosophy at Tokyo Imperial University, who held that the Uchimura incident in reality exposed the conflict between the Imperial Rescript on Education and Christian ethics, the former based on a particularistic patriotism and the latter on "indiscriminate" universal love.[28]

To this attack the Christian rejoinder was disappointingly weak. The majority tended to see the school ceremonies as acceptable social custom that could be distinguished from religious worship. Other responses, as for example that by the Christian minister Kashiwagi Gien, to the accusation about conflicting ethical principles defended the idea of Christianity's universal love and challenged the rescript. The majority, however, tried to show that Christianity actually conformed to the principles of the rescript. Various apologists cited the Hebrew Bible's premium on filial piety, the notion of rendering unto Caesar his due, and so on. They failed to recognize the challenge to the principle of religious freedom represented by the ceremonies for the rescript and by Inoue Tetsujirō's critique of Uchimura Kanzō.[29]

THE RELIGIOUS ORGANIZATIONS LAW

The state sought in 1899 to enact a legislative code that would standardize control of the operations of religious organizations. Having reserved to itself the authority to regulate the public practice of religion in the constitution, the stipulation of the scope of such regulation was a logical step. However, this proposed legislation repeatedly ran afoul of the constitutional provision for religious freedom. Attempts to pass it in 1899, 1927, and 1929 all failed, and it was not until 1940 that it was enacted.

The first draft of the Religious Organizations Law included the following provisions. It required religious organizations to give notice to government authorities of all public worship, and to seek government permission for altering their internal regulations and constructing buildings. The representatives of religious organizations were to be installed only with government approval. A special court was to be established to settle conflicts involving religion. Religious teachers could be suspended by the state from their posts if they were deemed a threat to social order, and they were prohibited from expressing political views or participating in political activities. Violation of these statutes was to be punishable by fine and imprisonment.[30]

The main sponsor of the bill was Yamagata Aritomo, one of the staunchest of the traditionalists in government, who was responsible for much other repressive legislation, such as the Peace Preservation Ordinance, the Press Code, and the Publications Ordinance. In general he was opposed to constitutionalism, as he asserted himself in a message of 1901 to the emperor:

My interpretation of the Constitution differs from that of Itō. . . . I am absolutely opposed to a party cabinet. My only hope is that Imperial authority will be extended and Imperial prestige will not decline.[31]

Yamagata could accept the idea of religious freedom only to the extent that it was harnessed to the goal of strengthening imperial authority, not as an inherent right of Japanese subjects. In essence his Religious Organizations Law was an attempt to establish the bureaucratic mechanisms by which religious organizations could be made to serve the state.

The bill came in for heavy fire when it was discussed in the House of Peers. The idea of a special court for religious affairs was criticized as infringing upon the autonomy of religious organizations. One councillor censured the provision allowing the state to prohibit proselytization activities deemed incompatible with social custom as tantamount to regulating the content of religious practice. A Shintō priest objected to punishments for those who slandered other religions because in his view propaganda of that kind was inseparable from advocacy of one's own religion, and that advocacy was an essential part of religious life.[32] The bill was defeated.

A revised version of the bill was submitted in 1900, but its proposed sphere of control over religious bodies was, if anything, even wider, limiting the tax-exempt status of religious organizations and expanding the role of the special court for religious affairs. This version of the bill was criticized for usurping the self-government of religious organizations. It was found to be contrary to the constitutional principle of religious freedom. The bill was again defeated.[33]

Discussion of the bill among religious leaders focused upon the advantage or disadvantage likely to accrue to a particular religion. Leaders of such major Buddhist schools and sects as the Rinzai, Sōtō, Tendai, and Jōdo schools, and the Nishi-Honganji sect of the Jōdo-Shin school all supported the bill on the grounds that incorporation would itself be beneficial. The Higashi-Honganji sect of the Jōdo-Shin school, the Nichiren school, and the Shingon school opposed the bill on the grounds that it was insulting to Buddhism to be put on the same footing with Christianity. Only a few Christians, Uemura Masahisa[34] among them, resisted the bill. Uemura opposed it because it limited the autonomy of religious organizations, restricted the civil rights of religious leaders by prohibiting their participation in political activities, and obstructed the freedom of religious association. Most leaders, however, failed to see the challenge to the principle of religious freedom and decided their position upon a narrow calculation of self-interest.[35]

Rejected a second time by the House of Peers, Yamagata was still not prepared to accept the verdict of the legislature. Instead, under Article 9 of the constitution, which empowered the government to issue ordinances, he promulgated regulations that effectively enacted the substance of the Religious Organizations Law. Thus he skillfully evaded the legislative process entirely. In these ordinances of 1900 and 1908, the police were granted broad powers of surveillance over religious activities. Specifically, they were empowered to supervise healing activities and to suspend such activities if they were deemed undesirable. Clearly, these ordinances represented a major challenge to the principle of religious freedom and established a strong system of bureaucratic control over religious bodies.[36]

The drafts of 1927 and 1929 for the Religious Organizations Law were essentially identical, and they were twice the size of the preceding bills. Many religious leaders lent their support to the bill because of its provisions for tax exemption and various benefits of incorporation. Few recognized its challenge to the principle of religious freedom. The bill's supporters in government defended it by referring to the government's right to regulate religious practice in public, just as it could control the press, publication, and association.[37] It was not until 1940, when the mood of the entire country had become pervasively militarized, and when many other systems of statist control were firmly in place, that the Religious Organizations Law was finally passed.

THE SUPPRESSION OF NEW RELIGIOUS MOVEMENTS

Both before and after the Meiji Restoration, nineteenth-century Japan witnessed a marked growth in popular religious movements outside the control of Shintō and Buddhist clergies. Groups founded before the Restoration, such as Tenrikyō, Kurozumikyō, and Konkōkyō, had by the 1890s spread nationwide, far beyond their rural origins. By the 1920s a group called Ōmotokyō had also grown rapidly, and in that decade such mass associations as Reiyūkai Kyōdan, Seichō no Ie, and Sōka Gakkai appeared and proselytized very successfully in the large cities.[38]

The rapid growth of these various religious associations was perceived as a potential threat by government bureaucrats. The clergies of Buddhism and Shintō also greatly disliked them because members often dissolved all former religious affiliations upon joining one of the new groups. To intellectuals these groups seemed reactionary and antimodern because of their frequently unsophisticated doctrine and pervasive faith healing and because they often appeared to contain more superstition than religion. Nor did their practices conform to the Protestant-inspired notions of religion then current. Thus in both bureaucratic language and the popular press it was common to refer to these new religious movements across the board as "pseudo-religions" (*ruiji shūkyō*).[39]

Under the broad powers of surveillance of religion granted the police by the Yamagata ordinances discussed above, and later under the Peace Preservation Law, many new religious associations were suppressed. In 1921 some 130 police descended upon the headquarters of Ōmotokyō, where they arrested leaders and destroyed buildings on charges of violation of the Newspaper Law and lèse majesté.[40] In 1926 Ōnishi Aijirō, the leader of a schism from Tenrikyō named Honmichi, taking the illness of his son as a heavenly warning of impending doom, published a pamphlet predicting that Japan would be defeated in a great war. He also denied the emperor's divinity and the truth of Japanese myth. In 1928 Honmichi leaders and believers across the nation were arrested and 179 charged with lèse majesté. Both Ōmotokyō and Honmichi were officially declared "evil religions" (jakyō).[41]

These suppressions were followed by massive suppression of Ōmotokyō in 1935, the suppression of a group called Hitonomichi in 1936, and a second suppression of Honmichi in 1938.[42] In the 1935 suppression of Ōmotokyō 550 police attacked the group's headquarters and reduced its buildings to pieces no larger than one Japanese foot, lest larger pieces be used to rebuild these edifices. Clearly the intent was to destroy the religion completely, again on charges of lèse majesté. The leader Deguchi Ōnisaburō was sentenced to life imprisonment, and he only regained his freedom after Japan's defeat in 1945. Hundreds of followers were arrested. Hitonomichi's fall came in spite of its attempts to toe the government line; the group was charged with holding a vulgar interpretation of the national mythology, was branded as an evil religion, and its leader Miki Tokuharu jailed. Honmichi had embraced pacifism, and its leader Ōnishi refused to let believers participate in war efforts in any capacity. When he issued a second pamphlet warning of impending disaster, he and a thousand of his followers were arrested. Ōnishi was put in jail and died there, and the group was proscribed. In 1930 Sōka Gakkai, a laymen's association attached to the Nichiren school of Buddhism, was suppressed for refusal to worship talismans from the Ise Shrines. Sōka Gakkai's leader Makiguchi Tsunesaburō was arrested and died in prison.[43]

These incidents are only the most spectacular examples of the suppression of new religious movements; there were many more on a smaller scale. New religious movements were not, however, the only forms of religious association to be suppressed. The Nichiren school of Buddhism was charged with lèse majesté because its doctrine described the sun goddess of imperial mythology as a protective deity of the Lotus Sutra, a position that implied that the goddess held lesser status than Buddhist divinities. The True Pure Land school of Buddhism was charged with weakness in its respect for government mythology. These incidents came about in spite of the Buddhist organizations' public declarations of allegiance to the state and its ideology.[44] The Holiness Church of Japan was forced to disband, and approximately fifty of its members were arrested. This group believed in a judgment day—time and place to be decided by Yahweh—a doctrine that contradicted the idea of the emperor's absolute authority.[45]

Although each of these incidents of suppression constituted an attack on the principle of religious freedom, there was only one direct challenge to the government's actions on those grounds. The case concerned a local leader of Hitonomichi who opened a place of worship without following the required registration procedure. For this, the leader was imprisoned for ten days. An intellectual of the day, Matsumoto Shigetoshi, appealed this case to the nation's highest court, on the grounds that the Hitonomichi leader's religious freedom had been violated; he had done nothing prejudicial to peace and order and hence should be left alone. Nevertheless, the high court upheld the lower court's verdict, saying that the city ordinance (violated when the new church was not properly registered) was itself established for the purpose of peace and order, and hence in failing to obey it the religious leader was not exercising religious freedom in conformity with peace and order. Thus while Matsumoto had read the constitutional guarantee with an emphasis on limitations implied for governing authorities—who should not abrogate religious freedom unless peace and order were clearly threatened—the high court emphasized the limitations placed upon the people's exercise of religious freedom. This precedent emboldened the state and the police to increase their surveillance of religious associations of all kinds.[46]

SHINTŌ'S ROLE IN RESTRICTING RELIGIOUS FREEDOM

Restrictions increasingly applied to the exercise of religious freedom as guaranteed in the Meiji Constitution were often rooted in the notion that shrine observances were a part of a subject's civic duty, and that as a consequence they had an obligatory character. Thus if a person refused a talisman from the Ise Shrines or doubted the truth of Shintō myth, or took umbrage at the Shintō trappings surrounding ceremonies for reading the Imperial Rescript on Education, such actions could be taken as a dereliction of civic duty, even though no national law required anyone to do any of these things. The definition of such Shintō observances as nonreligious facilitated their classification under the category of civic duty. This vague, assimilationist thinking did not come about only by bureaucratic fiat and sleight of hand. The Shintō priesthood had been active since the Restoration in the promotion of exactly this type of thought.

In earlier chapters we examined the motives drawing the Shintō priesthood closer to government: the desire to secure official sanction, the desire to lay claim to official status, the desire to use offical status to improve personal status. Priests were much better able to act effectively toward these goals when national and prefectural associations of shrine priests had been formed (by around 1900), when the training of priests was standardized through the creation of Kokugakuin University, and when leaders of national status had emerged. Shintō academics could act as spokesmen for priests because their university status transcended localized loyalties.

Through a variety of ingenious means, the priesthood tried to promote the idea that shrine participation was an integral part of communal life. A concerted effort on their part was necessary because the general populace had no such consciousness at the beginning of the twentieth century. The favored technique was to create ties with local schools, to bring children to the shrines at regular intervals for instruction by priests on patriotic themes, presented in such a way as to show that shrines were somehow at the center of patriotism. The national journal of the prewar priesthood, *Jinja kyōkai zasshi*, is replete with articles instructing priests how to deal with children and youth, and the many inquiries from priests on such points show that there was indeed a high level of commitment to this sort of outreach.

There were problems associated with the manner and content of the instruction priests offered to people in society at large. Since the priesthood had settled on the position that Shintō was not a religion, it was not possible to expound doctrines. Instead, the priests strove to create and strengthen attitudes of gratitude, respect, and reverence for the kami, without becoming more specific. In fact, the relation of religion to Shintō was still ambiguous, and public debate on this question continued.[47] As vague and amorphous as the priests' self-presentation was, they still succeeded in silencing challenges to Shintō's supposedly inviolate stature in national life, as the affair of Kume Kunitake shows.

This incident reflects more directly upon questions of academic freedom than upon the freedom of religion, but it reveals that by the 1890s Shintō figures were much more capable of engaging in public debate than they had been twenty years earlier when the discussion of Shintō's religiosity first appeared. Kume Kunitake (1839–1931) was a historian at Tokyo Imperial University. In 1891 he published an essay holding that Shintō represented the remains of an ancient worship of Heaven.[48] In other words, while Kume accepted the official Shintō line that Shintō was not a religion, his position was that it "was not even a religion," whereas the reading sanctioned by the priesthood held that Shintō transcended all religions and was something grander by far. As a result, Shintō ideologues raised a great hue and cry, and the minister of education removed Kume from his post in 1892. It would have been impossible for the priesthood to exert such pressure had their members not begun to organize in national and prefectural associations.

The Kanagawa Prefecture Shrine Priests' Association exemplifies patterns found nationwide. Founded in 1898, its principal activities included collection campaigns to raise money to send to the government during wartime, lectures on patriotic subjects, and a journal for the information of its members. In fact, fund-raising to contribute to Japan's various twentieth-century wars was universal among the prefectural associations of shrine priests. The Kanagawa branch also campaigned for government funding for the National and Imperial Shrines. Various local chapters undertook special public prayers and ceremonies to send soldiers off to war or compiled and distributed pamphlets on shrine rites and patriotic subjects.[49]

Writers and lecturers capable of rousing the priesthood to activity emerged. A lecturer named Suzuki Nobuhiko was particularly active in drumming up sentiment in rural areas to have the priesthood break all ties with the Shintō sects, lest these overlapping affiliations confuse the populace on the nonreligious character of Shintō.[50] Inasmuch as cutting those ties inevitably entailed a decrease in income, compliance meant a considerable sacrifice for shrine priests. Another wartime lecturer promoted the idea that all subjects must band together as a single body to escape domination by the West. Every deed must be performed in service to the nation. Every subject was a soldier. "A subject's duty is to have reverence for the gods from the bottom of one's heart and in that spirit to be sincere in every action."[51]

Suzuki Shirō, a priest who wrote and lectured widely in the 1930s and 1940s, traveled about urging priests to adopt novel techniques to attract the interest of their parishioners. He proposed that someone should make a film about Shintō, like the *King of Kings*, and include in it a treatment of shrine rites, thus bringing home to local people the close tie between rural life and Shintō, and promoting the "Japanese spirit," a term he was careful never to define. He also suggested that priests make comic-book versions of the classics to educate young children, and recommended that priests become writers of popular novels.[52] Suzuki was a skilled promoter of close relations between Shintō and the educational system. In 1932 he published a text for use by shrine priests in educating schoolchildren, and he recommended that each priest cultivate ties with local teachers and schools and give a course of lectures and presentations to each grade of elementary pupils every month. His text was divided into urban and rural sections, and each of these was further subdivided into six sections, according to school grades. For each monthly entry he prepared themes and questions, usually centering on the shrine rites performed at that time of year, supplemented by such items as "shrines and government," "shrines and national life," and "shrines and the colonies." An annotated bibliography suggested extra reading, and he encouraged priests to arrange for regular visits to the shrine by schoolchildren to clean the precincts and hear these lectures. Finally, Suzuki hammered home the idea that "the schools are Shintō's proselytization grounds," and suggested many ways by which priests could get their message across.[53]

Chapter 3 showed what great diversity existed among the Shintō priesthood. It would be misleading to suggest that with the formation of national and prefectural priests' associations members of the priesthood suddenly fell into lockstep. Nevertheless, one can say that there was no dissent on the desirability of presenting shrine participation as both patriotic and obligatory. Such a presentation achieved more credibility with the appearance of Shintō leaders in positions of national prominence. One example of Shintō's prewar leadership is Kōno Seizō.

Kōno was originally a priest of the Tamashiki District Shrine of Saitama Prefecture, located near the Hikawa Shrine and not far removed from the other Saitama shrines served by the diarists discussed in Chapter 3. Kōno graduated from Kokugakuin University, and that qualified him automatically to teach at normal school, middle-school, and women's high school. He took up a middle-school teaching post in Saitama upon his graduation. In 1929 he became director of Shintō Studies at Kokugakuin, though he still maintained close ties with educational circles in Saitama. The Ministry of Education appointed him in 1932 to its People's Spiritual Culture Institute (Kokumin seishin bunka kenkyūsho), and after he became president of Kokugakuin in 1935, he was appointed by the Ministry of Education to the editorial board of the highly influential ethics textbook, *The Fundamental Principles of the National Structure (Kokutai no hongi)*. He was also a member of the supervisory and investigative boards of national textbooks, and in 1941 he was appointed by the cabinet to investigate school curricula. In 1944 he was appointed by the Ministry of Education as the central director of wartime religious education. A noted scholar in addition to these public and administrative posts, Kōno provided a powerful model for the national priesthood, and his example proves that by the early decades of the twentieth century a Shintō figure could rise to a position of tremendous influence over the character of Japanese education.[54] While Kōno was hardly representative of the priesthood as a whole, priests increasingly achieved positions of prominence in local society in the twentieth century.

CONCLUSION

The Meiji Constitution's provision for freedom of religion and the idea that Shintō was not a religion emerged in tandem in an atmosphere of considerable diplomatic pressure on Japan to satisfy foreign governments on the question of religious freedom and under the burden of peculiarly Protestant notions of religion at odds with Japan's own religious history. The result for Shintō was its alignment with civic duty and patriotism, while the consequence for recognized religious associations was a tight circumscription of the exercise of religious freedom. In effect, Japanese subjects were free to believe in a religion but not necessarily to practice it publicly. Members of unrecognized religious associations frequently fell victim to suppression and persecution.

As Shintō drew closer to the state, its alliance with the nationalistic, chauvinistic patriotism of the times and its assumption of a pseudo-obligatory character increasingly divided the priesthood from parishioners, whose attachment to shrines continued to be religious in character. The members of the priesthood neither provided leadership for the popular religious life of shrines, nor did they understand the religious sentiments of the people in any depth. This situation yielded the paradoxical result that, while State Shintō was in many ways profoundly influential in prewar social life, it did not permeate the religious consciousness of the people very deeply.

7. Shintō and the State since 1945

JAPAN'S DEFEAT in World War II led to radical changes in Shintō and in Shintō's relation to the state. Like other Japanese religions, Shintō suffered greatly from postwar demographic changes, but, more than others, it seems to have been thoroughly discredited by its association with the prewar state. One of the first acts of the Allied Occupation was to end all state patronage of Shintō. The principle of religious freedom was combined with that of separation of religion and government in a single article of the postwar constitution, and as a result participation in shrine rites lost its formerly semi-obligatory character. Shrines were put on the same legal basis as any other religious organization and thus lost all financial support from public funds. As a result of these several changes, Shintō has ceased to link the populace to the prestige of the state, and hence it has lost much of its former popular appeal.

In the prewar era Shintō received state patronage in the many forms examined in detail in preceding chapters. Shintō contributed significantly to the legitimation of the prewar state and to state-sponsored myths of the cultural identity of the Japanese people, and nowhere was this symbolic presentation more effectively orchestrated than at the Yasukuni Shrine. When the emperor, the cabinet, and the military joined in paying tribute at the shrine's spring and autumn festivals, they illustrated the symbolic unity of the emperor with his subjects, the sacred sanction enjoyed by the political regime, and the highest value to which a Japanese subject could aspire: death in the nation's service, followed by apotheosis as a national deity. All the differences of gender, class, and ethnicity that weighed so heavily in determining an individual's access to opportunity and resources were buried in the symbolic harmony and unity thus presented.

The Allied Occupation's religious policies went far towards demolishing this symbolic edifice, and for some decades the secular government lacked a myth of legitimation that could anchor its own rule in some sacred source of authority and also set forth a compelling myth of Japanese cultural identity. Indeed, the exigencies of the early postwar decades demanded first the reconstruction of the nation's economic infrastructure.

With the achievement of a secure position as a global economic power and the tapering off of rapid economic growth since the oil shock of 1973, however, the government of Japan has achieved the leisure for the sort of introspection that produces a forceful statement of political legitimation. Stung by international criticism of the Japanese as rapacious "economic animals," the government since the 1970s has begun moving toward re-instituting the prewar symbolic unity of state and religion, centering again upon the Yasukuni Shrine. Whether specific individuals in government consciously intend this outcome cannot be known and is beside the point. In fact, nonetheless, we can see a clear reassertion of prewar patterns, indicating both the tenacity of the theme of a unity of religion and the state, and the inability of such secular ideals as democracy, capitalism, and rationalism to generate a symbolic order strong enough in its appeal to compete with those more deeply rooted in Japanese history and religious tradition. Also discernible is the desire to legitimate Japan's prewar and wartime regimes, to obliterate from the national memory incidents of persecution, suppression of individual liberties, and wartime atrocities in Asia. The state has pursued this end through its patronage of the Yasukuni Shrine and through a rewriting of history in the texts used in public schools. The political culture of postwar Japan is, however, highly pluralistic and open, and the state cannot institute these changes without encountering vigorous criticism from academics and the religious world.

SHINTŌ AND THE OCCUPATION

Before 1945, little was known about Shintō in the West, and the American directors of religious affairs within the Occupation had few guides. Coverage of Shintō in the Western popular press before 1945 had employed predictable wartime rhetoric, portraying Shintō as the "engine of war," responsible for the fanaticism of the kamikaze and possibly for all Japanese militarism.

The work of Daniel C. Holtom was highly influential in the Occupation's thinking on Shintō. Holtom was author of *The National Faith of Japan* (1938) and *Modern Japan and Shintō Nationalism* (1947). Six of the latter work's eight chapters were originally published in 1943. As these titles suggest, Holtom connected Shintō with nationalism, imperialism, and militarism, explaining that Shintō, originally a cult lacking political significance, had been perverted by militarists. He credited Shintō with imbuing prewar society with chauvinistic patriotism and unswerving loyalty to the emperor. The Occupation hoped to secure Holtom's services, but ill health prevented him from accepting this assignment.[1] Nevertheless, his views were much respected by Occupation personnel responsible for religious affairs.

While General Douglas MacArthur, supreme commander of the allied powers, played no direct role in administering religious affairs, his views were well publicized. According to William Woodward, foremost authority on Occupation religion policy, MacArthur "had something of a messianic complex—a consciousness of being called of God for the hour and a confidence that God was on his side!"[2] Shintō leaders seriously feared that he meant to Christianize Japan, by force if necessary.[3] Some of his more spontaneous remarks encouraged this anxiety. To Protestant leaders visiting Japan in the fall of 1945, he declared, "Japan is a spiritual vacuum. If you do not fill it with Christianity, it will be filled with Communism. Send me 1,000 missionaries."[4] In a radio message to Congress on 24 February 1947, MacArthur quite erroneously stated that some two million had been converted to Christianity, "as a means to fill the spiritual vacuum left in the Japanese life by collapse of their past faith."[5] Such statements angered Buddhists as well as Shintō leaders, but there was little need to fear that the nation could be converted so readily.

The Occupation established offices for administering religious affairs in the Civil Information and Education Section (CIES) of the Supreme Commander of the Allied Powers (SCAP). CIES, a special staff section of SCAP with the duty of advising MacArthur on matters of public information, education, religion and "sociological problems,"[6] was headed by Colonel (later Brigadier General) Ken R. Dyke.[7] CIES was to promote religious freedom and consult with religious organizations in order to secure their cooperation in the Occupation's objectives.

Within CIES a Religions Division was established in November 1945, headed by Lieutenant (later Lieutenant Commander) William Kenneth Bunce, United States Naval Reserve.[8] At its maximum strength the Religions Division had only seventeen Americans working for it.[9] It produced the Shintō Directive (Shintō shirei; see Appendix 2), and it cooperated with the Ministry of Education in drafting the Religious Juridical Persons Law (Shūkyō hōjin hō). It also investigated persecutions of religious persons and organizations before 1945, investigated claims of confiscation of property, studied the practices and management of the Yasukuni Shrine and other shrines for the war dead, assisted in the return of Christian missionaries, and investigated certain organizations suspected of being ultranationalists masquerading as religious groups.

The Religions Division had no detailed operational plan for establishing religious freedom, and a shortage of personnel also contributed to inconsistencies in policy implementation. Moreover, it did not have a high priority within the Occupation.[10]

Important changes were also taking place in the Japanese government. On 15 October 1945 a Religious Affairs Section was created within the Ministry of Education. The Shrine Board was abolished on 2 February 1946.

THE SHINTŌ DIRECTIVE

The Shintō Directive, issued on 15 December 1945, provided official notification of Occupation policy on religion. In October, however, John Carter Vincent, chief of the Division of Far Eastern Affairs of the State Department, had already announced on radio that Shintō was to be done away with, insofar as it was manipulated by the Japanese state, which would be required to end all patronage of Shintō. The broadcast caught Occupation authorities by surprise and they were hard pressed to answer the many inquiries about it from Japanese religious leaders.[11]

The purposes of the Shintō Directive were to relieve the Japanese people from any compulsion to believe in or practice any religion sponsored by the state, to free them from the duty of financially supporting such a religion, to prevent any future use of Shintō for nationalistic or militaristic ends, and to assist them in realizing the ideal of democracy. The directive banned all "propagation and dissemination of militaristic and ultranationalistic ideology" in anything connected with Shintō. It abolished all public educational institutions engaged in the study of Shintō or in training the priesthood. Thus, Kōgakkan University, a public university for priests' training, was abolished, but the private Shintō university Kokugakuin University was unaffected.[12] The educational system was purged of all "dissemination of Shintō doctrine in any forms and by any means," and thus all mention of Shintō was expunged from textbooks and teachers' manuals. School trips to shrines were forbidden, and the altars enshrining the imperial portrait and the Imperial Rescript on Education were removed.

The directive attempted to end debate on the question whether Shintō was a religion in a single pronouncement:

2.c. The term State Shintō within the meaning of this directive will refer to that branch of Shintō (Kokka Shintō or Jinja Shintō) which by official acts of the Japanese Government has been differentiated from the religion of Sect Shintō (Shūha Shintō or Kyōha Shintō) and has been classified a non-religious national cult commonly known as State Shintō, National Shintō, or Shrine Shintō. 2.d. The term Sect Shintō (Shūha Shintō or Kyōha Shintō) will refer to that branch of Shintō (composed of 13 recognized sects) which by popular belief, legal commentary, and the official acts of the Japanese Government has been recognized to be a religion.

2.e.(1) Sect Shintō will enjoy the same protection as any other religion.

2.e.(2) Shrine Shintō, after having been divorced from the state and divested of its militaristic and ultranationalistic elements, will be recognized as a religion if its adherents so desire and will be granted the same protection as any other religion in so far as it may in fact be the philosophy or religion of Japanese individuals.

The public reacted calmly to the directive. The Japanese press showed little concern for its implications for the shrines. Instead, the newspapers were most interested in its significance for the status of the imperial family and the educational system.[13]

Shintō priests were relieved to learn that the Shintō Directive did not require the destruction or closing of shrines. Nevertheless, loss of state patronage undermined the basis of Shintō's very existence, and, as we will see below, Shintō never really recovered from this blow. The priesthood had realized as early as the Vincent broadcast that Shintō would soon face a great crisis. Leaders of the major prewar Shintō organizations banded together and in January 1946 formed the Association of Shintō Shrines (Jinja Honchō), which continues to direct shrine affairs for the great majority of shrines today.[14]

The association named the Ise Grand Shrines the "Head Shrine" of Japan because of their close connection to the imperial house. Forsaking descriptions of shrines as responsible for the "rites of the nation," the association said this about their changed significance:

The true meaning of reverence for the shrines lies in the clarification and enhancement of the traditional faith which, following the great way of Shintō, clarifies the way of human relations, gives thanks for favors received from the *kami*, carries out the virtues of the ancestors, promotes the pure and faithful spirit and characteristics of the Japanese people, and thus contributes to the happiness and peace of humanity.[15]

RELIGIOUS FREEDOM AND THE SEPARATION
OF CHURCH AND STATE

As we have seen in Chapter 6, the Meiji Constitution had provided for religious freedom but not for the separation of church and state. The situation was radically changed by the postwar Constitution of Japan (1947), which forbids "discrimination in political, economic, or social relations because of . . . creed" (Article 14), provides in Article 19 that "freedom of thought and conscience shall not be violated," in a single article guarantees the freedom of religion and the separation of church and state (Article 20), and prohibits the use of public funds for religious purposes (Article 89).

Of these several provisions, Articles 20 and 89 have been most consequential in subsequent church-state relations.

Article 20: Freedom of religion is guaranteed to all. No religious organization shall receive any privileges from the state, nor exercise any political authority. No person shall be compelled to take part in any religious act, celebration, rite, or practice. The State and its organs shall refrain from religious education or any other religious activity.

Article 89: No public money or other property shall be expended or appropriated for the use, benefit or maintenance of any religious institution or association, or for any charitable, educational or benevolent enterprises not under the control of public authority.

Bunce and the staff of the Religions Division were not directly involved in the drafting of the constitution's provisions on religion, but Bunce was shown a preliminary draft and held discussions with the drafters before the final version was issued. The drafters consulted constitutions from a number of countries, and the Philippine constitution was most directly influential in the provisions above.

The drafters of Articles 20 and 89 were most concerned with the separation of church and state. They did not fully appreciate what effect their provisions would have on existing religious organizations, especially because they did not coordinate their project with the Religions Division. Then an officer of the Religions Division, William Woodward judged them harshly:

No member of the group was professionally informed on religion in Japan and none had any clear ideas as to how the principles enunciated would affect religious organizations. Their sole purpose was to separate religion and state. They were not motivated by any special philosophy regarding the place of religion in education. They had not the slightest idea as to how the government and religious leaders would react to such a drastic proposal as banning of all government grants to sectarian educational and social welfare institutions. Frankly their special concern was to prevent Shintō from ever again becoming entrenched in the government and the educational system of the country. They intended to purge Shintō from the state and they hewed to the line of complete separation without much regard to what would happen as a result of such a policy.[16]

Thus in Article 20 religious freedom and the separation of church and state are treated as inseparable, as two sides of the same coin.

Discussion in the Diet on these provisions was remarkably brief and confined to anxieties that religions were being allowed too much free-dom.[17] Reaction by religious leaders, including Shintō leaders, was gener-ally positive, but the ban upon religious education occasioned some contro-versy. It was not entirely clear whether teaching about religion as an aspect of human culture and as a force in Japanese history would be banned along with evangelism.[18]

Article 89 raised fears that religious organizations would lose their tax-exempt status and the ability to seek redress for confiscation of lands during the Meiji period. The status of religious charities also seemed doubtful in the absence of government subsidy.[19]

THE RELIGIOUS JURIDICAL PERSONS LAW

In Chapter 6 we saw how the Religions Bill was used to restrict religious freedom. The Religious Juridical Persons Law, promulgated 3 April 1951, was designed to supplant prewar legislation and to enable religious organi-zations to acquire legal capacity.[20]

Drafted with the cooperation of Japanese religious leaders and the Religious Affairs Section of the Ministry of Education, the law granted religious organizations tax-exempt status and specified the mechanisms of incorporation. The latter were formulated specifically to prevent the gov-ernment from using the fact of incorporation or nonincorporation as a litmus test for whether the organization was a religion or not. Several religious organizations actually requested some distinction between "true" and "false" religions, apparently in fear of the marked contemporary growth of new religious movements, but these requests were denied.[21]

Religious leaders' reactions were mixed. Buddhists and Christians wel-comed the new legislation, and the Union of New Religions (Shinshūren), representing many newly founded religions, was highly enthusiastic.[22] Shintō leaders objected that the new law gave too much authority to pa-rishioners when it should have reserved more prerogatives for the priest-hood.[23] Fear of the new religions remained strong even among Christians, as this critique by the Reverend Kozaki Michio, an official of the United Church of Christ in Japan, shows:

[In] principle, religion should not be supervised or controlled. . . . But in our country [people] do not discriminate between those religions that are good for society and the nation and those that are only for monetary gain. . . . From our own point of view, provisions should be made for the qualification of religious preachers. I think there should be some regulations regarding their character and educational background. . . . Just as the candidates for ministry are exam-ined for their qualifications so all religious bodies should be required by law to set standards for qualifying their preachers.[24]

THE IMPLEMENTATION OF THE OCCUPATION'S
POLICY ON RELIGION

Implementation of the Shintō Directive and the separation of religion and state was a complex task but achieved with a minimum of rancor. The "decontamination" of the schools was the first order of business for the Occupation. Teachers understood that shrine and temple visits were forbidden, but these places were sites of the highest cultural and historical significance. Students deprived of a knowledge of them would lack fundamental appreciation of their history and culture. Ethics courses were also ended in December 1945 as part of the separation of church and state, but both these courses and school visits to temples and shrines were reinstated after the end of the Occupation.

Local officials were empowered to decide such matters as whether Shintō and Buddhist clergy could be allowed to teach in the public schools and whether religious organizations could be permitted to use school facilities when classes were not in session.[25]

The Religions Division particularly objected to veneration of the Imperial Rescript on Education in the schools because it was viewed as Confucian and hence antidemocratic, made the emperor an absolute standard of morality, and was used in a way to suggest that the emperor was divine and that the document itself was sacred. The Imperial Household Ministry had the imperial portraits, worshiped in connection with the rescript, removed. On 8 October 1946 the Ministry of Education withdrew the rescript from the schools, and it was formally rescinded by the Diet on 19 June 1948.[26]

The custom of bowing to the palace, universalized in 1937 and called "worship from afar" (*yōhai*), was not abolished until June 1947. The Ministry of Education did not, however, unequivocally renounce the practice:

Henceforth school-sponsored or school-directed ceremonies of bowing to the imperial palace and school-sponsored or school-directed shouting "Long live the emperor" will cease. In instructing students, principals and teachers will not insist on outward manifestations of belief in the divinity of the emperor or lead the students to so believe. Needless to say, this does not prevent spontaneous expressions of respect for the emperor on the part of the students and school children.[27]

In view of the use of war memorials in prewar society by militaristic elements, the Religions Division was determined to root out this practice. Between late 1946 and May 1948, it had 5,613 monuments and 354 statues eliminated; 890 monuments and 17 statues moved to different locations; and the wording on 908 monuments and 29 statues altered to remove objectionable elements.[28]

Bunce enunciated a consequential distinction when he said that no government or public official acting in his *official capacity* should attend funerals of the war dead or make condolence speeches. This policy was especially painful since the ashes of fallen combatants were being returned to Japan in large numbers and national sentiment for memorializing them in some way ran high. An important exception to this policy was made for the handling of ashes of victims of the bombing of Tokyo. They were interred in the Tomb for Unidentified War Victims (Mumei Senshisha Byō) at Chidorigafuchi, in the Chiyoda Ward of Tokyo, completed in 1959. Because of its ambiguous relation to the Yasukuni Shrine, Chidorigafuchi later became the subject of much controversy.

The treatment of the Ise Grand Shrines and the Yasukuni Shrine deserves special attention. Both were reconstituted as Religious Juridical Persons and lost all public funding. Thus they were put on the same footing as any shrine, temple, or church. The Religions Division expressed a position on the Yasukuni Shrine as follows:

Although many have regarded it as equivalent to the Tomb of an Unknown Soldier, Yasukuni Shrine differs from that mausoleum in a number of important aspects. There is no tomb on Kudan Hill [site of the Yasukuni Shrine], and there are no mortal remains or ashes anywhere in or adjacent to the shrine's precincts. The purpose of the shrine is not to provide symbolically an appropriate burial for the unknown dead. The enshrined are not unknown; each one is listed with his name, rank, unit, and the date and place of his last action.

Yasukuni Shrine is a religious institution. The enshrined are individual spirits to whom prayers of gratitude and petitions for protection and assistance are offered. Instead of being devoid of religious symbolism, Yasukuni is a Shintō shrine, served by professional Shintō priests who daily perform rites according to the Shintō tradition. It presents to all the bereaved families a miniature shrine for home use in which to place an amulet, the symbol of the shrine itself and the enshrined kami. In speaking to the bereaved families, the Chief Priest, General Takao Suzuki said, "I wish to have this shrine placed in the home at a sacred spot where it is convenient to pay daily homage when you worship other kami. Think of it as the guardian of the family."[29]

Former Prime Minister Nakasone Yasuhiro was fond of likening the Yasukuni Shrine to the Arlington National Cemetery. There are significant differences, however, between a national memorial cemetery and a religious institution. Perhaps the most important of these is that while a cleric of any religion may freely enter the Arlington National Cemetery and perform memorial or any other sort of rites for the war dead buried there, Yasukuni Shrine is exclusively a Shintō institution, and it is unthinkable that a cleric of any other religion would perform rites there.

The Japanese institution that most nearly approximates the Arlington National Cemetery or other similar national war memorials in other nations is the Tomb for Unidentified War Victims at Chidorigafuchi. This memorial is completely nonreligious in character, is not registered as a religious institution, and anyone may freely enter and perform rites there. It has been constructed on such a small scale, however, that many feel it lacks the grandeur appropriate to a national memorial.[30]

SHINTŌ SINCE WORLD WAR II

Since 1945 Shintō has experienced significant decline, and "decay" is a word used by major studies to describe its situation.[31] The decline results from a combination of factors, some of which impinge on all Japanese religions. The greatest of these is demographic change. The urbanization of the population has increased markedly since 1945, and since 1955 a majority of the population has resided in urban areas, but temples and shrines have historically been far more concentrated in rural areas. Postwar construction of urban shrines and temples has not compensated for the imbalance.

New immigrants to the cities have been disproportionately younger than those remaining in the countryside, and this means that an increasingly aging population is left to care for the temples and shrines in rural Japan. The disappearance of youth from festivals has turned these once-exuberant events into much less attractive gatherings, further dampening enthusiasm for participating in or supporting shrine life. Furthermore, rural income is generally not as high as in urban areas, leaving fewer resources for shrine upkeep.[32]

Prewar urban parishes have, meanwhile, not succeeded well in integrating new immigrants. Never a democratic organization, the parish offers little attraction to younger in-migrants, who find that they can participate in festivals without taking ongoing responsibility for shrine maintenance, and increasingly this is the tendency. Because Shintō's ties to the state have been so reduced, parish membership no longer offers either a means of access to the prestige of the state or the opportunities for self-promotion and entrepreneurship seen before 1945.[33]

An important factor contributing to Shintō's postwar decline is the sense that it has been discredited by the loss of World War II, that it has been exposed as bankrupt and as an empty shell in the absence of state patronage. This attitude finds confirmation in the increasingly secular disposition of the society, the growing prestige of science (seen by most as antithetical to religion of any kind), and the media's tendency to ignore or ridicule religion. The efforts of the priesthood to meet these various challenges have been feeble and ineffectual.[34]

Many of the same forces have produced a decline in temple Buddhism also, but on the whole the Buddhist clergy has been better able to respond. As always, the Buddhist clergy's level of education remains higher than Shintō's, having available to it more and better educational institutions. Kokugakuin University, Kōgakkan University (reopened as a private institution in 1962), and the tiny seminaries attached to the Shintō sects are the Shintō priesthood's main training facilities. Priests currently number about twenty thousand, and most serve more than one shrine and hold some kind of by-employment. Now, as in the past, it is generally impossible to earn a living from the priesthood alone.[35]

Shrines have had to create commercial enterprises to survive in the absence of state patronage and virtually compulsory parishioner support. Larger shrines have frequently opened wedding halls, featuring Shintō weddings, often performed in sequence with Christian or Westernized ceremonies for the same couple. Combined with a lack of effective proselytization, this commercialization of the shrines contributes to society's impression of Shintō as ethically and intellectually bankrupt.

The big winners in this whirlwind of postwar social change have been the new religions. The most impressive sociological factor in their rise and supersession of the established religions has been their incorporation of the religious aspirations of women. Providing significant outlets for the energies and talents of women, the new religions have succeeded in attracting large numbers of female adherents. Neither temple Buddhism nor Shintō has been able to duplicate this achievement, and if anything, Shintō seems the less able of the two. Until Shintō can extend some recognition to this majority of the Japanese population, there is no reason to expect its decline to be reversed.

POSTWAR CHALLENGES TO RELIGIOUS FREEDOM AND TO SEPARATION OF STATE AND RELIGION

Since the establishment of the postwar constitution, there have been several notable challenges to its provisions on religion, and the most celebrated of these involves the Yasukuni Shrine. Other cases, equally consequential if less well known outside Japan, concern a Shintō grounds purification ceremony (*jichinsai*) performed at public expense in the city of Tsu, Mie Prefecture, and the apotheosis of a member of the Self-Defense Force in a prefectural Nation-Protecting Shrine in defiance of the wishes of his Christian widow. The grounds purification case has established guidelines for the scope of religious activity permitted to the state, and the apotheosis case has indirectly encouraged the Yasukuni Shrine to continue apotheosizing persons against the will of their survivors by ruling this matter irrelevant to religious freedom.

These cases are intimately related and build upon each other in such a way that it is impossible to treat them as entirely separate. The longest-lived is the case of the Yasukuni Shrine, and the others can best be examined in the course of legal decisions involving the shrine.

Much of the controversy concerning the Yasukuni Shrine focuses on

143

its martial character. Directly administered before 1945 by the Ministries of the Army and Navy, this shrine houses the nation's only public military museum, opened in 1872. The museum displays weapons and military memorabilia, including planes, cannons, and tanks. Outside the museum large stone lanterns marking the approach to the shrine are decorated with metal plaques in relief eulogizing the exploits of Japanese military personnel at various Asian, mostly Chinese, sites. In these various ways the shrine symbolically glorifies war.

Before 1945 the cabinet and the emperor customarily attended the spring and autumn festivals of the Yasukuni Shrine. All prime ministers of the Liberal Democratic Party since 1945, except Takeshita Noboru (for reasons to be discussed below), have continued to attend these festivals. Prime Minister Miki Takeo (in office from December 1974 to December 1976) added the further practice of paying tribute at the shrine on 15 August, the anniversary of Japan's surrender.

Each year members of the Diet have challenged the government to demonstrate that its tribute at the Yasukuni Shrine does not violate Articles 20 and 89 of the constitution. The issue centers on the distinction between cabinet visits in official and nonofficial capacities, a distinction first introduced by Bunce. If the prime minister acts as a representative of state, then he violates the principle of separation of religion and state by paying tribute at a religious institution, and if he further makes an offering from public funds, then he violates Article 89. If, however, the prime minister visits a religious institution as a manifestation of his personal religious beliefs, then he is merely exercising his constitutional right to religious freedom. The problem, therefore, is how to distinguish between the prime minister's actions in his private and public capacities.

From roughly 1972 to the present, Diet members and the media have questioned every prime minister in order to clarify this distinction and the government's intentions. Did the prime minister use a private or a public car in traveling to the shrine? Did he make an offering to the shrine from his private or public funds? Did he sign the shrine registry with his personal name, or did he add his official title? The government was considerably aided by the inherent ambiguity and vagueness, referred to in the Introduction, of symbolism at the shrine and despite the questioning managed to continue its visits until 1985.

Miki's manner of paying tribute was the least ambiguously "private," in that he used a private car, private funds, signed only his personal name, and, significantly, went to the shrine alone, unaccompanied by other members of the cabinet. Subsequent prime ministers have increasingly used official cars and titles and have encouraged the cabinet to pay tribute with them. In this way the government's patronage of the Yasukuni Shrine has assumed an increasingly official character.

It is difficult to regard visits for formal tribute at the Yasukuni Shrine on the anniversary of the surrender, by nearly the entire cabinet, attired in morning coats, as the action of private individuals. Whatever explanation is given of personal intention remains highly subjective, while the outward symbolism adopted is that of an official affair of state. The distinction between private and official capacity is by nature difficult to maintain in the case of public officials, and it breaks down entirely in the case of the emperor, whose every move outside the palace inevitably has a public character. All these points have been repeatedly and vigorously debated in the Diet, and the issue of cabinet tribute at the Yasukuni Shrine has become inextricably linked to the question of reviving state support for this religious institution.[36]

THE ATTEMPT TO REESTABLISH STATE SUPPORT FOR THE YASUKUNI SHRINE

The Yasukuni Shrine occupies a central position in government revival of prewar Shintō symbolism, and the shrine in turn is central to an emerging myth of the national identity, encompassing the legitimation of the state. Essentially, the government seeks to revive the prewar pattern in which the unity of the populace was asserted symbolically, thus excusing the state from action to remove gender, class, and ethnicity as barriers to access to resources and opportunity. The state, headed by the emperor in a liturgical capacity, had the function of presiding over this cozy union. A major difference between the state's prewar appropriation of Shintō symbolism and the postwar situation lies in the open, pluralistic political culture of contemporary Japan, in which the state now meets strong opposition to its symbolic reconstructions.

In 1956 the Bereaved Society of Japan (Nihon Izokukai) began to petition for renewed state support of the Yasukuni Shrine. Although the shrine had been registered as a Religious Juridical Person, the petitions proposed to make it a special entity eligible for this support. Conservative Diet members joined the Bereaved Society in calling for the Self-Defense Force, the prime minister, and the emperor to attend the spring and autumn festivals as in the prewar era. They desired that the shrine be made a public institution where the imperial house, the government, and the military could pay tribute in concert, thus reviving the prewar pattern intact.

The initiatives of the Bereaved Society and conservative Diet members were opposed by the Union of New Religions, which maintained that state support of the shrine would violate Articles 20 and 89. It held that commemoration of the war dead should be performed in a manner consonant with the individual faith of the deceased.

The union foresaw that both religious freedom and the separation of religion and state would be endangered by yielding on the Yasukuni question. Furthermore, it feared that persecution of religious associations on the prewar model might follow if the state were not monitored vigilantly. Since the union included a number of groups persecuted before 1945, this fear was based on actual experience.

To justify state support for the Yasukuni Shrine, the Legal Bureau of the Lower House of the Diet commissioned a study of measures necessary to make that support permissible under the postwar constitution. The report specified that the shrine would have to forego all religious education and cease to act as a base for proselytization of Shintō. Major changes in shrine rites would also be required to purge them of a religious character. For example, swords and mirrors would have to be removed as objects of worship and Shintō prayers deleted from ritual. Shintō rites of purification and invoking the kami, sacred dance (*kagura*), use of the title "Shintō priest" (*shinshoku*), use of Shintō vestments, divination practices, and the characteristic gate (*torii*) of the shrine would all have to be abolished. If and only if these changes were made, the study opined, state support would be permissible. It was obvious, however, that these changes would also dismantle the shrine's symbolic presentation and render it useless to the state.[37]

Nevertheless, conservative politicians of the Liberal Democratic Party in 1969 introduced a bill known as the Yasukuni Shrine Bill (Yasukuni hōan) to grant state support to the shrine. This bill had the strong support of the Bereaved Society, the Association of Shintō Shrines, patriotic and right-wing groups, and right-leaning new religions such as Reiyūkai Kyōdan and Seichō no Ie.[38]

The first article of the bill specified that the shrine's purpose was to offer rites and ceremonies (*gishiki gyōji*) for the souls of the war dead as an expression of reverence (*sonsu*) for them. Article 2 stated that the shrine would not be classified as a religious institution. Since the Religious Juridical Persons Law stated that a defining purpose of religious organizations was precisely to offer rites and ceremonies (the same terms were used), the Yasukuni Shrine Bill directly conflicted with it, and thus the bill sought to have Yasukuni reclassified as nonreligious while yet retaining the defining characteristic of a religious institution.[39]

The Union of New Religions saw in this contradiction between the Yasukuni Shrine Bill and the Religious Juridical Persons Law the same casuistry characteristic of prewar legislation, which declared shrines nonreligious and then used that designation as a pretext to make support for them and participation in their observances semicompulsory. For this reason in 1969 the union circulated a petition in opposition to the Yasukuni Shrine Bill and collected 3,277,405 signatures. Partly as a result of this strong opposition, the bill was defeated on that occasion and on four subsequent attempts to pass it: in 1970, 1971, 1972, and 1974.[40]

That the government could be handed five humiliating defeats on the question of funding for the Yasukuni Shrine illustrates clearly its determination to utilize the shrine in its symbolic self-presentation, and it shows how, in the open political culture of postwar Japan, its ability to do so is limited by the opposition of the populace, led by an association of religious organizations. The contrast with prewar Japan is striking indeed.

Five resounding defeats have not, however, deterred conservative efforts to reinstate government patronage of the Yasukuni Shrine. A major purpose of the bill was to permit formal, public tribute or worship at the shrine (*kōshiki sanpai*) by public officials, a continuing issue in Japanese politics. Conservative Diet members of the Liberal Democratic Party formed a Society for Honoring the Glorious War Dead (Eirei ni kotaeru kai), and in concert with the Bereaved Society, this group has steadily pushed for a return to the prewar pattern of regular, formal worship by the cabinet and the emperor at the Yasukuni Shrine.

Anxious to establish that this goal was not in violation of the constitution, the Liberal Democratic Party again commissioned the Legal Bureau of the Lower House of the Diet to give a judgment on the matter but was most disappointed with the result. On 18 December 1980 the Legal Bureau found that paying formal tribute at the Yasukuni Shrine was unambiguously in violation of Article 20, and it stated further that arguments drawn from the use of private cars and private funds did not alter the unconstitutionality of the matter. In spite of this clear statement, however, the party has persisted in efforts to reinstate both formal cabinet tribute and public support for the shrine.

The opposition to these government moves has not been idle. The Union of New Religions is spearheaded by Risshōkōseikai, the principal financial backer of the organization. The member organizations of the union are in many cases quite wealthy and have regularly been approached by politicians seeking election for campaign contributions. Until the early 1980s, partly out of some vague fear of reprisal, member organizations tended to fund more or less any conservative politician. Now, however, at Risshōkōseikai's initiative, they have begun to withhold funds from candidates favoring state patronage of Yasukuni. Their position has provoked a few calls for revoking the tax-exempt status of religious organizations, but for the moment the union is standing its ground.

Whether in the form of financial support or formal tribute by the cabinet, the Self-Defense Force, and the emperor, state patronage of the Yasukuni Shrine inevitably gives the appearance of state sanction of the shrine, its history, and its traditions. Because the shrine has repeatedly been charged with violating the principle of religious freedom since 1945, state patronage necessarily implicates the state in these accusations, which have taken several forms.

Suppose that the Yasukuni Shrine apotheosizes as one of its deities an individual who was a Christian. To treat any human being, living or dead, as a deity is a clear violation of Christian tenets, but of course that individual is no longer in a position to protest this treatment. Should the survivors be able to compel the shrine to remove their relative's name from its register of deities? Or suppose that not the deceased but the survivors are Christians, and that the apotheosis is offensive to them, should they have the power to compel the shrine to remove their relative's name? What about the case of survivors of war dead from Japan's former colonies, who protest that the apotheosis, far from being an honor, is a humiliating and degrading reminder of their country's former colonial status?

All these situations have arisen many times since 1945, and in every case the shrine has rejected requests to remove names from the register of deities.[41] The shrine's position remains unchanged since the prewar era: those who have died in military service have become "glorious war dead" (*eirei*) and have been absorbed into the national polity (*kokutai*), and their survivors have no further authority over the posthumous care of these souls. The war dead no longer "belong" to their families as an ancestral spirit does. Because of its ties to the state, Yasukuni Shrine is uniquely authorized to perform liturgy for them, and survivors simply have no rightful say in the matter.[42]

The government has patronized the Yasukuni Shrine in other, less obvious ways. The shrine has continued to apotheosize war dead since 1945, down to the present day. In fact, the majority of those enshrined there have been installed since 1945. Among those apotheosized in recent years were fourteen convicted war criminals, including seven Class A war criminals, among them Tōjō Hideki, on 17 October 1978. These war criminals were given a special designation by the shrine: "Martyrs of the Shōwa Era."[43] In order to register these and other persons as deities of the shrine, however, priests must have access to information regarding such matters as the date and place of birth of each individual and the circumstances of death. The Yasukuni Shrine made a private request to the Ministry of Welfare for aid in collecting this information, and the ministry transmitted these data on thousands of war dead, free of charge. When the same services were requested by the religious organization Perfect Liberty Kyōdan, however, the request was denied. This practice continued until 1971.[44]

In this way the government assisted the shrine, gratis, in applying its own standards for the apotheosis of individuals, regardless of their religious beliefs or those of their survivors. While tax monies of course underwrite the labor invested in this undertaking, and while weighty constitutional issues of religious freedom are involved in the shrine's practices, none of these matters was made public; they came under scrutiny only through the vigorous inquiries of members of the Diet. Thus the government has become deeply involved in this covert patronage in such a way as possibly to violate Article 89 and to lend support and approval to practices that may violate Article 20. Further, in assisting the shrine in these various ways, it lends its approval to the apotheosis of Class A war criminals, individuals who have been convicted of the grossest crimes against humanity. The latter practice in particular casts the prewar regime, and the military in particular, in a benign light and attempts to erase the issue of war guilt from the national memory.

THE TSU GROUNDS PURIFICATION CASE

The most consequential postwar court case bearing on religious freedom and the separation of religion and state was ruled upon by the Supreme Court by 1977, and it has had direct consequences for the Yasukuni Shrine issue.[45]

In 1965 citizens of Tsu City in Mie Prefecture brought suit against the mayor, saying that he violated Article 89 when he paid local shrine priests to perform a grounds purification ceremony (*jichinsai*) preceding the city's construction of a gymnasium. The city's defense of the mayor's actions was based on the claim that the ceremony was not religious in character and that it was not, therefore, prohibited to the state, while the plaintiff's claim held both that the ceremony was a religious activity and that all religious activity was prohibited to the state.

Grounds purification was originally a rite to pacify the spirits of the earth, supposedly disturbed by new construction. The rite exists in both Buddhist and Shintō forms, but in modern times it has been performed almost exclusively in the latter form. When the Supreme Court ruled upon this case, it specified that grounds purification was now performed so routinely that few people were aware of its original significance. In this sense it had been thoroughly secularized (*sezokuka*) and could not any longer be said to be religious. Therefore the Tsu City mayor did not violate Article 89 when he paid Shintō priests to perform it.

The Court further ruled that not all religious activity was prohibited to the state. Instead, only activity that by intention or in its effect (intended or not) gave support and patronage to a particular religious institution or that hindered or did harm to a religious institution was prohibited.[46]

The Supreme Court's interpretation of the scope of religious activity permitted the state emboldened the government to proceed further in its patronage of the Yasukuni Shrine. Although the five defeats of the Yasukuni Shrine Bill made it clear that it would not be possible to institute direct state financial support, conservatives in the Liberal Democratic Party came to believe that the Tsu verdict would sanction formal cabinet tribute.

The opposition parties are united against formal tribute, and they are joined by *burakumin*[47] and liberally inclined groups of all persuasions, including important sectors of the Jodō Shinshū school of Buddhism and Christian societies concerned with the bereaved of World War II.[48] Up until 1985, the Liberal Democratic Party's own publicly stated position was that formal tribute at the Yasukuni Shrine by the cabinet was unconstitutional, but with the advent of the Nakasone cabinets, that is from 1982, conservative factions of the party began agitating for reversal of the party's position.

CABINET TRIBUTE AT THE YASUKUNI SHRINE

In April 1983 Nakasone paid tribute at the Yasukuni Shrine on the occasion of its spring festival, and at that time, although he refused to clarify whether his was a private or an official visit, he signed the register with his official title. This seemingly minor detail was in fact an important gesture, a signal to hard-line conservatives and to the right wing that the government shared their desire to reinstitute state patronage.

In November 1983 the Liberal Democratic Party formed an internal committee to study the shrine issue again. Drawing upon the Tsu case, it held that formal cabinet tribute was constitutional, thus contradicting the party's stated policy to the contrary, still in force at that time.[49]

In August 1984 the cabinet secretary convened a fifteen-member advisory committee to study the Yasukuni issue. Unlike the previous committee, this advisory committee was composed mainly of persons outside government, including scholars, authors, businessmen, jurists, and former high-ranking bureaucrats, representing opinions on both sides of the issue. Although it met on twenty-one occasions over the course of a year, the committee was unable to produce a unified report.

During this interval, opposition politicians and others opposed to cabinet tribute questioned the status of the advisory committee, pointing out that while it could not be considered representative of public opinion, neither had it any qualifications to render a judicial verdict. What significance could the resulting report possibly have?[50]

The writers of the report split three ways: those favoring cabinet tribute, those opposed to it, and a faction advocating the construction of an entirely new national memorial for the war dead, one that would be free of the religious and political implications bound up with the Yasukuni Shrine.[51] Receiving this divided report on 9 August 1985, the government was evidently already determined to use it as justification for formal cabinet tribute on the anniversary of the surrender on 15 August. It ignored the report's failure to reach a consensus and the problems raised by the opposition with respect to the committee's doubtful qualifications, and tagged on to the end of the report this sentence, which henceforth became official party policy: "Based upon the findings of this advisory committee, the government intends to take appropriate measures toward formal tribute by the cabinet at the Yasukuni Shrine."

Lamely claiming the advisory committee's report as warrant for its actions, and in defiance of its own legal experts, on 15 August 1985 the Nakasone cabinet paid formal tribute at the Yasukuni Shrine. In a feeble effort to rid the observance of religious overtones, the prime minister and cabinet members offered flowers instead of the standard Shintō offering of sakaki branches upon the altar and bowed fewer times than is ordinarily prescribed by shrine liturgy.

The cabinet's first postwar formal tribute at the Yasukuni Shrine was greeted by strong domestic opposition from the same groups that had always opposed state patronage of the shrine, but their opposition could not compare with the outrage of other Asian nations.[52] The press in Japan's former colonies protested that Japan's actions showed gross insensitivity towards Asian nations, for whose people Yasukuni Shrine represents a symbol of Japanese militarism and aggression, existing only to glorify war. They interpreted Japan's actions as an affirmation of prewar militarism, a repudiation of war guilt, and as a green light to forces in Japan eager to exploit the former colonies again.

China was strongest in its opposition. Demonstrations by thousands in China's major cities showed forcefully the depth of Chinese resentment against Japanese actions before the surrender. The Chinese press pointed to the metal sculpture on the stone lanterns on the approach to Yasukuni, described above, which glorify, among other things, the massacres committed by the Japanese military in Nanjing, where from two to three hundred thousand Chinese civilians were slaughtered. How, the Chinese press demanded, could the Japanese government ally itself with a religious institution that so blatantly glorified war and eulogized Japanese aggression in Asia? How could the government lend its support to a shrine that had apotheosized Class A war criminals, and what did the government think the phrase "glorious war dead" meant to the Chinese?

The Nakasone government had no answer to these criticisms, and it was so shocked and unprepared for such stinging international condemnation that it suspended all further tribute at the Yasukuni Shrine, and the succeeding government of Takeshita Noboru followed suit. Nevertheless, the government has declared its intention to move forward to gain domestic and international consensus for formal tribute at the Yasukuni Shrine by the emperor, the cabinet, and the Self-Defense Force. In other words, the government has expressed its desire to reinstitute the prewar symbolic unification of religion and state.

In response to domestic criticism, the government has said that whatever Yasukuni's past may have been, it regards the shrine now as a symbol of peace and international understanding in the context of what the government calls a "new nationalism." Needless to say, this claim fails to convince either the domestic or the foreign opposition, and a further question concerns the timing of Nakasone's ill-fated formal tribute.

In May 1985 President Ronald Reagan accompanied Helmut Kohl, chancellor of West Germany, to the German military cemetery at Bitberg, where members of the *Schutzstaffel* (ss), Hitler's infamous secret police, are buried, and laid a wreath of tribute there. An anthropologist, David Kertzer, has analyzed this symbolic act as follows:

The value to Kohl of the rites lay in dispelling the discomfiting hold the Nazi symbolic legacy had on his countrymen. In doing so it would bolster his own stature and that of his party. The very staging of the rites demonstrated Kohl's power, all the more so when Reagan, by coming, showed he valued his commitments to the German chancellor above the passionate pleas of American congressmen and the American people. Reagan, for his part, was repaying Kohl in this ritual currency for a variety of both symbolic and material expressions of support that Kohl's government had given Reagan in the past. The most notable of these involved stationing a new battery of nuclear missiles on German soil. . . . Defending his planned visit to honor the German war dead, Reagan told an American audience that the dead German soldiers were "victims of Nazism also, even though they were fighting in the German uniform, drafted into service to carry out the hateful wishes of the Nazis. They were victims, just as surely as the victims in the concentration camps." The evils perpetrated by Nazi Germany, in other words, were the responsibility of a tiny group of leaders who forced the German population to do their wicked bidding. Although this was the message Reagan hoped his cemetery ceremonies would send, he ran afoul of the symbolic construction his listeners had already placed on the events of the past.

For many Germans, by contrast, the rites were a satisfying vindication of their view that Germans had been unfair victims of malicious propaganda, that the Second World War was but another in a long line of European conflicts for which no one people could be singled out for blame.[53]

There is a remarkable similarity between the Bitberg visit and Nakasone's formal tribute at Yasukuni, and perhaps a connection between them.[54] Kohl was clearly seeking to present the Nazi regime in a benign light, and, while such a move would have had little credibility if he had presented a wreath at an ss cemetery alone, Reagan's tribute with him lent the prestige of the United States to the undertaking and to Kohl personally. Thus Kohl was able to appease that part of the German population that would like to erase the issue of war guilt.[55]

Nakasone's tribute at the Yasukuni Shrine shared the aims of rewriting the past and of appeasing the Japanese right wing. It is of a piece with changes in the Ministry of Education's policies approving for use in the public schools only those history textbooks that present the actions of the prewar regime in a positive, affirming tone. Both are actions geared to appease the Liberal Democratic Party's traditionally conservative constituency in a symbolic coin, now that the party is unable to deliver continued economic protectionist policies for domestic markets.[56]

Nakasone was a great admirer of Ronald Reagan and consistently sought to bolster his own image by presenting himself as the friend and confidant of the American president. It seems highly likely that Nakasone took his cue from Reagan's tribute at Bitberg and was emboldened by it to override the advice of his own party's legal counsel, brave domestic opposition, and march on to Yasukuni with his cabinet. Had the foreign opposition not been so strong, succeeding prime ministers would probably still be doing so.

THE SELF-DEFENSE FORCE APOTHEOSIS CASE

In 1973 Nakaya Takafumi, a serving member of the Self-Defense Force, died in a traffic accident.[57] His widow Yasuko entrusted his remains to a Yamaguchi Prefecture Christian church of which she was a member. Several years later Yasuko was approached by the prefectural Veterans' Association (Taiyūkai Yamaguchiken shibu rengōkai) of the Self-Defense Force, which sought copies of Takafumi's death certificate and the domiciliary record from which his name had been deleted after his decease. The Veterans' Association wanted these documents for use in arranging for a ceremony of apotheosis (*gōshi*). This was precisely the same rite as apotheosis in the Yasukuni Shrine, and in it Takafumi and twenty-six other deceased Self-Defense Force members from Yamaguchi Prefecture were to be enshrined as deities in the prefectural Nation-Protecting Shrine. The prefectural Veterans' Association had been sponsoring such apotheosis rites since 1964, when they were initiated at the request of the survivors of deceased Self-Defense Force members from the prefecture.

Yasuko refused to provide the requested documents and declined to give her assent to the proposed apotheosis of her husband, on the grounds that such a ceremony violated her religious beliefs. She was a Christian; Takafumi was not. The Veterans' Association carried out the apotheosis ceremony over her protests. She sued the state, specifically the Self-Defense Force, for violating her right to religious freedom. She was awarded the sum of a million yen by a lower court, and this ruling was upheld on appeal.

The Veterans' Association is a registered corporate body (*shadanhōjin*), and while it is not an official organ of government, it has its headquarters in the Ministry of Defense and receives bureaucratic and clerical aid from the ministry and its prefectural branches. Specifically, the Self-Defense Force and its provincial branches provide records of such things as the dates, places, and circumstances of death of Self-Defense Force members whom the Veterans' Association seeks to apotheosize in prefectural Nation-Protecting Shrines, the prewar provincial branches of the Yasukuni Shrine.[58]

In this case, the Yamaguchi Prefecture branch of the Self-Defense Force also investigated the practice of prefectural Veterans' Associations sponsoring apotheosis ceremonies in the prefectures of the island of Kyushu and provided the head of the Yamaguchi Prefecture Veterans' Association with access to this information. Investigative reporting revealed that this ceremony was widely sponsored by the Veterans' Associations of fifteen prefectures in western Japan. Between the end of World War II and June 1988, they had apotheosized some 465 souls. In at least three cases lawsuits had been brought against the Veterans' Association, but the apotheosis rites had been carried out nevertheless.[59]

The importance of this case lies in the analogy it provides to issues surrounding the Yasukuni Shrine. The Nation-Protecting Shrines are performing the same rites of apotheosis as the Yasukuni Shrine, and, as discussed above, citizens have frequently protested that these violate their right to religious freedom. Thus the verdict in the Self-Defense Force apotheosis case bears important implications for future litigation against the Yasukuni Shrine. Furthermore, a judicial finding that the rite of apotheosis is religious in character would bear on the constitutionality of state patronage of the shrine, since the apotheosis of the war dead is the shrine's principal raison d'tre.

The state appealed the ruling of the lower court, and the Supreme Court of Japan rendered its verdict on 1 June 1988, Chief Justice Yaguchi Kōichi presiding. Four points were at issue in the Supreme Court's ruling. First, was the constitutional provision for separation of religion and state (Article 20, Section 3) violated by the actions of the Yamaguchi Prefectural Branch of the Self-Defense Force when it assisted the Veterans' Association in the bureaucratic arrangements for the ceremony of apotheosis? The two lower courts had held that the Self-Defense Force lent aid and comfort to a *specific* religion—Shintō—and that hence it had violated Article 20 of the constitution. The Supreme Court overturned these verdicts and ruled that the Veterans' Association had acted alone when it engaged in religious activity, and that hence no violation of Article 20 had occurred, since the Veterans' Association was not an organ of the state.

Second, was the action taken by the Self-Defense Force religious? The Supreme Court ruled that the wish and intention of the Self-Defense Force was only to raise its own social prestige and to promote a martial spirit; its consciousness of any religious significance was quite shallow. The Self-Defense Force itself did not directly encourage the Yamaguchi Nation-Protecting Shrine to carry out the apotheosis. It was the Veterans' Association that approached the shrine, paid for the ceremony, and lent its name to the proceedings. The Self-Defense Force's actions, neither by intention nor in their effect, caused harm to any religion, nor did they serve to promote or patronize any religion. Hence the Self-Defense Force's actions did not fall into the category of religious activity prohibited to the state (this following the Tsu case).

In a minority report, however, Justice Itō stated his view that the Self-Defense Force had acted to patronize Shintō by assisting the Veterans' Association to have the apotheosis ceremony carried out, and that the Self-Defense Force's actions were precisely of the sort prohibited to the state and all its organs. Justice Itō maintained that the court had interpreted too narrowly the sphere of religious activities prohibited to the state, and that the Self-Defense Force had exceeded the terms permitted to it in its cooperation with the Veterans' Association. In individual comments, Justices Shimaya Rokurō and Satō Tetsurō said the action of the Self-Defense Force and the Veterans' Association was nothing other than religious activity, but that no one's individual rights were violated.

The Tsu grounds purification case had established a precedent for the first and second points of this case. In the Tsu case the issue centered on the religious or nonreligious character of the rite in question; if the Supreme Court had chosen to apply that standard in this case as well, it would have had to admit that apotheosis epitomized religious action. It sidestepped this issue by focusing on the nonofficial character of the Self-Defense Force's surrogate organization, the Veterans' Association.

The Tsu case also focused much attention on the intention of the person or organization performing or sponsoring religious action, but how can the intention of an official organ of state of the size of the Self-Defense Force be known? When the Court focused on intention, which by nature is highly complex and not susceptible to verification, it chose to ignore the historical question of the meaning of the rite in Japanese religious history. By that standard it is absolutely clear that apotheosis is religious, and that when it is performed by one religion, that religion receives the patronage of the state to the exclusion of other religions that might also have been asked to perform it.

Third, does the constitutional separation of religion and state guarantee the rights and freedoms of individuals? The Court ruled that even when the state or its organs performed unconstitutional religious activities, the state was not violating the religious rights of any individual unless it coerced individuals to perform some religious activity or limited their religious freedom.

The problem here derives in part from the wording of Article 20, which says, "Freedom of religion is guaranteed to all"; "No person shall be compelled to take part in any religious act, celebration, rite, or practice";

and "The State and its organs shall refrain from religious education or any other religious activity." Thus this article tries to include both the issue of religious freedom (and state coercion) and the further issue of separation of religion and state. As discussed above, its drafting was undertaken without full consultation with the Religions Division of CIES during the Occupation, and it would have been more prudent to separate these issues in different articles.

However that may be, the constitution as presently worded clearly does make a single guarantee of religious freedom and separation of religion and state. Here the Court has produced a highly convoluted, even casuistic interpretation of Article 20, saying that the state shall not be held accountable for violations of religious freedom resulting from its own unconstitutional religious actions unless coercion is involved. This extension of state prerogative will surely be taken as an ominous sign of the state's intent to perform such action by the domestic opposition to state patronage of the Yasukuni Shrine.

Fourth, Nakaya Yasuko claimed that her "religious human rights" (*shūkyōjō no jinkakuken*) were violated in that the apotheosis of her husband's soul disrupted her own memorialization of him according to Christian rites and disturbed her peace of mind. Does the notion of religious human rights have legal status? The Supreme Court ruled that when one seeks legal redress against the religious actions of another, which may conflict with one's own, those proceedings may actually violate the religious freedom of the other party. "The guarantee of religious freedom demands toleration of the actions of those whose faith may not agree with one's own, so long as there is no coercion or violation of religious freedom. Everyone is free to memorialize anyone else according to personal belief, and this goes for the memorialization or veneration of a spouse as well." Thus one cannot, on the basis of the constitution's demand for religious toleration, recognize the idea of religious human rights as having legal status.

In his minority report, however, Justice Itō held that the right not to have one's peace of mind violated was protected under the Civil Code. Because this peace of mind is protected by law, one may sue if it is violated. This is a recognition of the plaintiff's claim for religious human rights.

The idea of "religious human rights" is quite novel, but this fourth point bears on a very ancient theme in Japanese religious history, the memorialization of the dead and of ancestral spirits. According to common understanding of this ancient substratum of religious practice and sentiment, a kin, occupational, or territorial group worships its own ancestors and no others, and conversely, no one but members of the group worships its ancestors. Retaining exclusive claim to these rites establishes the boundaries of the group.

An exception to the rule of exclusivity in ancestor worship is found in the purely sentimental placing in the domestic ancestral altar of a photo or ancestral tablet of some person unrelated by any of the usual ties. When this is done for private devotional reasons, it is generally unknown to the group to which the soul of the deceased "belongs" and is of no consequence to them, because of its purely private character.

We have seen also that, in previous eras and in the colonies, to worship the ancestors of a conqueror was the mark of submission to a new overlord. Part of the symbolic presentation of the Yasukuni Shrine has always been the claim that because of its unique ties to the state it is empowered to take charge of the posthumous care of the war dead, who, when apotheosized at Yasukuni, are absorbed into the national polity and are severed from all connection with their survivors, who thus lose the "right" to exclusive memorialization of them as ordinary ancestral spirits. In accepting this arrangement, subjects/citizens symbolically affirm the religious hegemony of the state.

Generally, kinship-based ancestor worship is performed by household (*ie*) units, not by the nuclear family. Following the household's patrilateral tendency, it is not the widow but the deceased's parents who would normally have first claim on their son's spirit. Nakaya Takafumi's parents were not Christians, and his widow did not reside with them. Pointing out that the deceased's parents had favored the apotheosis, Justice Sakagami questioned why their wishes should not carry as much weight as the widow's. Whatever mental anguish this apotheosis might cause the widow was, he wrote, within the scope of what she could rightfully be expected to bear.

In effect, the Court has ruled that anyone may memorialize anyone else. This is a matter that would inevitably lead to litigation when a public body—in this case the state in the form of its surrogate, the Veterans' Association—sought symbolic hegemony over the religious claims of a private citizen. In the Court's ruling on the apotheosis case, the state has achieved precisely that, and the implications for the Yasukuni Shrine issue are clear: the shrine may now continue its apotheosis procedures without fear of legal challenge on the basis of religious freedom, and the state is free to patronize the shrine without fear of violating Article 20. Thus Nakaya Yasuko's two previous victories in lower courts were entirely overturned by the Supreme Court. She was ordered to pay the state one million yen.

CONCLUSION

Before 1945 Japanese society was so dominated by the state, and opposition so intimidated, that the nation's political culture was monolithic in character. The state enjoyed virtual hegemony in articulating the meaning of the symbols of State Shintō such as the Yasukuni Shrine. In those decades no one dared oppose the state's claim that apotheosizing fallen combatants as "glorious war dead" in the Yasukuni Shrine was simply a continuation of tradition from time immemorial, though in fact this practice ran roughshod over the customs of ancestor worship.

In the postwar period, however, political culture has become much more pluralistic, and a voice opposing the state's past and present policies on religion has developed, with the Yasukuni Shrine as a central symbol of contention. The Japanese left, spearheaded by an academic intelligentsia, has consistently opposed moves to reinstate state support for the shrine.[60] Similarly, the Union of New Religions has been consistent in its opposition to such support. Both these groups have seen a resurgence of nationalism and a constriction of personal liberties, especially religious freedom, in state efforts to revive the Yasukuni Shrine. Another powerful force in the opposition to the shrine is the new religion Sōka Gakkai and its associated political party Kōmeitō. Opposition to the Yasukuni Shrine by these three groups is not systematically coordinated but springs from a common history of persecution in the prewar period. To them the shrine is a symbol of persecution and the suppression of religious freedom. Far from representing tradition, to these opposition groups, the shrine represents nothing other than the perversion of every laudable element of the national identity.

In the postwar decades the state has lost its symbolic hegemony of the prewar period, and there is now an active competition to formulate the meaning of such national symbols as the Yasukuni Shrine, the national flag, and the national anthem. The state has vigorously sought to regain its former prerogatives, as we have seen, by introducing a bill to give the Yasukuni Shrine state support no less than five times. It has covertly given the shrine administrative support by supplying it, gratis, with information on deceased combatants of World War II, while denying these services to other religious organizations that have requested them. Most recently, in the Self-Defense Force apotheosis case, the Japanese Supreme Court ruling clearly indicated the state's intention to uphold what it claims as its own prerogatives in manipulating the symbolism of the war dead, even where the violation of religious freedom is involved.

Since 1985 domestic opposition to the state's support for the Yasukuni Shrine has been joined by that of foreign nations, most of them Japan's former colonies. These nations, led by China, have opposed state visits to the shrine by the prime minister and the cabinet. The first attempt by former Prime Minister Nakasone Yasuhiro and his cabinet to reinstate regular formal tribute at the shrine by the cabinet aroused such violent foreign opposition that it has not yet been repeated.

Thus the issue of Shintō continues to preoccupy contemporary Japanese domestic and international politics. The issue is increasingly obscure and associated with rightist political sentiments and a resurgence of nationalism. It is debated now, however, in a pluralistic political culture, one in which no single party has hegemony in formulating the content of tradition or the meaning of its symbols.

Some have dismissed the entire Yasukuni issue as no more than a question of memorializing the war dead. If that were the only problem, however, the government could quickly put the matter to rest by turning its attention to the real national war memorial, the Tomb for Unidentified War Victims at Chidorigafuchi, or to the Peace Park at Hiroshima. If the state only wished, as is the right of every sovereign nation, to memorialize its war dead in some fitting way, it could do so with no controversy at either place. There are no objections when the prime minister lays a wreath at Hiroshima or Chidorigafuchi, and because neither is a religious institution, no constitutional problems arise. If the present construction of either institution is insufficiently grand, that can easily be remedied.

Unlike the Yasukuni Shrine, Chidorigafuchi and Hiroshima symbolize the suffering of war, its pointless sacrifice; neither glorifies it in any way. The government's reluctance to focus its memorials for the dead upon their sacrifice and suffering lends credibility to the claims of Asian nations and of the domestic opposition that the Japanese government's real intent is to glorify war and to justify past aggression.

Epilogue

EXCEPT POSSIBLY for contemporary socialist states, it would be difficult to identify a political regime that has not sought to legitimate itself by forging symbolic links to a sacred realm and claiming to be based on cosmological principles. Likewise, most religions have, at one time or another, claimed authority to make their doctrines the foundation of secular government. Indeed many have obligingly provided divine mandates for particular regimes. Shintō's relation to the state from 1868 to 1988 is a Japanese expression of this general rule.

Whereas many political regimes have sought legitimation from established religions, the Japanese state looked to Shintō, and as we have seen, the question whether Shintō was a religion was vigorously debated. During this period of 120 years, one of the most conspicuous themes to emerge was the clash between indigenous Japanese constructions of religious life and Western definitions of religion. Both secular intellectuals and Shintō ideologues have maintained that Shintō was not a religion. These positions have been reached, however, by different, indeed opposing, chains of reasoning. Western assumptions about religion have influenced Japanese jurisprudence throughout the period and have significantly affected legal thought regarding religion's relation to the state and such constitutional questions as religious freedom. Before 1945, the idea that Shintō was not a religion allowed it to be viewed as a suprareligious entity and its rites as obligatory civic duties. Shintō was taken to be an incontrovertible orthodoxy, based upon a nebulous purported connection with the imperial house. Nonconforming individuals and organizations were repeatedly sup-

160

pressed, usually on charges of lèse majesté. This resulted in the stifling of academic freedom, persecution of religious groups, and suppression of religious freedom.

While shrines were officially considered nonreligious, by the creation of a cult of the war dead Shintō nevertheless tapped Japan's oldest and most affectively laden area of religious life, the cult of the dead and the ancestors. The people sought religious explanations for the multitudinous deaths in war of Japanese youth. Officiating at public memorial rites, Shintō priests, in their capacity as government spokesmen, inevitably affirmed and glorified Japan's wars. Thus it was not that Shintō itself became an "engine of war," as some studies have implied, but that it idealized as the highest good a role as the state's obedient servant. And its greatest service to the state has concerned memorialization of the war dead.

Shrines took on a distinctively militaristic aura in the early twentieth century that they retained until 1945. This aura continues to characterize some shrines even at the end of the twentieth century, particularly the Yasukuni Shrine and its provincial branches, the Nation-Protecting Shrines. It was precisely by establishing this link between shrines and the cult of the war dead, and thereby imbuing the shrines with a martial ambience, that the Japanese state has been most effective in its manipulation of Shintō. This is the area, moreover, in which Shintō has been least successful in maintaining its autonomy.

In its desire to remove Shintō influence from public education, and on the basis of observing kami-worship at shrines, the Allied Occupation decided to treat Shintō like any other religion and thus severed its ties to the state. Since 1945, although Shintō has been declared religious in character, the old argument to the contrary has been used to reestablish links between the state and the Yasukuni Shrine. The Japanese Supreme Court's verdict on the Tsu City Grounds Purification case has perpetuated Western-influenced, nineteenth-century ideas of religion. The rite in question was declared nonreligious, in part because it lacked any doctrinal basis, and this has paved the way for closer ties between religion and state. The Self-Defense Force apotheosis case has laid the groundwork for further state patronage of the Yasukuni Shrine, which the government seems likely to initiate as soon as it judges that the international climate is safe and that it will not encounter significant criticism.

Not only does the central government seek to make connections with shrines, but similar cases on a smaller scale have repeatedly arisen at the levels of prefectural and city government. Since the prewar style of connecting Shintō and the state was so intimately connected with the suppression of individual liberties and religious organizations, these initiatives are vigorously opposed by religious organizations under the leadership of the Union of New Religions.

The various cases of lower-level administrations in Japan seeking to reestablish connections with shrines show clearly that the desire of governments to seek religious legitimation operates at all levels of politics. Most of these cases have arisen in the 1970s and 1980s and have been made possible by the Supreme Court ruling on the Tsu City case.

During the 1970s the Nation-Protecting Shrines of many areas were revived and became sites for war memorials and memorial rites by local governments. The Yasukuni Shrine has itself been eager to exert influence over prefectural governments, and so it financed and hosted a government-sponsored training session for members of prefectural governments, held at the Yasukuni Shirne in 1971.[1]

Some recent cases of the revival of government connections with Yasukuni and the Nation-Protecting Shrines are worth examining. In 1976 Watanabe Hironao, a Christian minister of Kitakami City in Iwate Prefecture, learned that the local ward tax included a levy for support of the prefectural Nation-Protecting Shrine, on the theory that all prefectural residents were automatically members of its Shrine Support Group and had a duty to maintain it financially. It came to light that this association was headed by the prefectural governor and that its officers included all mayors of the prefecture. Because the prefectural Nation-Protecting Shrine was registered as a Religious Juridical Person, city-government contributions to it from public funds were clearly unconstitutional. On that basis Watanabe raised a formal complaint. He asserted further that it was a violation of religious freedom for a government to take tax money from people who had no real connection to the shrine or who might in fact oppose it on religious grounds. The city promised to stop collecting and disbursing funds to the shrine, but there is no evidence that it has actually done so.[2]

On 4 and 5 June 1978, Asahikawa City in Hokkaidō carried out a formal tribute, complete with military music, to the local Nation-Protecting Shrine. The prefectural governor, the city mayor, and a company of the Self-Defense Force paid tribute together, thus aligning the shrine with prefectural and local governments and the military.[3] In many areas there have been reports of companies of the Self-Defense Force paying tribute at Nation-Protecting Shrines in uniform.[4] The governor of Yamanashi Prefecture presided over memorial services at the Kōfu Nation-Protecting Shrine on 15 August 1985 in his capacity as head of the Shrine Support Group.[5]

On 30 January 1982 the Kyōdō News Service reported that seven prefectures were making donations to both the Yasukuni Shrine and prefectural Nation-Protecting Shrines from public funds. In order to put a stop to these unconstitutional uses of public revenue, civil suits were brought in Iwate, Ehime, Gunma, Hyōgo, and Tochigi Prefectures. All these cases are still in the lower courts. The Ehime case illustrates well the characteristic attitudes of both plaintiff and defendant.

The suit was brought by a coalition of citizens and religious leaders that seeks the restitution of funds expended for shrines—37,000 yen was paid out over five occasions from April 1981 to April 1982. The defendant is Prefectural Governor Shiraishi Haruki, who is president of the prefectural Society of the Bereaved of World War II, prefectural President of the Society for Honoring the Glorious War Dead, and prefectural organizer of the Society to Protect Japan, a patriotic group. When the case was initiated, Shiraishi led all seventy members of the prefectural legislature to make formal tribute at the Yasukuni Shrine. He ignored repeated requests for meetings from the plaintiffs and went on record as saying, "As long as I'm the governor of this prefecture, I'll pay tribute at the Yasukuni Shrine and the Nation-Protecting Shrine and make offerings to both of them. It's a matter of course!" Meanwhile, the plaintiffs were repeatedly harrassed by members of the prefectural Society of the Bereaved, who shouted at them, "People like you shouldn't be allowed to live in Japan. How can you say that you are Japanese?"[6] Thus Shintō memorialization of the war dead still arouses conflicting and deeply felt religious emotions that for many people take precedence over the constitutional issues of separation of religion and state or religious freedom.

It seems clear that since 1945 Shintō and the state have succeeded in reconstructing parts of the symbolic edifice that united them before the reforms of the Allied Occupation. Politicians at all levels seek to legitimate themselves and their administrations by appearing to honor the most profound religious sentiments of the people, embodied in the desire to memorialize the war dead.

Shrines, having lost state support in 1945, seek to regain it. In part, this is because individually they have been rather unsuccessful in sustaining the type of mass religious attraction that drew people before 1868, and there is much truth in the observation that without the reintroduction of the element of coercion present before 1945 many shrines would be completely ignored by their parishioners. Many now are largely neglected except on the occasion of annual festivals and subsist by providing wedding parlors and sites for tourism. Created in its modern form by the state, Shintō continues to work towards establishing substantive links to the state. It seems likely that both central and local-level administrations will comply, so long as it is expedient and inexpensive, appeases highly conservative elements, and serves the purpose of their own legitimation to do so—and to the extent that Japanese citizens do not oppose it vigorously.

Appendixes

1. GOVERNMENT EXPENDITURES FOR SHRINES IN COMPARATIVE PERSPECTIVE

THIS APPENDIX presents the categories and quantity of Japanese national government outlays for shrines and related expenditures during the period 1868 to 1945, insofar as they can be known, and compares them with similar expenditures by European states in the same period.

What aspects of Shintō were deemed to be of sufficient national importance to justify support from public funds, and which were not? How do these compare with the investment made in religion by European nations, from which Japan borrowed so much of the machinery of its modern statecraft? Although in the nineteenth century a number of European states confiscated land and other property from Christian churches, most had accepted a principle of religious toleration, and only a few spent public funds to support religious institutions. Examining the 1876 edition of the *Statesman's Yearbook*, we find no religious expenditures in the national budgets of Austria, Denmark, Germany, Great Britain and Ireland, Spain, Portugal, Switzerland, and Turkey.[1] The following nations specified no religious expenditures but maintained a department or ministry of "education and worship": Hungary, the German states of Bavaria and Wurtemburg, and Greece.

In those nations making expenditures from the national budget for religion, the only category of expenditure was support of clerical salaries. For example, Belgium and France paid salaries to Roman Catholic, Protestant, and Jewish clerics. The total of these expenses amounted in 1875 to 1.9 percent of the total of Belgium's expenditures, and to 2.1 percent of France's. Similarly, Prussia and Italy gave state pensions to clerics, Prussia only to archbishops and bishops, while in Italy monks and nuns were entitled to pensions. The Netherlands paid the salaries of some ministers from public funds.

The only nation where strong state financial support for religious institutions survived into the twentieth century was Russia.[2] Until 1917 Russia included in its national budget an annual appropriation to the Holy Synod of the Eastern Orthodox Church. The figures given in Table 7 suggest that while gross appropriations to the Holy Synod consistently rose, they did so in stable and predictable proportion to the national budget.

By comparison with the situation in Europe, the Japanese case shows much more elaborate state support of religious institutions. There were many categories of national expenditures for Shintō. The most consistent of these was an annual appropriation for the Ise Shrines, rising from 50,000 yen in 1902 to 230,000 yen in 1944. In addition, there were special appropriations for the regular rebuilding of the Ise Shrine every twenty years,[3] to assist the shrine after a fire, and other occasional appropriations. The Imperial and National Shrines consistently received appropriations, but these never paid more than a fraction of the expenses of those shrines. From 1902 to 1909 the state contributed to the preservation of temples and shrines, but the amount dwindled over these years. The Ministry of the Army made an annual appropriation for the Yasukuni Shrine. From 1910 to 1936 the state supported the training of Shintō priests, but the appropriations were extremely erratic, suggesting that there was no clear policy on or commitment to this expenditure. The state granted funds to specific shrines that had suffered fire or other national disaster, and it bore much of the cost of constructing shrines built at state initiative, such as the Meiji Shrine.

7. Payments to the Holy Synod from the Russian Imperial Budget, as Percentage of Total National Expenditures, 1873–1916 (in rubles)

	Total Expenditures	Payments to Holy Synod	Percent
1873	517,322,162	9,559,438	1.8
1878	600,398,425	10,100,830	1.7
1883	778,505,423	10,369,929	1.3
1888	888,082,110	11,030,477	1.2
1893	946,955,000[a]	12,309,000[a]	1.3
1898	4,470,149,923	20,374,941	0.4
1903	2,071,667,472	28,388,049	1.4
1908	2,656,682,804	29,763,662	1.1
1913	3,431,204,786	45,664,696	1.3
1914	3,613,569,398[b]	53,093,225[b]	1.5
1915	3,308,561,986	52,564,695	1.6
1916	3,250,915,197[b]	53,965,767[b]	1.7

SOURCE: *Statesman's Yearbook* (London: Macmillan, 1873–1916).
[a] Figures available only in thousands of rubles.
[b] Estimated appropriations.

When we examine the aggregated expenditures of the state on Shintō as a proportion of the national budget, it is difficult to draw clear conclusions. These figures are available for the years 1902 to 1944, and over that period the proportion of the national budget taken up by Shintō-related expenditures declines from .43 percent in 1902 to .01 percent in 1944. (See Table 1, p. 24) Moreover, the overall pattern is one of decline in the proportion of the total national budget and highly erratic decreases and increases in total annual Shintō-related expenditures. The lack of stability in annual appropriations seems to signal the lack of clear and consistent state commitment to Shintō and its various institutions.

By comparison with Russia, and measured by proportion of the national budget appropriated, the fiscal commitment of the Japanese state to Shintō was only a fraction of Russia's to the Eastern Orthodox Church. While Russian appropriations were made directly to the Holy Synod, the Japanese state did not simply hand over the appropriation to an institution like the Holy Synod that then disbursed the funds autonomously. Instead, the Japanese state retained much more minute control over the annual appropriations. Rather than direct grants to shrines or the priesthood, public appropriations were largely controlled by the Home Ministry. This, combined with the erratic fluctuation of funds for priests' training and the aggregated annual Shintō-related outlays, suggests that the state did not see Shintō priests as appropriate, competent executors for all Shintō affairs.

2. THE SHINTŌ DIRECTIVE

1. In order to free the Japanese people from direct or indirect compulsion to believe or profess to believe in a religion or cult officially designated by the state, and

In order to lift from the Japanese people the burden of compulsory financial support of an ideology which has contributed to their war guilt, defeat, suffering, privation, and present deplorable condition, and

In order to prevent a recurrence of the perversion of Shintō theory and beliefs into militaristic and ultranationalistic propaganda designed to delude the Japanese people and lead them into wars of aggression, and

In order to assist the Japanese people in a rededication of their national life to building a new Japan based upon ideals of perpetual peace and democracy,

It is hereby dictated that:

a. The sponsorship, support, perpetuation, control and dissemination of Shintō by the Japanese national, prefectural, and local governments, or by public officials, subordinates, and employees acting in their official capacity are prohibited and will cease immediately.

b. All financial support from public funds and all official affiliation with Shintō and Shintō shrines are prohibited and will cease immediately.

(1) While no financial support from public funds will be extended to shrines located on public reservations or parks, this prohibition will not be construed to preclude the Japanese government from continuing to support the areas on which such shrines are located.

167

(2) Private financial support of all Shintō shrines which have been previously supported in whole or in part by public funds will be permitted, provided such private support is entirely voluntary and is in no way derived from forced or involuntary contributions.

c. All propagation and dissemination of militaristic and ultranationalistic ideology in Shintō doctrines, practices, rites, ceremonies, or observances, as well as in the doctrines, practices, rites, ceremonies, and observances of any other religion, sect, creed, or philosophy, are prohibited and will cease immediately.

d. The Religious Functions Order relating to the Grand Shrine of Ise and the Religious Functions Order relating to State and other Shrines will be annulled.

e. The Shrine Board (Jingi-in) of the Ministry of Home Affairs will be abolished, and its present functions, duties, and administrative obligations will not be assumed by any other governmental or tax-supported agency.

f. All public educational institutions whose primary function is either the investigation and dissemination of Shintō or the training of a Shintō priesthood will be abolished and their physical properties diverted to other uses. Their present functions, duties and administrative obligations will not be assumed by any other governmental or tax-supported agency.

g. Private educational institutions for the investigation and dissemination of Shintō and for the training of priesthood will be permitted and will operate with the same privileges and be subject to the same controls and restrictions as any other private educational institution having no affiliation with the government; in no case, however, will they receive support from public funds, and in no case will they propagate and disseminate militaristic and ultranationalistic ideology.

h. The dissemination of Shintō doctrines in any form and by any means in any educational institution supported wholly or in part by public funds is prohibited and will cease immediately.

(1) All teachers' manuals and textbooks now in use in any educational institution supported wholly or in part by public funds will be censored, and all Shintō doctrine will be deleted. No teachers' manual or textbook which is published in the future for use in such institutions will contain any Shintō doctrine.

(2) No visits to Shintō shrines and no rites, practices or ceremonies associated with Shintō will be conducted or sponsored by any educational institution supported wholly or in part by public funds.

i. Circulation by the government of *The Fundamental Principles of the National Structure* (*Kokutai no Hongi*), *The Way of the Subject* (*Shinmin no Michi*), and all similar official volumes, commentaries, interpretations, or instructions on Shintō are prohibited.

j. The use in official writings of the terms "Greater East Asia War" (*Dai Tōa Sensō*), "The Whole World under One Roof" (*Hakko Ichi-u*), and all other terms whose connotation in Japanese is inextricably connected with State Shintō, militarism, and ultranationalism is prohibited and will cease immediately.

k. God-shelves (*Kamidana*) and all other physical symbols of State Shintō in any office, school, institution, organization, or structure supported wholly or in part by public funds are prohibited and will be removed immediately.

l. No official, subordinate, employee, student, citizen, or resident of Japan will be discriminated against because of his failure to profess and believe in or participate in any practice, rite, ceremony, or observance of State Shintō or any other religion.

m. No official of the national, prefectural, or local government, acting in his public capacity, will visit any shrine to report his assumption of office, to report on conditions of government or to participate as a representative of government in any ceremony or observance.

2. a. The purpose of this directive is to separate religion from the state, to prevent misuse of religion for political ends, and to put all religions, faiths, and creeds upon exactly the same basis, entitled to precisely the same opportunities and protection. It forbids affiliation with the government and the propagation and dissemination of militaristic and ultranationalistic ideology not only to Shintō but to the followers of all religions, faiths, sects, creeds, or philosophies.

b. The provisions of this directive will apply with equal force to all rites, practices, ceremonies, observances, beliefs, teachings, mythology, legends, philosophy, shrines, and physical symbols associated with Shintō.

c. The term State Shintō within the meaning of this directive will refer to that branch of Shintō (*Kokka Shintō* or *Jinja Shintō*) which by official acts of the Japanese Government has been differentiated from the religion of Sect Shintō (*Shūha Shintō*) and has been classified a non-religious cult commonly known as State Shintō, National Shintō, or Shrine Shintō.

d. The term Sect Shintō (*Shūha Shintō* or *Kyōha Shintō*) will refer to that branch of Shintō (composed of 13 recognized sects) which by popular belief, legal commentary, and the official acts of the Japanese Government has been recognized to be a religion.

e. Pursuant to the terms of Article 1 of the Basic Directive on "Removal of Restrictions on Political, Civil, and Religious Liberties" issued on 4 October 1945 by the Supreme Commander for the Allied Powers in which the Japanese people were assured complete religious freedom.

(1) Sect Shintō will enjoy the same protection as any other religion.

(2) Shrine Shintō, after having been divorced from the state and divested of its militaristic and ultranationalistic elements, will be recognized as a religion if its adherents so desire and will be granted the same protection as any other religion in so far as it may in fact be the philosophy or religion of Japanese individuals.

f. Militaristic and ultranationalistic ideology, as used in this directive, embraces those teachings, beliefs, and theories which advocate or justify a mission on the part of Japan to extend its rule over other nations and peoples by reason of:

(1) The doctrine that the Emperor of Japan is superior to the heads of other states because of ancestry, descent, or special origin.

(2) The doctrine that the people of Japan are superior to the people of other lands because of ancestry, descent, or special origin.

(3) The doctrine that the islands of Japan are superior to other lands because of divine or special origin.

(4) Any other doctrine which tends to delude the Japanese people into embarking upon wars of aggression or to glorify the use of force as an instrument for the settlement of disputes with other peoples.

3. The Imperial Japanese Government will submit a comprehensive report to this Headquarters not later than 15 March 1946 describing in detail all action taken to comply with all provisions of this directive.

4. All officials, subordinates, and employees of the Japanese national, prefectural, and local governments, all teachers and education officials, and all citizens and residents of Japan will be held personally accountable for compliance with the spirit as well as the letter of all provisions of this directive.

Notes

INTRODUCTION

1. Shils, *Tradition*, 247–49.

2. Eric Hobsbawm, "Introduction: Inventing Traditions," in *Invention of Tradition*, ed. Hobsbawm and Ranger, 1–14.

3. Marilyn R. Waldman has provided useful qualifications to Hobsbawm's notion of invented traditions and has identified how the idea of tradition can be used to facilitate social change. See her "Tradition as a Modality of Change."

4. Kuroda Toshio, "Shinto in the History of Japanese Religion."

5. The political uses of symbolic ambiguity are treated in Kertzer, *Ritual, Politics, and Power*, Chap. 4.

6. This practice is exemplified in the collection of studies by Shintō scholars, *Meiji ishin Shintō hyakunen shi*, 5 vols., ed. Shintō bunkakai, hereafter referred to as MISH.

7. See, for example, the works of Murakami Shigeyoshi and Yasumaru Yoshio, cited below.

8. Holtom, *Modern Japan*.

9. Lokowandt, *Entwicklung des Staats-Shintō*.

10. This trend is exemplified in MISH and Ashizu, *Kokka Shintō*.

11. The works of Murakami and Yasumaru exemplify this approach.

12. See Chap. 5 of Kertzer, *Ritual, Politics, and Power*, on the way ritual discourages critical thinking and on its persuasiveness precisely because it has no contrary and hence cannot be directly challenged by rational argument.

13. State Shintō during the 1930s and its connection to the suppression of popular religious movements is documented in Murakami, *Modern Century*, Chap. 3. Other works treating this important era are Smethurst, *Social Basis for Japanese Militarism*; Mitchell, *Thought Control*; and Maruyama Masao, *Thought and Behavior*.

14. On the related subject of postwar Japanese nationalism, see Ivan Morris, *Nationalism and the Right Wing in Japan: A Study of Post-war Trends* (London: Oxford University Press, 1960).

15. Wach, *Comparative Study of Religions*.

16. For a discussion of the various ways the word *Shintō* has been used, see Kuroda Toshio, "Shinto in the History of Japanese Religions."

17. This classification omits purely private shrines, such as those on the grounds of a family dwelling, and the informal shrines of the crossroads, fields, and mountains. It should be admitted at the outset, however, that Shintō was so diverse during this period that some of its manifestations are bound to elude this attempt at simple classification for the purpose of conveying background information.

18. See Haga Shōji, "Meiji jingikansei no seiritsu," for a discussion of rites performed at court at the end of the period.

19. Ellwood, *The Feast of Kingship*.

20. Bock, *Engi-Shiki*.

21. The *Shosha negi kannushi hatto*.

22. These deities are Kamimusubi no kami, Takamimusubi no kami, Tamatsumemusubi no kami, Ikumusubi no kami, Tarumusubi no kami, Omiya no mekami, Miketsu no kami, Kotoshironushi no kami.

23. Murakami, *Kokka Shintō*, 52–56.

24. Murakami, *Tennō no saishi*, 38–39.

25. Fukaya, "Kinsei no shogun to tennō," 50.

26. *Ibid.*, 50–63.

27. Ono, *Jinja Shintō*, 86.

28. Weinstein, "Usa Hachiman Shrine," "Tsurugaoka Hachiman Shrine," and "Iwashimizu Hachiman Shrine."

29. At Ise there are actually several shrines, of which the most prominent are called the Inner and the Outer Shrines. It is conventional to refer to the whole complex as the Ise Shrines.

30. On the development of pilgrimage during the Tokugawa period, see Shinjō, *Shaji to kōtsū*.

31. An important exception to this generalization is the True Pure Land school of Japanese Buddhism, whose founder Shinran (1173–1262) did not recognize the cult of kami as legitimate and therefore discouraged his followers from participating in it.

32. Yoneji, *Sonraku saishi*, 60.

33. *Ibid.*, 11–23.

34. Umeda, *Nihon shūkyō seido shi* 3: 38.

35. Murakami, *Kokka Shintō*, 60.

36. On the *honji-suijaku* theory, see Matsunaga, *Buddhist Philosophy of Assimilation*.

37. Nishigaki, *O-Ise mairi*, 85–90.

38. Fujitani, *Shintō shinkō*, 39–40.

39. *Ibid.*, 70–71; see Shinjō, *Shaji to kōtsū*, 125–28, for a slightly different estimate.

40. Nishigaki, *O-Ise mairi*, III, 154.

41. Fujitani, *Shintō shinkō*, 70–71.

42. Shinjō, *Shaji to kōtsū*, 122.

43. For cogent discussion of Shintō theories during the Tokugawa period, see Ooms, *Tokugawa Ideology*.

44. On National Learning see Nosco, "Nostalgia for Paradise," and Harootunian, *Toward Restoration*. For a concise account of the activities of National Learning figures at the end of the Tokugawa era, see Matsumoto, "Bakumatsu kokugaku."

45. See Harootunian, *Things Seen and Unseen*.

46. See the writings of Mutobe Yoshika and Ōkuni Takamasa as two representative figures, collected in *Nihon shisō taikei*, Vol. 50, *Hirata Atsutane, Ban Nobutomo, Ōkuni Takamasa*, ed. Haga Noboru et al. (Tokyo: Iwanami shoten, 1973), and Vol. 51, *Kokugaku undō no shisō*, ed. Matsumoto Sannosuke and Haga Noboru (Tokyo: Iwanami shoten, 1971).

47. Sakamoto Ken'ichi, *Meiji Shintō*, 424–69.

48. On Tamamatsu, see Itō, *Fukko no sekishi Tamamatsu Misao*.

49. Sakamoto Koremaru, "Meiji Jingikan."

50. *Ibid.*, 39–47.

51. See Kuroda Toshio, "Shinto in the History of Japanese Religion," for a treatment of the changes in the meaning of the word *Shintō* before the Meiji period.

CHAPTER I

1. For example, Ōnishi Aijirō, founder of the new religion Honmichi, was investigated along with 385 members of the associated group Tenri Kenkyūkai in 1928.

2. On the separation of Buddhism from Shintō, see Tamamuro, *Shinbutsubunri*, and Grapard, "Japan's Ignored Cultural Revolution."

3. Yasumaru, *Kamigami*, 145–59.

4. Fridell, "Shrine Shintō," 154.

5. Yoneji, "Saishi soshiki to ujiko seido."

6. *Ibid.*, 411.

7. Haga Shōji, "Meiji jingikansei no seiritsu," Pt. 1, 36–37.

8. *Ibid.*, passim.

9. *Ibid.*, Pt. 2, 97.

10. The personal and theological differences of these two factions are detailed at length in the diary of one participant in the Department of Divinity and Great Promulgation Campaign, Tokoyo Nagatane, reprinted in Uno, "Shinkyō soshiki monogatari."

11. Jinja shinpō seikyō kenkyū kai, *Kindai jinja Shintō shi*, 42, hereafter cited as KJSS.

12. Murakami, *Tennō no saishi*, 53–54.

13. *Ibid.*, 56.

14. *Ibid.*, 68.

15. *Ibid.*, 71.

16. *Ibid.*, 73.

17. *Ibid.*, 132, and Tamamuro, "Meiji ki no shūkyō seisaku."

18. Yasumaru, *Kamigami*, 140–41, 186ff.

19. Ariizumi, "Meiji kokka to shukusaibi."

20. Nishida, "Meiji ikō jinja hōseishi no ichidanmen," 62–63.

21. KJSS, 65–67.

22. This budgetary decision underlined a division of the shrines into two main categories: the National and Imperial Shrines, collectively known as *kankoku heisha*, "government shrines," and the shrines below those ranks, collectively known as *minsha*, "civic shrines."

23. This act was carried out in anticipation of the opening of the Diet in 1890 and in fear of what might happen to public support of the shrines if the matter were left to the political process.

24. KJSS, 77–79.

25. *Ibid.*, 84.

26. The history of these terms is discussed fully in Chap. 3.

27. The growth of new religions in relation to Shintō is discussed in Chap. 2.

28. More shrines began to receive financial support from local administrations in the twentieth century, a phenomenon that is discussed in Chap.4.

29. *Ibid.*, 67–72.

30. This issue was debated at length in the Pantheon Dispute (*saijin ronsō*). See Fujii, *Meiji kokugaku.*

31. Traditionally, in the pre-Meiji temple-shrine complexes, and with few exceptions, funerals had been performed only by Buddhist priests.

32. *Ibid.*, and KJSS, 67–72.

33. KJSS, 47–49.

34. *Ibid.*, 83ff.

35. *Ibid.*, 87.

36. *Ibid.*, 87–89.

37. *Ibid.*, 90, 93. As for where in the structure of government the Department of Divinity should be located, some held that it should be an autonomous, free-floating organ unattached to any ministry, while others believed it should be placed within the Imperial Household Ministry. The argument for making it autonomous was that in this way it would have maximum impact upon the whole nation. On the other hand, if it were not protected by some powerful ministry, others warned, it could easily be rendered impotent by bureaucrats who considered shrines useless, just as in early Meiji.

38. Nevertheless, in spite of vigorous lobbying, the priesthood was unable to have a higher level of shrine support instituted at this time.

39. KJSS, 102.

40. Murakami, *Modern Century*, 65–67.

41. *Ibid.*, 113–14.

42. *Ibid.*, 68–69.

43. Miyachi, *Nichirō sengo seijishi no kenkyū*, 89–91.

44. See Fridell, *Shrine Mergers.*

45. Abe, "Religious Freedom," Pt. 1.

46. Miyachi, *Tennōsei no seijishiteki kenkyū*, 161–81.

47. Murakami, *Modern Century*, 110–11.

CHAPTER 2

1. The thirteen sects are: Kurozumikyō, Konkōkyō, Tenrikyō, Shinrikyō, Fusōkyō, Misogikyō, Ontakekyō, Jikkōkyō, Taishakyō, Shūseikyō, Shinshūkyō,

Taiseikyō, and Shintō Taikyō. Another group, called Jingūkyō, was previously counted as one of the Shintō sects, but is not now.

2. Toyota, *Nihon shūkyō seido*, 216.

3. Uno, "Shinkyō soshiki monogatari," 207.

4. Hirai, "Sekkyō katsudō," 45.

5. Uno, "Shinkyō soshiki monogatari," 271.

6. Meiji hennenshi hensankai, ed., *Meijihen nenshi* 2: 270–71.

7. One could cite many examples of this kind, but these from the newspaper *Chōya shinbun* of 1874 and 1875 are representative.

8. Toyota, *Nihon shūkyō seido*, 206–7.

9. *Ibid.*, 207–9.

10. Fujii, "Yamagata-ken no chūkyōin," and "Chūkyōin no kenkyū."

11. Fujii, "Fukushima-ken chūkyōin no kenkyū."

12. Hirai, "Sekkyō katsudō," 47–48.

13. Yasumaru, *Kamigami*, 186ff.

14. Toyota, *Nihon shūkyō seido*, 207–9.

15. Nakajima, "Taikyō senpu undō," 41.

16. Toyota, *Nihon shūkyō seido*, 209, 216.

17. *Ibid.*, 247.

18. Nakajima, "Taikyō senpu undō," 34–38.

19. Kanzaki, *Meiji ikō ni okeru Shintō shi no shosō*, 253–54.

20. Fujii, *Meiji kokugaku*, is the most complete source for documents pertaining to the Pantheon Dispute.

21. Inoue Nobutaka, "Shintō-kei kyōdan ni kansuru shūsenzen no kenkyū jōkyō ni tsuite."

22. Tokoyo Nagatane records these protests in Uno, "Shinkyō soshiki monogatari," 45, and they are also discussed in the diaries of such National Evangelists as Satō Norio (see below).

23. Fukuzawa, *Bunmeiron no gairyaku*, 195. This passage is also discussed and translated in part in Muraoka, *Studies in Shintō Thought*, 210. See also Fukuzawa, *Encouragement of Learning*.

24. Akaiwagun, *Akaiwagun shi*, 30; Chayamachi, *Chayamachi shi*, 211; Jōtōgun, *Jōtōgun shi*, 726ff; Uno, "Chiiki shakai ni okeru Shintō kyōha no denpa to teichaku," 67.

25. Miyake Shigezō, "Jūshichi setsu mondai" (1872). This document is preserved as Document 66 in the Okayama Kenritsu Sōgō Bunka Sentaa Kyōdo Shiryō Shitsu, in a special collection on Kurozumikyō, hereafter referred to as OKSS.

26. Yamano Sadayasu's diary is preserved in the Munetada Shrine of Kurozumikyō.

27. OKSS Document 81, "Kyōdōshoku kokoroe" (1878?).

28. Nagamitsu, *Okayama no shūkyō*, 140–42.

29. This information is drawn from a collection of letters and documents preserved by Kurozumikyō's Kamogata church.

30. This deity represents a renaming of the deity of the Northeast, Konjin, traditionally believed to possess or cause misfortune to those who offend him.

31. Morikawa, "Honkyō josei kyōshi ni tsuite"; Tabuchi, "Okayama itō chiiki ni okeru kyōso jidai no dendō jōkyō."

32. While most of the founder's direct disciples came from southern Okayama, those of his disciple Saitō Ju'emon (1823–1895), who headed the Kasaoka church, were 60 percent from Hiroshima and 36 percent from southern Okayama. From 1865 Saitō kept a record of followers showing a total of 13,667 who came for prayers.

33. Sugihara, "Konjinsha kō."

34. Sawada, "Shinshin, fukyō, seiji—Konkō Daijin Oboesho."

35. Misogikyō, known at first as Toho kamikō, was founded between 1830 and 1844 by Inoue Masakane (1790–1849). This group was later counted among the thirteen Shintō sects.

36. Shinrikyō, founded in 1880 by Sano Tsunehiko (1834–1906), was counted among the thirteen Shintō sects.

37. Hashimoto, "Deyashiro no seiritsu to sono tenkai." The *Omichi Annai* was Konkōkyō's only written scripture until 1887.

38. Yamada Jitsuo, "Shintō Mihashira kyōkai no seiritsu to hokai."

39. Satō recorded his participation in the Great Promulgation Campaign in the first volume of his autobiography, *Shinkyō kaiyō rokujūgonen*. On the creed Satō composed, see Fujio, "Fukyō to kyōgika no mondai—Shinjō o megutte."

40. In 1885 the group became known as the Shintō Konkōkyōkai and became attached to the Office of Shintō Affairs (after 1887 to the Shintō Honkyoku). There was a period when all ministers had to be approved by the office in order to proselytize. However, by 1888 the local churches were linked directly to the headquarters and a system of churches was firmly established. Muta, "Shintō Konkōkyōkai ni tsuite," 53–54.

41. Like Kurozumikyō, Konkōkyō continued to use the ranking system of the Great Promulgation Campaign even after its abolition. The figures given here cover the years 1880 to 1889. Of the 222, 199 were men and 23 were women. Satō Mitsutoshi, "Gitai," 87ff.

42. Yamada Jitsuo, "Junkyō no yōsō to sono mondaisei," 57.

43. After 1890 Satō and other Konkōkyō ministers turned their attention to sermons on the Imperial Rescript on Education. *Ibid.*, 58–60.

44. Tsuji, *Meiji Bukkyōshi no mondai*, Chap. 3.

45. Satō Mitsutoshi, "Gitai," 77.

CHAPTER 3

1. Hirata Atsutane (1776–1843) was the most influential National Learning figure of the late Tokugawa period. In him the philological study of Motoori Norinaga and earlier National Learning scholars was superseded by loyalist thought and criticism of Confucian and Buddhist thought.

2. Ōkuni Takamasa (1792–1871) of Tsuwano played a leading role in making National Learning the official ideology of his domain. Taking much from Hirata, he had many followers among the shrine priests of western Japan. He served briefly in the Bureau of Rites, retiring because of old age.

3. Haga Noboru presents a fascinating case of this kind in Satō Kiyotomi from Mino. Satō expected that the fulfillment of the Restoration would make National Learning or Shintō the state religion, and to further that end he founded a school, preached vigorously, and promoted cults of local tutelary deities as a means to instill

in the populace reverence for the kami. See Haga Noboru, *Meiji kokka to minshū*, 28–49.

4. Haga Shōji, "Meiji jingikansei no seiritsu," Pt. 2, 96.

5. *Ibid.*, 97.

6. A system of shrine ranks, loosely modeled on the tenth-century *Engishiki* was created, and a rank assigned to each shrine. From the top down the ranks were Imperial Shrine (*kanpeisha*), National Shrine (*kokuheisha*)—there were Major, Middle, and Minor grades of both—Prefectural Shrine (*kensha*), District Shrine (*gōsha*), Village or Town Shrine (*sonsha, chōsha*), and Unranked Shrine (*mukakusha*). District and Unranked categories had no ancient precedent. In addition, there was a category of Special Shrines (*bekkakusha*), newly created shrines for the war dead, enshrining famous loyalists, and other patriotic purposes.

7. This shrine and Yasukuni were Special Shrines.

8. KJSS, 66.

9. Collcutt, "Buddhism."

10. Founded between 1830 and 1844 by Inoue Masakane. Misogikyō's founder died in exile after being banished for predicting the downfall of the shogunate. The group was reconstituted after the Restoration.

11. See Chap. 2.

12. See Chap. 2.

13. See Yasumaru, *Kamigami*, 119–30.

14. For a discussion of this term, see Koizumi, *Meiji shisōka no shūkyōkan*, 16–18, and Ouchi, *Shūkyōgaku jiten*, 255–56.

15. On the history of translating the English word *religion* in Japan, see Katō, *Shūkyōgaku seiyō*, and Aihara, "Yakugo *shūkyō* no seiritsu." Aihara notes that the term *shūkyō* does not appear in early Meiji dictionaries. Its first use outside of treaties is in 1877; its first appearance in a book title comes in 1880. In *Meiji shūkyō shichō no kenkyū*, Suzuki Norihisa notes that an 1867 government document concerning the Urakami Christians (see below) uses the word *shūkyō* to mean Christianity (pp. 14–15). In fact, one possible reading of government documents that use *shūkyō* is to understand them as meaning Christianity, not a generic phenomenon of religion.

16. See Koizumi, *Meiji shisōka no shūkyōkan*, for a succinct overview.

17. Kiyozawa Manji (1863–1903), a priest of the True Pure Land school and graduate of Tokyo Imperial University, was instrumental in effecting significant reforms within Buddhism.

18. Shimaji Mokurai (1838–1911), a priest of the True Pure Land school, traveled widely in Europe in 1872 and 1873 to survey religious affairs. He was mainly responsible for withdrawing Buddhist priests from joint proselytization with Shintō in the Great Promulgation Campaign and was later a strong advocate of freedom of religion.

19. Ouchi Seiran (1845–1918) was a priest of the Sōtō Zen school who later laicized and began publishing a journal for Buddhist lay people, *Meikyō shinshi*. He also founded an ecumenical group for Buddhists of various schools.

20. Inoue Enryō (1858–1919) was a Buddhist philosopher and critic of Christianity. He preached a sort of Buddhist patriotism and the need for reform within Buddhism. He founded the Tetsugakkan in 1887 to promote the study of Asian philosophy and was instrumental in founding the journal *Nihonjin*.

21. For a general treatment of these writers, see Ikeda, *Meiji no shinbukkyō undō*.

22. For example, Fukuzawa Yukichi said Shintō lacked a doctrine (4: 156), that it seemed to be in a daze (19: 711), and that its priests were more like antiquarians than religious leaders (*Fukuzawa Yukichi zenshū*, ed. Keiogijuku, 21 vols. [Tokyo: Iwanami shoten, 1958–64]). Nishimura Shigeki said that Shintō was a Way (*dō, michi*), which he distinguished from religion (*Jishikiroku*, quoted in Koizumi, *Meiji shisōka no shūkyōkan*, 112); Katō Hiroyuki said in his *Kokutai shinron* (1874) that scholars of National Learning were liars who turn their backs on the truth (quoted in Koizumi, *ibid.*, 320–24).

23. See Ōkuni's "Hongaku kyōyō."

24. *Nihon kokugo daijiten* (Tokyo: Shōgakkan, 1973). Confusingly, the word *Shintō* was used by some early Meiji writers, such as the educator Katō Hiroyuki, as a translation for *religion*, proving that in this period not only the general public, but also philosophers, educators, and social thinkers did not understand *Shintō* to refer to shrines, their priests, and kami cults. That understanding of the term did not achieve ubiquity or hegemony until the early twentieth century *even among the priesthood*. See Koizumi, *Meiji shisōka no shūkyōkan*, 19. For a historical survey of premodern understandings of the term *Shintō*, see Kuroda Toshio, "Shinto in the History of Japanese Religion."

25. The text of the memorial is reproduced as No. 174 in Irokawa et al., *Meiji kenpakusho shūsei*, Vol. 3.

26. I have been unable to locate the term *kokkyō* in government directives on shrine or temple affairs in this period.

27. See *Meiroku zasshi*. In the journal's fourth issue (undated but probably 1872 or 1873), Nishi Amane wrote as follows: "What about a religion that interferes with the national structure (*kokutai*)? He may wonder whether a religion may eventually injure the national structure if . . . the government leaves religion to individual preference. . . . I would respond that the powers of government are really not in the same sphere as the path of religion" (p. 51).

28. These stalwart believers' ancestors must have been converted in the sixteenth century and then gone underground when Christianity was proscribed in the early seventeenth century. Their unexpected appearance was a crisis of the first magnitude for Shintō administrators, a dramatic exposure, from their point of view, of "the enemy within." See Tokushige, *Ishin seiji shūkyōshi kenkyū*, 168–73.

29. Fujii, *Meiji kokugaku*, 556ff.

30. For a general study of Motoori Toyokai, see Suzuki Atsushi, "Motoori Toyokai-den," in *Ishin zengo ni okeru kokugaku no shōmondai* (Tokyo: Kokugakuin daigaku Nihon bunka kenkyūsho, 1983), 387–443. In later life Motoori lectured widely on National Learning at Tokyo Imperial University and at the Institute for the Study of the Classics. On changes at the Kanda Shrine under Motoori's tenure, see Ogi Shinzō, *Tokyo shomin seikatsushi kenkyū* (Tokyo: Nihon hōsō shuppan kyōkai, 1979), 563–65.

31. Created in 1858 and abolished in 1868, this post had simultaneously as many as ten incumbents. It ranked below the Council of Elders and carried a stipend of 2,000 *koku* (1 *koku* = approximately 5 bushels of rice) and 300 *ryō* in cash. *Nihonshi jiten* (Tokyo: Kadokawa shoten, 1982), 175.

32. *Gokajō no seimon*. Taking the form of a vow by the emperor to the kami, the Charter Oath proclaimed the intention of the new state to establish public assemblies, seek knowledge throughout the world, and other items.

33. Fujii, *Meiji kokugaku*, 490ff.

34. *Shintō jinmei jiten*, 254.

35. This important post (Kyōtō shōshidai) combined the duties of a regional governor, civil inspector, and judge, carrying responsibility for all civil cases in shogunal lands in the Kyoto area, oversight of *daimyō*, supervision of the Kyoto nobility, and other duties. The post was abolished in 1867. *Nihonshi jiten*, 267.

36. *Shintō jinmei jiten*, 37–38.

37. Fujii, *Meiji kokugaku*, 56, 383, 434.

38. *Shintō jinmei jiten*, 69–70.

39. Itō Hirobumi (1841–1909) was arguably the most powerful political leader of the 1880s.

40. Inoue Kowashi (1843–1895) drafted the Imperial Rescript on Education and played a central role in the drafting of the Meiji Constitution.

41. *Shintō jinmei jiten*, 278. See also Maruyama Sueo, *Kokugaku shijō no hitobito*, 752–816.

42. Fujii, *Meiji kokugaku*, 621.

43. It goes without saying that Taishakyō, Ontakekyō, Jingūkyō, and Shintō Taikyō were fundamentally different in character from groups originating in a founder's revelations, although the same administrative term, "sect" (*kyōha, shūha*), was applied to both types.

44. The main business of the Nagasaki Teaching Institute was in fact to dispose of the Urakami Christians.

45. The text of Tokoyo's memoirs is reproduced in Uno, "Shinkyō soshiki monogatari," 179–272.

46. National Learning identified deities appearing in the first three chapters of the *Kojiki* as creators of the universe (*zōka no sanjin*): Takamimusubi no kami, Amenominakanushi no kami, and Kamimusubi no kami.

47. This latter point divided the Shintō world irrevocably, exploding in the Pantheon Dispute of the early 1880s. See Fujii, *Meiji kokugaku*.

48. Founded in 1838 by Nakayama Miki (1798–1887), Tenrikyō was one of the fastest-growing new religious groups of the period. However, its founder despised the shrine priesthood and refused to have anything to do with National Teaching. It was only after her death, in 1908, that the group was recognized as a sect of Shintō.

49. See Hardacre, "Creating State Shintō: The Great Promulgation Campaign and the New Religions," *Journal of Japanese Studies* 12 (January 1986): 29–63, on the participation of sects in the Great Promulgation Campaign.

50. Uno, "Shinkyō soshiki monogatari," 206.

51. The closed character of National Learning schools was specifically criticized by Fukuba Bisei, himself a disciple of Ōkuni Takamasa. See *ibid.*, 196.

52. Such was the immediate reaction of Sano Tsunehiko when he learned that Tokyo priests preached in this way.

53. In fact, an identification of Shintō with everything Japanese was one way the term was used by Motoori Norinaga (quoted in Kuroda Toshio, "Shinto in the

History of Japanese Religion," 2), who asserted that even Buddhism and Confucianism were part of the Shintō of a certain age. Shintō priests in the Meiji era, under the influence of National Learning after Motoori, would not have extended the Shintō label to Buddhism or Confucianism, but might instead have claimed that Buddhist ideas originated in Shintō.

54. Mutobe Yoshika was one of the influential writers on this theme in the late Tokugawa period. See his "Ubusunasha kōdenshō."

55. Tanaka Sen'ya, a priest of a shrine in rural Chichibu during the early Meiji period (whom I discuss in more detail below), started local confraternities for worship of the tutelary deities. Nor was promotion of the cult of these deities limited to the shrine priesthood; it was advocated among sect leaders also, as demonstrated in the diary of Sano Tsunehiko, founder of Shinrikyō.

56. In only a few cases did the public funds spent on shrines provide salaries adequate to allow priests to forego secondary employment. Although statistics on the proportion of the priesthood serving more than one shrine or taking by-employments do not exist before the twentieth century, the lament over shrine priests' economic situation is voiced loudly beginning in 1868 in diaries, memorials, and histories of the priesthood. See KJSS, passim.

57. Some might also place Shinrikyō in this group.

58. The *Tanaka Sen'ya Nikki* was published in 1977 in Saitama by the Saitama Shinbun Shuppansha. Covering the years 1850 to 1898, it is a collection of eight manuscripts, of which seven comprise the diary proper. The eighth manuscript is a separate account of the Chichibu Uprising of 1884–1885. The years 1878 to 1880 are missing.

59. Tanaka spent almost his entire life in Chichibu, venturing only occasionally beyond its borders on shrine business, making a trip to Nikkō, to the Ise Shrines, to the Hikawa Shrine in present-day Ōmiya City, and to Tokyo to make the rounds of shrines there. He owned enough land to rank among the "middling sort." His land was largely forest and upland fields with only a fraction of an acre in paddy. His rice harvest was about ten bushels annually, raised for domestic consumption. He hired labor seasonally but had no tenants. He attended village council meetings before and after becoming a priest and kept the books of the primary school and several rotating credit associations (*mujinkō, tanomoshikō*). He also kept the accounts of the local Office of Shintō Affairs. He was a small-scale moneylender (lending at about six percent), and he also kept funds on deposit in this era before the development of rural banking.

60. His diary (p. 30) shows that he performed pilgrimage to Kannon (Skt. Avalokitesvara) temples (his town of Shimoyoshida was located in the area of a famous pilgrimage route of temples dedicated to Kannon) and *goma* (Skt. *homa*) ceremonies to cast out disease deities (p. 40), prayers for the successful maturation of silkworms (p. 52), rites for lifting the postpartum taboo (p. 71), and other rites.

61. *Hi-machi*, literally "awaiting the sun," is thought to be a very ancient custom. The practice consists of an all-night vigil, generally conducted in a shrine, after purification. It is connected in some places with the worship of Koshin, but not necessarily so, and elsewhere climaxes with dawn worship of the rising sun. Tanaka's diary shows that he participated frequently in this rite, and that it was often

connected with meetings of the rotating credit associations he joined (pp. 65, 118).

62. Tanaka founded a confraternity to promote the worship of tutelary deities, and also a confraternity to prevent the spread of Christianity (p. 390).

63. *Tanaka Sen'ya Nikki*, 276.

64. For the first ten years of his priesthood (1873–1882), Tanaka never performed kitō. From 1883, however, the performance of such rites, especially healing, became an important activity. Furthermore, he became involved in exorcism. Having only performed one rite to exorcise a fox before 1882, he performed several in succeeding years, performing in all thirty-eight kitō rites and five fox-spirit exorcisms, all in violation of prefectural and central prohibitions and repeated warnings on such practices. He performed rites of purification and blessing at small, unofficial shrines on private land, also a questionable practice in Tokyo's eyes. Some of these were ancestral shrines, while others were dedicated to the rice god Inari. Tanaka also officiated at a variety of folk rites to make rain, stop sleet, protect silkworms, and purify domestic dwellings.

65. Yamada's diary was published privately as *Asahi no yado nikki, Kawagoe Hikawa Jinja Shikan Yamada Morii nikkishū* at Kawagoe City in 1979. Six manuscripts have been preserved, covering the years 1872–1874 (sixth month), 1880 (eighth month)–1883, and 1886, for a total of 307 pages.

66. Tanaka's main post was the Muku Shrine, but he also served as main priest of another, smaller local shrine, the Kibune Shrine. He frequently assisted priests of other shrines in rites and festivals, and he preached widely in Chichibu. Tanaka was second-in-command at the Muku Shrine until 1893, when he became its head priest (*Tanaka Sen'ya Nikki*, 4).

67. Tanaka constantly bought books by mail from Tokyo on a variety of historical and literary subjects, in addition to his unstinting interest in National Learning. He presented memorials to the state in 1872 and 1881.

68. However, Yamada was acquainted with many local National Learning enthusiasts (*Asahi no yado nikki*, 309). Both he and Tanaka were involved in a brisk circulation of manuals on Shintō funerals, though Yamada actually performed funerals very seldom.

69. Tanaka performed ancestral memorial rites, funerals, purifications, rites connected with small shrines on private land, and miscellaneous prayer services.

70. Tanaka helped found a literary journal around 1881. This monthly poetry journal, *Meirin zasshi*, ran to at least 143 issues.

71. I would like to thank Marius Jansen for useful information on *fukko yamato-e*. Yamada received numerous commissions for portraits of Jinmu. His availability to comply with these repeated requests suggests both that there was a demand for these scrolls and that Yamada helped stimulate the demand. When lay people purchased these items, the pictures and, presumably, related Shintō ideas were incorporated into domestic rites.

72. *Asahi no yado nikki*, 252. Yamada also officiated (p. 216) at Buddhist rites devoted to Yakushi, the healing Buddha (Skt. Bhaisajyaguru).

73. However, this question became an issue again in the 1890s, spawning many publications and much argument both inside and outside the priesthood.

74. The first Meiji official use of this term occurred in a directive of 14 May 1871, in which it was stated that hereditary succession to the priesthood was prohibited because shrines were not the possession of private individuals but represented the national rites (*kokka no sōshi*).

CHAPTER 4

1. See Tamamuro, *Shinbutsu-bunri*, 175–205.

2. Busō shiryō kankō kai, *Musashi kuni Sōhara gun Taishidō mura goyō todome*, 1.

3. Information on the Miwa Shrine is drawn from the major history of the shrine, Ōmiwa Jinja shiryō henshū iinkai, *Ōmiwa Jinja shi*.

4. Yasumaru, *Kamigami*, 145–59.

5. Yoneji, "Meiji shoki ni okeru sonraku shozai jinja to kokka tōsei," 75. The legal prescriptions for this system are Dajōkan tasshi 322 and 323.

6. Yoneji, "Saishi soshiki to ujiko seido."

7. Yoneji, *Sonraku saishi*, 49.

8. *Ibid.*, 31.

9. Yoneji, "Saishi soshiki to ujiko seido," 395–96.

10. Yoneji, *Sonraku saishi*, 293–305.

11. Gomazuru, "Jingū hyakunen no ayumi," 432–33.

12. On the administrative systems devised at the Ise Shrines to manage the distribution of talismans, see Kubota, "Jingū kyōin to jingū hōsaikai."

13. An 1874 document from a village near Tokyo directed priests to charge no more than two sen for the Ise talisman. From their total collections they were to retain twenty sen per collector (one or two collectors were permitted per 100 households) and send the rest to the ward government, which may have taken a further cut for its services in the distribution. See Busō shiryō kankō kai, *Musashi kuni Sōhara gun Taishidō mura goyō todome*, 91, Document 200.

14. *Ibid.*, Document 198, 90–91.

15. *Ibid.*, 38.

16. This Buddhist school did not recognize kami worship; it was also the one that most vigorously resisted *shinbutsu bunri*.

17. Fujii, "Jingū to Meiji seifu no kyōka katsudō," 130. Urata's plan resembled the ancient idea of *kokubunji*, assigning a Buddhist temple for monks and one for nuns to each province.

18. Okada, "Daijingū sūkei."

19. Mosaka, *Niigata Daijingū no goyuisho*, 12–13.

20. Okada, "Daijingū sūkei," 249.

21. *Ibid.*

22. Mosaka, *Niigata Daijingū no goyuisho*, 10–11.

23. *Ise Yama Kōtai Jingū yuisho*, unpaginated.

24. Okada, "Daijingū sūkei," 250.

25. *Ibid.*, 255.

26. *Ibid.*, 233.

27. *Ibid.*, 256–65.

28. Okada, *Tokyo Daijingū enkakushi*, 2.

29. Murakami, *Tennō no saishi*, 85.

30. Ōe, *Yasukuni Jinja*, 104–6. Before 1879 the Yasukuni Shrine was called the Tokyo Shōkonsha. It was operated by the ministries of the Army and Navy after 1887, before which time the Home Ministry shared its control with those ministries.

31. *Ibid.*, 112–27, 136–37.

32. *Ibid.*, 127–28.

33. *Ibid.*, 130–35.

34. This editorial was printed in the *Asahi shinbun*, 6 Nov. 1898. The preceding events in this paragraph are also drawn from the *Asahi shinbun*.

35. Ohama, "Eirei sūhai," 141–42.

36. *Ibid.*, 147.

37. Ōe, *Yasukuni Jinja*, 160–61.

38. Ohama, "Eirei sūhai," 150.

39. Ōe, *Yasukuni Jinja*, 168–69, 182. See also Ohama, "Eirei sūhai," 149–50.

40. Ohama, "Eirei sūhai," 149–50. After 1908 the Home Ministry sought to limit the performance of rites for the war dead at shrines and temples, though the reason for and extent of this policy is unclear.

41. The shrine's history is exhaustively documented in Meiji Jingū Gojūnenshi Hensan iinkai, *Meiji Jingū gojūnenshi* (Tokyo: Meiji Jingū, 1980).

42. Only the construction of headquarters of new religious groups like Tenrikyō and Konkōkyō rivaled the building of the Meiji Shrine, and that work did not benefit from state approval.

43. This incident is discussed in detail in Morioka, "Jinja o meguru jūmin kanjō to kanryōteki gōrishugi" 1–49.

44. Nakano, *Tennōsei kokka*, 87.

45. *Ibid.*, passim.

46. *Ibid.*, 90, 278.

47. Taiwan Sōtokufu, *Taiwan ni okeru*, 1–5.

48. *Zenkoku shinshoku kaikaihō* 143 (September 1910): 51–55.

49. *Jinja kyōkai zasshi* 35 (1936): 43.

50. Taiwan Sōtokufu, *Taiwan ni okeru*, 1.

51. *Jinja kyōkai zasshi* 6 (January 1907).

52. Nakano, *Tennōsei kokka*, 257–59.

53. *Asahi shinbun*, 9 Sept. 1894.

54. Nakano, *Tennōsei kokka*, 282–91.

55. Yoshii, *Jinja seido shi*, 91.

56. In the ancient pattern, *shinsen* were offerings of food and drink for the deities, while *heihaku* were offerings of cloth, clothing, and implements. Until 1874 National Shrines only received tribute twice a year.

57. Yoshii, *Jinja seido shi*, 91–93. This work contains a useful chart showing the amount specified for each shrine rank. All of these offerings originated in public funds: monies for the Imperial Shrines came from the imperial house, funds for the National Shrines came direct from the national treasury, money for the Prefectural and District Shrines came from the prefectural government, while money offerings made at town and village shrines came from the town or village government.

58. Since we know that the level of funding for priests' salaries varied widely by prefecture (see Yoshii, *Jinja seido shi*, 267–71), it seems likely that the level of support for shrines themselves was also subject to similar regional variation. The criteria used

in deciding among shrines of the same rank were numerous, but in general shrines with longer histories, more abundant facilities, and more numerous parishioners were favored. In cases where more than one shrine seemed equally qualified on all these criteria, the choice was usually made in favor of the shrine with the more powerful, politically influential parishioners. Sakurai, "Shinsen heihaku ryō kyūshin sha no shitei o meguru shō mondai."

59. Yoshii, *Jinja siedo shi*, 98–99.

60. Naimushō, *Naimushōshi* 2: 15.

61. As of 1923, the average shrine's yearly income from all sources combined was 179 yen. Yoshii, *Jinja seido shi*, 264. The state assumed the burden of supporting the Ise Grand Shrines and the Imperial Shrines in the early 1870s. It did not promulgate a decree of support for National Shrines until 1902.

62. Kodama, *Jinja gyōsei*, 297.

63. Kōmoto, "Jinja gasshi—kokka Shintōka seisaku no tenkai," 72–74.

64. The standard work on this topic is Fridell, *Shrine Mergers*; see particularly pp. 18–22.

65. *Ibid.*, 13.

66. *Ibid.*, 18–21.

67. *Zenkoku shinshoku kaikaihō* 6 (January 1900): 19–22.

68. *Jinja kyōkai zasshi* 11 (May 1912): 48–50.

69. Sakurai, "Jinja gappei to sonraku no henka," 226.

70. Miyachi, *Nichirō sengo seijishi no kenkyū*, 94.

71. Yoneji, *Sonraku saishi*, 478.

72. Yanagita, "Shintō to minzokugaku."

CHAPTER 5

1. Hagiwara, "Sekku."

2. Ariizumi, "Meiji kokka to shukusaibi."

3. See Murakami, *Tennō no saishi*, 139–40 for a chart showing how each rite was observed at the palace, Ise, and government shrines.

4. Ariizumi, "Meiji kokka to shukusaibi."

5. Murakami, *Tennō no saishi*, 38–39.

6. *Ibid.*, 53–59.

7. *Ibid.*, 65–73.

8. *Ibid.*, 76–94.

9. *Ibid.*, 132 and passim.

10. Fukuba began life as a samurai from Tsuwano, a stronghold of National Learning thought. As a high-ranking early-Meiji Shintō administrator, he exerted great influence in the formation of early government policy on shrine affairs.

11. A subplot of the episode concerns the participation of geisha. The Nihonbashi and Yanagibashi geisha had agreed to participate, but the Shinbashi geisha refused. They were persuaded to take part when a Konkōkyō believer, Hata Tokusaburō, went and urged them to do so. Direct negotiations with Fukuba were then held, and the geisha contributed 150 yen. They arranged to arrive in carriages dressed in identical jackets and provide entertainment. Apparently the Konkōkyō connection was the source of some confusion, because a week later the committee

published a notice saying that it was not necessary to be a member of Konkōkyō to participate in the rites for Kōmei.

12. This account is based on the *Asahi shinbun*.

13. The account of Urakabe Masaka's amusement park is taken from the *Asahi shinbun* of November and December 1888.

14. *Asahi shinbun*, 3 Nov. 1895.

15. *Asahi shinbun*, 1 May 1889 and 25 Jan. 1893.

16. All references in this paragraph are from the *Asahi shinbun*.

17. *Asahi shinbun*, 14 Oct. 1892 and 8 Dec. 1892.

18. For other examples of activity aimed at raising a shrine's rank, see *Asahi shinbun*, 14 Oct. 1892, 27 Oct. 1895, and 11 Apr. 1898.

19. Yamamoto and Imano, *Kindai kyōiku no tennōsei ideorogii*, 24, 60–61.

20. *Ibid.*, 71, 83–89.

21. *Ibid.*, 75–77.

22. *Ibid.*, 93–104.

23. *Asahi shinbun*, 9 Apr. 1889.

24. Kubota, "Jingū kyōin to jingū hōsaikai," 53.

25. Yamamoto and Imano, *Taishō, Shōwa*, 28, 276–94.

26. Kōmoto, "Shisō kokunan to jinja," 321.

27. Yamamoto and Imano, *Taishō, Shōwa*, 311.

28. Kōmoto, "Shisō kokunan to jinja," 333.

29. See the *Jinja kyōkai zasshi* 6 (June and Aug., 1907), 49, 65. According to the *Asahi shinbun*, 27 Oct. 1894, there were even incidents of desecration of the imperial photo in schools.

30. The material in this section is based in large part on extended conversations during June and July 1986 with Professor Hirai Naofusa, head of Shintō Studies at Kokugakuin University.

31. The traditional age for girls was thirteen and fifteen for boys. Since 1945 young people have been legally considered adults at twenty.

32. Kōmoto, "Jinja gasshi—kokka Shintōka seisaku no tenkai," 93.

CHAPTER 6

1. In the sixteenth century, rebellious followers of the True Pure Land school were put down after protracted struggles known as the *ikkō ikki*. The practice of Christianity was proscribed in the seventeenth century. The Fujufuse sect of the Nichiren school of Buddhism had also been suppressed in the Edo period.

2. Abe, "Religious Freedom," Pt. 1, 299. On the hidden Christians see Urakawa, *Urakami Kirishitanshi*, and Kataoka, *Nihon Kirishitan junkyōshi*, Chap. 4.

3. On the role of the question of religious freedom in the revision of the unequal treaties, see Inada, *Meiji kenpō*, Vol. 1, Chap. 4, Pt. 3.

4. Abe, "Religious Freedom," Pt. 2, 60; Nakajima, "Dainihon."

5. Abe, "Religious Freedom," Pt. 2, 60–63; Nakajima, "Dainihon," 15–19.

6. Inada, *Meiji kenpō* 1: 204–10, 291–92, 318–19.

7. For a full discussion of constitutional drafts produced by the Council of Elders, see Inada, *Meiji kenpō*, Vol. 1, Chap. 7.

8. *Ibid.*, 1: 437–39, and Abe, "Religious Freedom," Pt. 2, 65–67.

9. Quoted in Abe, "Religious Freedom," Pt. 2, 68–69.

10. The People's Rights Movement of the 1870s and 1880s aimed at the formation of a national legislative assembly, the creation of a constitution, and other democratic reforms. Spreading over the country, the movement spawned many groups for discussion and research, and some of these produced draft constitutions.

11. Translated in Irokawa, *Culture of the Meiji Period*, 111.

12. Abe, "Religious Freedom," Pt. 2, 74–75. See Inada, *Meiji kenpō*, Vol. 1, Chap. 8, for a full survey of the constitutional drafts produced by the People's Rights Movement.

13. Gneist (1816–1895) was a professor at the University of Berlin.

14. Stein (1815–1890) was a professor at the University of Vienna.

15. Abe, "Religious Freedom," Pt. 2, 78.

16. *Ibid.*, 79–81.

17. Inoue entered government after studying law in Germany and France. As we have seen, he drafted many important documents besides the constitution, including the Imperial Rescript on Education.

18. Siemes, "Hermann Roesler's Commentaries," 55–57.

19. Translated in Abe, "Religious Freedom," Pt. 2, 86–87. On the evolution of Inoue's views on religion see Nakajima, "Meiji kokka to kenpō."

20. Translated in Abe, "Religious Freedom," Pt. 2, 91.

21. *Ibid.*, 94–95.

22. Yamagata Aritomo (1838–1922) was one of the most powerful of the Meiji oligarchs, holding nearly absolute power after Itō's death. He served as minister of the army, and was twice prime minister.

23. *Ibid.*, Pt. 3, 185–86.

24. For a study of the social impact of the Imperial Rescript on Education, see Yamazumi, *Kyōiku chokugo*.

25. *Ibid.*, 109ff., and Gluck, *Japan's Modern Myths*, 128–29.

26. Abe, "Religious Freedom," Pt. 3, 187–90.

27. Translated *ibid.*, 192–93.

28. *Ibid.*, 197.

29. *Ibid.*, 196–99.

30. *Ibid.*, Pt. 4, 27–30.

31. *Ibid.*, 35.

32. *Ibid.*, 37–38.

33. *Ibid.*, 42–43.

34. Uemura Masahisa (1857–1925) was a leader of the Japan Christian Church and a vocal social critic.

35. *Ibid.*, 47–49.

36. *Ibid.*, 51–52.

37. *Ibid.*, Pt. 5, 76.

38. Murakami, *Nihon hyakunen no shūkyō*, 59–60.

39. Abe, "Religious Freedom," Pt. 6, 225–26. On the state's motives for the suppressions of religious associations, see Garon, "State and Religion in Imperial Japan." The term *ruiji shūkyō* was used in government documents to refer to all religious organizations other than shrine and sectarian Shintō, Buddhism, and

Christianity, and to any sect of one of the religions that had not been recognized by the state. See Inoue Egyō, *Shūkyō hōjin hō no kisoteki kenkyū*, 30–31.

40. On the suppression of Ōmotokyō, see Miyachi, "Ōmotokyō fukei jiken," 273–304, and Nadolski, "Omoto Suppressions in Japan."

41. Murakami, *Nihon hyakunen no shūkyō*, 97–107.

42. Miyachi, "Hitonomichi kyōdan fukei jiken," in *Nihon seiji saiban shiroku*, Vol. 4, *Shōwa-zen*, ed. Wagatsuma Sakae (Tokyo: Daiichi hōki shuppansha, 1970).

43. *Ibid.*, 125–30, 139.

44. *Ibid.*, 134.

45. Abe, "Religious Freedom," Pt. 6, 245.

46. *Ibid.*, 226–41.

47. The debate on Shintō's religiosity was especially prominent in 1882, 1894, and 1929, but it was by no means limited to these years. The policy of shrine mergers stimulated such discussion among leading intellectuals. Yanagita Kunio, founder of folklore studies in Japan and a bureaucrat as well, denounced the idea that Shintō was not religious in "Shintō shikan," first published in 1932. The journals of priests at both prefectural and national levels before 1945 reveal that the question of Shintō's religiosity was by no means clearly settled, even among the priesthood.

48. Kume Kunitake, "Shintō wa saiten no kozoku," first published in *Shigaku zasshi* 2 (Oct.–Dec. 1891): 636–49, and then reprinted for a wider audience in *Shikai* (June 1892). A sampling of newspaper editorial reaction can be consulted in Miyachi et al., *Meiji nyūsu jiten* 4: 177. The Shintō reaction is presented in MISH 3: 83–94.

49. This information was compiled from issues of the *Kanagawa shinshoku kaihō*, the journal of the Kanagawa Prefecture Shrine Priests' Association.

50. Komuro, *Jingikan fukkō undō*, 15ff.

51. Kohama, *Kokumin soshiki to ujiko seido*, 5–11.

52. See Kanagawa ken shinshoku kai, *Jinja to kyōdokyōiku*.

53. Suzuki Shirō, *Jinja to kyōdo kyōiku*.

54. Kōno, *Waga mi no sugata*. This work is a compilation of Kōno's diaries covering the years 1905–1913.

CHAPTER 7

1. Woodward, *Allied Occupation*, 26.

2. *Ibid.*, 241.

3. Shibukawa, "Sengo, Shintō no ayumi."

4. Woodward, *Allied Occupation*, 243.

5. *Ibid.*, 244.

6. *Ibid.*, 22–23.

7. Prior to this assignment, Dyke's career had been limited to sales and marketing.

8. Bunce held the Ph.D. in history from Ohio State University and taught in the Matsuyama Higher School in Japan from 1936 to 1939, in which year he became professor at the New Mexico State Teacher's College.

9. The staff were recruited through regular military and Department of the Army civilian channels, without regard to their personal religious affiliations.

10. Woodward, *Allied Occupation*, 32.

11. *Ibid.*, 14–15.

12. The university itself continued to exist, but its wartime president, Kōno Seizō, whose career was discussed in Chap. 6, was dismissed.

13. The *Asahi* and *Yomiuri* newspapers carried related stories on 15, 16, and 17 December.

14. Creemers, *Shrine Shintō*, 67–77.

15. *Ibid.*, 76.

16. Woodward, *Allied Occupation*, 78.

17. Kenpō chōsakai jimukyoku, *Kokkai ni oite okonawareta rongi* 1: 187–90; 2: 157–58; 3: 39–40.

18. Woodward, *Allied Occupation*, 80.

19. *Ibid.*, 80–81.

20. The law also replaced the short-lived Religious Corporations Ordinance of 1946. See *ibid.*, 82–92.

21. *Ibid.*, 93–102.

22. *Ibid.*, 101–2.

23. Shibukawa, "Sengo, Shintō no ayumi," 317ff.

24. Quoted in Woodward, *Allied Occupation*, 102, n. 1.

25. *Ibid.*, 110–13. The Occupation undertook surveys in some areas of the proportion of school teachers who were also clergy members and found that they numbered no more than 10 percent (pp. 117–18).

26. *Ibid.*, 164–69.

27. *Ibid.*, 169–71.

28. *Ibid.*, 152–53.

29. *Ibid.*, 158–59.

30. This view has been forcefully expressed by Sono Ayako, a contemporary novelist and member of the 1984–1985 Cabinet Secretary's Advisory Committee on the Yasukuni Shrine. See her "Shūkyō o tokutei shinai aratana kinen byō no setsuritsu o."

31. See Norbeck, *Religion and Society in Modern Japan*, 54–63, and Morioka, *Religion in Changing Japanese Society*, Chap. 9.

32. Morioka, *Religion in Changing Japanese Society*, 159–60.

33. *Ibid.*

34. Norbeck, *Religion and Society in Modern Japan*, 57–59.

35. *Ibid.*, 61–62.

36. Sangiin, *Naikaku iinkai kaigiroku*, 1974–1980; Shūgiin, *Naikaku iinkai kaigiroku*, 1974–1980, and especially 21 February 1980, 22ff.

37. Shinshūren, *Shinkyō no jiyū tokuhon*, 35–36.

38. On Shrine Association support for the Yasukuni Shrine, see Iguchi, "Sengo Yasukuni Jinja no kokueika 'undō' ni tsuite."

39. Murakami, *Gendai shūkyō to seiji*, 148–58.

40. Shinshūren, *Shinkyō no jiyū tokuhon*, 30–37. See also Kokuritsu kokkai toshokan, *Yasukuni Jinja mondai shiryōshū*, Pt. 3, for a collection of drafts of the Yasukuni Shrine Bill and other documents relating to the bill, and Pt. 2 for the text of Diet discussion of the shrine from 1952 to 1975.

41. See Diet discussion of this problem in Shūgiin, *Shūgiin naikaku iinkai kaigiroku* 103, No. 3 (6 December 1985), 89ff, and also Murakami, *Shūkyō no shōwashi*, 153.

42. The Yasukuni Shrine has repeatedly expressed this point of view; one easily consulted instance is *Asahi shinbun*, 16 April 1978.

43. Murakami, *Shūkyō no shōwashi*, 154, and Murakami, *Yasukuni Jinja*, 46–47.

44. Sangiin, *Sangiin shakai*, 17. Documents explaining the Ministry of Welfare's involvement with the Yasukuni Shrine are collected in Kokuritsu kokkai toshokan, *Yasukuni Jinja mondai shiryōshū*, 231–34.

45. This case has been exhaustively treated by Ernst Lokowandt in *Zum Verhältnis von Staat und Shintō im Heutigen Japan.*

46. Hayashi, "Kakuryō no Yasukuni Jinja sanpai mondai." See also Lokowandt, *Zum Verhältnis von Staat und Shintō im Heutigen Japan*, 145–53.

47. *Burakumin* are a traditionally stigmatized class in Japan who originally were engaged in tanning, slaughtering of animals, and other occupations considered ritually polluting. They are now politically active in an effort to abolish the discrimination they face.

48. Wada Shigeshi, *Shin no kaifuku* (Kyoto: Higashi Honganji Dōbō sensho, 1975) describes the Buddhist opposition to state support for Yasukuni, and Christian opposition is described in Takahashi, *Kirisuto kyōtō no Yasukuni Jinja yōgoron*, and in Ogawa, *Heiwa o negau izoku no sakebi*. The opposition by *burakumin* is described in Nakao, *Yasukuni: inga to sabetsu.*

49. Saitō Norishi, "Yasukuni Jinja mondai kankei nenpyō."

50. These and similar criticisms of the committee were voiced in the anonymous *Yasukuni kōshiki sanpai o hihan suru.*

51. The Advisory Committee's report is reprinted in *Jurist* 848 (November 1985): 110–15.

52. A Tokyo man brought suit against Nakasone, claiming that formal tribute was unconstitutional; *Kyoto shinbun*, 16 Aug. 1985, p. 16. A survey of regional newspapers shows that most prefectures held nonreligious memorial services to commemorate the surrender. Christian groups were particularly active.

53. Kertzer, *Ritual, Politics, and Power*, 93–94.

54. Annette Aronowicz, in her review of Geoffrey Hartmann, ed., *Bitburg in Moral and Political Perspective* (Bloomington: Indiana University Press, 1986) in *Religion* 18 (July 1988): 287–92, also notes the striking parallel between Kohl and Reagan's Bitburg visit on the one hand, and Nakasone's Yasukuni tribute on the other.

55. Nakasone's favored phrase for ending all discussion of the issue of war guilt was "a complete resolution of postwar government" (*sengo seiji no sōkessan*). See Saitō Kenji, "Sengo no Yasukuni Jinja mondai no suii."

56. On the issue of textbook revision, see Kuroda Kōichirō, "Kyōkasho kentei no gendankai," and Kagotani, "Monbushō 'kokki, kokka' tsūchi ni tsuite."

57. At present the only sources available to document this case are newspaper reports. The following composite account is based on articles from June 1988 in the *Asahi shinbun*, *Mainichi shinbun*, and *Yomiuri shinbun*.

58. The National Assembly of Nation-Protecting Shrines (Zenkoku gokoku jinja

kai), composed of the head priests of these shrines, has its offices in the Yasukuni Shrine. These shrines are still, in effect, prefectural branches of the Yasukuni Shrine.

59. *Mainichi shinbun*, 1 June 1988, p. 1.

60. For an example of academic opposition to formal tribute, see the declaration of the Japanese Historical Association in Nihonshi kenkyūkai iinkai, "Nakasone shushō oyobi kakuryō no Yasukuni Jinja e no 'kōshiki sanpai' ni kōgi suru."

EPILOGUE

1. Sangiin, *Sangiin shakai*, 17.
2. Watanabe, *Kusa no ne no sakebi*, 7–30.
3. Ogawa, *Heiwa o negau izoku no sakebi*, 173–74.
4. Sangiin, *Naikaku iinkai kaigiroku*, 22 May 1979, p. 5.
5. *Yamanashi shinbun*, 15 Aug. 1985, p. 2.
6. Nada, "Ehime tamagushi ryō kisō."

APPENDIX I

1. *Statesman's Yearbook* (London: Macmillan, 1873–1916).
2. I am indebted to my father, Professor Paul H. Hardacre, for the discovery of these comparative data and the sources from which they derive.
3. Ise was the only shrine complex periodically razed and rebuilt in this way to preserve its purity.

Selected Sources

Abe, Yoshiya. "Religious Freedom Under the Meiji Constitution." Parts 1–6. *Contemporary Religions in Japan* 9 (December 1968): 268–338; 10 (March–June 1969): 57–97; 10 (September–December 1969): 181–203; 11 (March–June 1970): 27–53, 54–79; 11 (September–December 1970): 223–96.

Aihara Ichirōsuke. "Yakugo *shūkyō* no seiritsu." *Shūkyōgaku kiyō* 5 (1938): 1–6.

Akaiwagun Kyōikukai. *Akaiwagun shi*. Okayama: Akaiwagun, 1912.

Ariizumi Sadao. "Meiji kokka to shukusaibi." *Rekishigaku kenkyū* 341 (October 1968): 61–70.

Ashizu Uzuhiko. *Kokka Shintō to wa nan datta no ka*. Tokyo: Jinja shinpōsha, 1987.

Bock, Felicia. *Engi-Shiki: Procedures of the Engi Era, Books I–V*. Tokyo: Sophia University Press, 1970.

Busō shiryō kankō kai. *Musashi kuni Sōhara gun Taishidō mura goyō todome*. Tokyo: Busō shiryō kankō kai, 1965.

Chayamachi yakuba. *Chayamachi shi*. Okayama: Chayamachi, 1964.

Chōya shinbun.

Collcutt, Martin. "Buddhism: The Threat of Eradication." In *Japan in Transition*, edited by Marius Jansen and Gilbert Rozman, 143–67. Princeton: Princeton University Press, 1986.

Creemers, Wilhelmus H. M. *Shrine Shintō After World War II*. Leiden: E. J. Brill, 1968.

Date Mitsumi. *Nihon shūkyō seido shiryō ruishūkō*. Tokyo: Ganshōdō shoten, 1930.

Ellwood, Robert. *The Feast of Kingship: Accession Ceremonies in Ancient Japan*. Tokyo: Sophia University Press, 1973.

Fridell, Wilbur. "The Establishment of Shrine Shintō in Meiji Japan." *Japanese Journal of Religious Studies* 2 (June-September 1975): 137–67.

_____. *Japanese Shrine Mergers 1906–1912*. Tokyo: Sophia University Press, 1973.

Fujii Sadafumi. "Chūkyōin no kenkyū." *Shintōgaku* 91 (November 1976): 1–20.

———. "Fukushima-ken chūkyōin no kenkyū." *Shintōgaku* 93 (May 1977): 1–22.

———. "Jingū to Meiji seifu no kyōka katsudō." *Shintō shi kenkyū* 6 (November 1958): 127–40.

———. *Meiji kokugaku hassei shi no kenkyū*. Tokyo: Yoshikawa kōbunkan, 1974.

———. "Yamagata-ken no chūkyōin." *Shintōgaku* 92 (February 1977): 1–14.

Fujio Setsuaki. "Fukyō to kyōgika no mondai—Shinjō o megutte." *Konkōkyōgaku* 11 (1971): 40–67.

Fujitani Toshio. *Shintō shinkō to minshū, tennōsei*. Kyoto: Hōritsu bunkasha, 1980.

Fukaya Katsumi. "Kinsei no shogun to tennō." In *Kōza Nihonrekishi*, Vol. 6, *Kinsei 2*, edited by Rekishigaku kenkyūkai, 45–75. Tokyo: Tokyo daigaku shuppankai, 1985.

Fukuzawa Yukichi. *Bunmeiron no gairyaku*. 18th ed. Tokyo: Iwanami shoten, 1983.

———. *An Encouragement of Learning*. Translated by David Dilworth and Umeyo Hirano. Tokyo: Sophia University Press, 1969.

Garon, Sheldon. "State and Religion in Imperial Japan, 1912–1945." *Journal of Japanese Studies* 12 (Winter 1986): 273–302.

Gluck, Carol. *Japan's Modern Myths*. Princeton: Princeton University Press, 1985.

Gomazuru Hiroyuki. "Jingū hyakunen no ayumi." In *Meiji ishin Shintō hyakunen shi*, edited by Shintō bunkakai, Vol. 1, pp. 361–510. Tokyo: Shintō bunkakai, 1966.

Grapard, Allan G. "Japan's Ignored Cultural Revolution: The Separation of Shintō and Buddhist Divinities in Meiji (*shinbutsu bunri*) and a Case Study: Tonomine." *History of Religions* 23 (February 1984): 240–65.

Hackworth, Green Haywood. *Digest of International Law*. Washington, D.C.: United States Government Printing Office, 1943.

Haga Noboru. *Meiji kokka to minshū*. Tokyo: Yūzankaku, 1974.

Haga Shōji. "Meiji jingikansei no seiritsu to kokka saishi no saihen." Parts 1–2. *Jinbun gakuhō* 49 (1981): 33–46; 50 (1982): 51–100.

Hagiwara Tatsuo. "Sekku." In *Nihon minzoku jiten*, edited by Otsuka Minzoku gakkai, 384–85. Tokyo: Kōbundō, 1975.

Harootunian, Harry. *Things Seen and Unseen*. Chicago: University of Chicago Press, 1988.

———. *Toward Restoration*. Berkeley and Los Angeles: University of California Press, 1970.

Hashimoto Masao. "Deyashiro no seiritsu to sono tenkai." *Konkōkyōgaku* 5 (1962): 24–63.

Hayashi Shūzō. "Kakuryō no Yasukuni Jinja sanpai mondai kondankai no hōkokusho ni tsuite." *Jurist* 848 (November 1985): 40–44.

Hikaku shisōshi kenkyūkai, ed. *Meiji shisōka no shūkyōkan*. Tokyo: Daizō shuppansha, 1975.

Hirai Naofusa. "Taikyō senpu undō ni okeru sekkyō katsudō." *Shintō shūkyō* 58 (May 1970): 44–48.

Hobsbawm, Eric, and Terence Ranger, eds. *The Invention of Tradition*. New York: Cambridge University Press, 1983.

Holtom, Daniel C. *Modern Japan and Shintō Nationalism*. Rev. ed. New York: Paragon, 1943.

———. *The National Faith of Japan*. New York: E. P. Dutton and Company, 1938.

Iguchi Kazuki. "Sengo Yasukuni Jinja no kokueika 'undō' ni tsuite." *Nihonshi kenkyū* 126 (April 1972): 1–25.

Ikeda Eishun. *Meiji no shinbukkyō undō*. Tokyo: Yoshikawa kōbunkan, 1976.

Inada Masatsugu. *Meiji kenpō seiritsushi*. 2 vols. Tokyo: Yūhikaku, 1960–62.

Inoue Egyō. *Shūkyō hōjin hō no kisoteki kenkyū*. Tokyo: Daiichi shobō, 1969.

Inoue Nobutaka. "Shintō-kei kyōdan ni kansuru shūsenzen no kenkyū jōkyō ni tsuite." *Nihon bunka kenkyūjo kiyō* 51 (March 1983): 246–304.

Irokawa Daikichi. *The Culture of the Meiji Period*. Translation edited by Marius B. Jansen. Princeton: Princeton University Press, 1985.

Irokawa Daikichi, Makihara Norio, and Gabe Masao, eds. *Meiji kenpakusho shūsei*. 8 vols. Tokyo: Chikuma shobō, 1986.

Ise Yama Kōtai Jingū yuisho. Yokohama: Ise Yama Kōtai Jingū, 1925.

Itō Takeo. *Fukko no sekishi Tamamatsu Misao*. Tokyo: Privately published, 1927.

Jingū gojūnen hensan iinkai. *Meiji Jingū gojūnenshi*. Tokyo: Meiji Jingū, 1980.

Jinja kyōkai zasshi.

Jinja shinpō seikyō kenkyū kai. *Kindai jinja Shintō shi*. Tokyo: Jinja shinpōsha, 1976.

Jōtōgun Kyōikukai. *Jōtōgun shi*. Okayama: Jōtōgun, 1975.

Kagotani Jirō. "Monbushō 'kokki, kokka' tsūchi ni tsuite." *Nihonshi kenkyū* 279 (November 1985): 119–24.

Kanagawa ken shinshoku kai. *Jinja to kyōdokyōiku*. Yokohama: Privately published, 1935.

Kanagawa shinshoku kaihō.

Kanzaki Issaku. *Meiji ikō ni okeru Shintō shi no shosō*. Tokyo: Yoshikawa kōbunkan, 1937.

Kataoka Yakichi. *Nihon Kirishitan junkyōshi*. Tokyo: Jiji tsūshinsha, 1979.

Katō Genchi. *Shūkyōgaku seiyō*. Tokyo: Nishikiseisha, 1944.

Kenpō chōsakai jimukyoku. *Kokkai ni oite okonawareta rongi*. 3 vols. Tokyo: Kenpō chōsakai, 1958.

Kertzer, David. *Ritual, Politics, and Power*. New Haven: Yale University Press, 1988.

Kodama Kyuichi. *Jinja gyōsei*. Tokyo: Jiji gyōsei sōsho, 1934.

Kohama Yoshio. *Kokumin soshiki to ujiko seido*. Miyagi: Miyagi kennai seibu gakka, 1943.

Koizumi Takashi et al. *Meiji shisōka no shūkyōkan*. Tokyo: Daizō shuppansha, 1975.

Kokuritsu kokkai toshokan chōsa rippō kōsakyoku. *Yasukuni Jinja mondai shiryōshū*. Tokyo: Kokuritsu kokkai toshokan, 1976.

Kōmoto Mitsuru. "Jinja gasshi—kokka Shintōka seisaku no tenkai." In *Nihonjin no shūkyō*, Vol. 3. *Kindai to no kaikō*, edited by Tamaru Noriyoshi, Miyata Noboru, and Muraoka Sora, 67–112. Tokyo: Kōsei shuppansha, 1973.

———. "Shisō kokunan to jinja—Taishōki o chūshin ni shite." In *Nihon ni okeru kokka to shūkyō*, edited by Shimode Sekiyo hakushi kanreki kinenkai, 315–35. Tokyo: Daizō shuppansha, 1978.

Komuro Norio. *Jingikan fukkō undō*. Mito: Privately published, 1939.

Kōno Seizō. *Waga mi no sugata*. Kisaichō, Saitama Prefecture: Kisaichō shihensan shitsu, 1985.

Kubota Osamu. "Jingū kyōin to jingū hōsaikai." In *Meiji ishin Shintō hyakunen shi*, edited by Shintō bunkakai, Vol. 4, pp. 3–58. Tokyo: Shintō bunkakai, 1966.

Kume Kunitake. "Shintō wa saiten no kozoku." *Shigaku zasshi* 2 (October–December 1891): 636–49.

Kuroda Kōichirō. "Kyōkasho kentei no gendankai." *Nihonshi kenkyū* 123 (January 1972): 66–68.

Kuroda Toshio. "Shinto in the History of Japanese Religion." *Journal of Japanese Studies* 7 (Winter 1981): 1–21.

Lokowandt, Ernst. *Die rechtliche Entwicklung des Staats-Shintō in der ersten Hälfte der Meiji-Zeit (1868–1890)*. Wiesbaden: Otto Harrassowitz, 1978.

———. *Zum Verhältnis von Staat und Shintō im Heutigen Japan*. Wiesbaden: Otto Harrassowitz, 1981.

McMullin, Neil. *Buddhism and State in Sixteenth-Century Japan*. Princeton: Princeton University Press, 1984.

Maruyama Masao. *Thought and Behavior in Modern Japanese Politics*. Edited by Ivan Morris. London: Oxford University Press, 1963.

Maruyama Sueo. *Kokugaku shijō no hitobito*. Tokyo: Yoshikawa kōbunkan, 1979.

Matsumoto Sannosuke. "Bakumatsu kokugaku no shisōteki igi." In *Nihon shisōshi taikei*, Vol. 51, *Kokugaku undō no shisō*, edited by Matsumoto Sannosuke and Haga Noboru, 633–61. Tokyo: Iwanami shoten, 1971.

Matsunaga, Alicia. *The Buddhist Philosophy of Assimilation: The Historical Development of the Honji-Suijaku Theory*. Tokyo: Sophia University Press, 1969.

Meiji hennenshi hensankai, ed. *Meijihen nenshi*. 14 vols. Tokyo: Rinsensha, 1940.

Meiroku zasshi. Translated and with an introduction by William Braisted. Tokyo: University of Tokyo Press, 1976.

Mitchell, Richard H. *Thought Control in Prewar Japan*. Ithaca, N.Y.: Cornell University Press, 1976.

Miyachi Masato. *Nichirō sengo seijishi no kenkyū*. Tokyo: Tokyo daigaku shuppankai, 1973.

———. "Ōmotokyō fukei jiken: Shinkō shūkyō to tennōsei ideorogii." In *Nihon seiji saiban shiroku*, Vol. 3, *Taishō*, edited by Wagatsuma Sakae. Tokyo: Daiichi hōki shuppansha, 1969.

———. *Tennōsei no seijishiteki kenkyū*. Tokyo: Kokura shobō, 1981.

———. "Tenri Kenkyūkai fukei jiken." In *Nihon seiji saiban shiroku*, Vol. 4, *Shōwa-zen*, edited by Wagatsuma Sakae, 258–90. Tokyo: Daiichi hōki shuppansha, 1970.

Miyachi Masato et al., eds. *Meiji nyūsu jiten*. 9 vols. Tokyo: Mainichi communications, 1984.

Morikawa Machiko. "Honkyō josei kyōshi ni tsuite." *Konkōkyōgaku* 22 (1982): 76–95.

Morioka Kiyomi. "Jinja o meguru jūmin kanjō to kanryōteki gōrishugi." *Nihon jōmin bunka kiyō* 2 (December 1975): 1–49.

———. *Religion in Changing Japanese Society*. Tokyo: University of Tokyo Press, 1975.

Mosaka Kiyomatsu. *Niigata Daijingū no goyuisho*. Niigata: Privately published, 1974.

Murakami Shigeyoshi. *Gendai shūkyō to seiji*. Tokyo: Tokyo daigaku shuppankai, 1978.

———. *Japanese Religion in the Modern Century*. Translated by Byron Earhart. Tokyo: Tokyo University Press, 1980.

———. *Kokka Shintō*. Tokyo: Iwanami shoten, 1970.

———. *Nihon hyakunen no shūkyō*. Tokyo: Kōdansha, 1968.

———. *Shūkyō no shōwashi*. Tokyo: Mitsumine shobō, 1985.

———. *Tennō no saishi*. Tokyo: Iwanami shoten, 1977.

———. *Yasukuni Jinja*. Iwanami booklet No. 57 (Tokyo: Iwanami shoten, 1986).

Muraoka Tsunetsugu. *Studies in Shintō Thought*. Translated by Delmer Brown and James Araki. Tokyo: Ministry of Education, 1964.

Muta Michimasa. "Shintō Konkōkyōkai ni tsuite." *Konkōkyōgaku* 8 (1951): 40–74.

Mutobe Yoshika. "Ubusunasha kōdenshō." In *Nihon shisōshi taikei*, Vol. 51, *Kokugaku undō no shisō*, edited by Matsumoto Sannosuke and Haga Noboru, 221–30. Tokyo: Iwanami shoten, 1971.

Nada Takashi. "Ehime tamagushi ryō kisō." *Dentō to gendai* 79 (Spring 1984): 69–74.

Nadolski, Thomas Peter. "The Socio-Political Background of the 1921 and 1935 Omoto Suppressions in Japan." Ph.D. dissertation, University of Pennsylvania, 1975.

Nagamitsu Norikazu. *Okayama no shūkyō*. 2d ed. Okayama: Okayama bunkō, 1983.

Naimushō. *Naimushōshi*. 4 vols. Tokyo: Naimushō, 1970–71.

Nakajima Michio. "Dainihon teikoku kenpō dainijūhachi-jō, shinkō jiyū, kitei seiritsu no zenshi." *Nihonshi kenkyū* 168 (August 1976): 1–32.

———. "Meiji kokka to kenpō." *Rekishigaku kenkyū* 10 (October 1974): 29–43.

———. "Taikyō senpu undō to saijin ronsō." *Nihonshi kenkyū* 126 (June 1972): 26–67.

Nakano Kyōtoku. *Tennōsei kokka to shokuminchi dendō*. Tokyo: Kokusho kankōkai, 1976.

Nakao Shunpaku. *Yasukuni: inga to sabetsu*. Kyoto: Nagata bunshodō, 1985.

Nihonshi kenkyūkai iinkai. "Nakasone shushō oyobi kakuryō no Yasukuni Jinja e no 'kōshiki sanpai' ni kōgi suru." *Nihonshi kenkyū* 278 (October 1985): 94–95.

Nishida Hiroyuki. "Meiji ikō jinja hōseishi no ichidanmen." In *Meiji ishin Shintō hyakunen shi*, edited by Shintō bunkakai, Vol. 4, pp. 59–143. Tokyo: Shintō bunkakai, 1966.

Nishigaki Seiji. *O-Ise mairi*. Tokyo: Iwanami shoten, 1983.

Norbeck, Edward. *Religion and Society in Modern Japan*. Houston: Rice University, 1970.

Nosco, Peter. "Nostalgia for Paradise: Nostalgic Themes in Japanese Nativism." Ph.D. dissertation, Columbia University, 1978.

Ōe Shinobu. *Yasukuni Jinja*. Tokyo: Iwanami shoten, 1984.

Ogawa Takemitsu. *Heiwa o negau izoku no sakebi*. Tokyo: Shinkyō shuppansha, 1983.

Ohama Tetsuya. "Eirei sūhai to tennōsei." In *Nihonjin no shūkyō*, Vol. 3, *Kindai to no kaikō*, edited by Tamura Noriyoshi, Miyata Noboru, and Muraoka Sora, 113–78. Tokyo: Kōsei shuppan, 1973.

Okada Yoneo. "Daijingū sūkei no chihōteki hatten." In *Jingū—Meiji hyaku nen shi*, edited by Jingūjichō, Vol. 3, pp. 233–68. Ise: Jingūjichō bunkyōbu, 1970.

———, ed. *Tokyo Daijingū enkakushi*. Tokyo: Eibunsha, 1965.

Ōkuni Takamasa. "Hongaku kyōyō." In *Nihon shisōshi taikei*, Vol. 50, *Hirata Atsutane, Ban Nobutomo, Ōkuni Takamasa*, edited by Haga Noboru et al., 403–57. Tokyo: Iwanami shoten, 1973.

Ōkurashō, ed. *Meiji Taishō zaiseishi*. 20 vols. Tokyo: Keizai Ōraisha, 1956.

Ōmiwa Jinja shiryō henshū iinkai. *Ōmiwa Jinja shi*. Nara: Ōmiwa Jinja, 1975.

Ono Sokyō. *Jinja Shintō no kiso chishiki to kiso mondai*. Tokyo: Sanpōsha, 1963.

Ooms, Herman. *Tokugawa Ideology*. Princeton: Princeton University Press, 1985.

Ouchi Eiji. *Shūkyōgaku jiten*. Tokyo: Tokyo daigaku shuppankai, 1973.

Saitō Kenji. "Sengo no Yasukuni Jinja mondai no suii." *Jurist* 848 (November 1985): 83–90.

Saitō Norishi. "Yasukuni Jinja mondai kankei nenpyō, 1945–1985." *Jurist* 848 (November 1985): 167–87.

Sakamoto Ken'ichi. *Meiji Shintō shi no kenkyū*. Tokyo: Kokusho kankōkai, 1984.

Sakamoto Koremaru. "Meiji Jingikan no saiki katei." *Shintō shūkyō* 94 (July 1979): 33–59.

Sakurai Haruo. "Jinja gappei to sonraku no henka—Hokusei chihō no jirei." *Kōgakkan daigaku kiyō* 14 (January 1976): 224–41.

————. "Shinsen heihaku ryō kyōshin sha no shitei o meguru shō mondai." *Shintō shūkyō* 117 (December 1984): 61–90.

Sangiin. *Naikaku iinkai kaigiroku*. 1974–1980.

————. *Sangiin shakai rōdō iinkai kaigiroku* 16 (3 July 1973).

Satō Mitsutoshi. "Gitai toshite no soshika." *Konkōkyōgaku* 18 (1978): 62–112.

Satō Norio. *Shinkyō kaiyō rokujūgonen*. 2 vols. Konkōmachi: Konkōkyō, 1971.

Sawada Shigenobu. "Shinshin, fukyō, seiji—Konkō Daijin Oboesho." *Konkōkyōgaku* 9 (1961): 93–114.

Shibukawa Ken'ichi. "Sengo, Shintō no ayumi." In *Meiji ishin Shintō hyakunen shi*, edited by Shintō bunkakai, Vol. 1, pp. 247–359. Tokyo: Shintō bunkakai, 1966.

Shils, Edward. *Tradition*. Chicago: University of Chicago Press, 1981.

Shinjō Tsunezō. *Shaji to kōtsū*. Tokyo: Chibundō, 1960.

Shinshūren shinkyō no jiyū ni kansuru tokubetsu iinkai, ed. *Shinkyō no jiyū tokuhon*. Tokyo: Shinshūkyō shinbunsha, 1984.

Shintō bunkakai, ed. *Meiji ishin Shintō hyakunen shi*. 5 vols. Tokyo: Shintō bunkakai, 1966.

Shintō jinmei jiten. Tokyo: Jinja shinpōsha, 1986.

Shūgiin. *Naikaku iinkai kaigiroku*. 1974–1980.

————. *Shūgiin naikaku iinkai kaigiroku*. 1980.

Siemes, Johannes. "Hermann Roesler's Commentaries on the Meiji Constitution," *Monumenta Nipponica* 17, Nos. 1–4 (1962): 1–66.

Smethurst, Richard J. *The Social Basis for Japanese Militarism: The Case of the Imperial Military Reserve Association*. Berkeley: University of California Press, 1974.

Smith, Robert A. *Philippine Freedom, 1946–1958*. New York: Columbia University Press, 1958.

Sono Ayako. "Shūkyō o tokutei shinai aratana kinen byō no setsuritsu o." *Jurist* 848 (November 1985): 32–34.

Sugihara Shin'ichi. "Konjinsha kō." *Konkōkyōgaku* 2 (1948): 55–64.

Suzuki Norihisa. *Meiji shūkyō shichō no kenkyū*. Tokyo: Tokyo daigaku shuppankai, 1979.

Suzuki Shirō. *Jinja to kyōdo kyōiku*. Tokyo: Kaitsūsha, 1932.

Tabuchi Noriyuki. "Okayama itō chiiki ni okeru kyōso jidai no dendō jōkyō." *Konkōkyōgaku* 4 (1949): 137–50.

Taiwan Sōtokufu Kyōkyoku shakaika. *Taiwan ni okeru jinja oyobi shūkyō*. Taipei: Yamashina shoten, 1941.

Takahashi Fujio. *Kirisuto kyōtō no Yasukuni Jinja yōgoron*. Tokyo: Dainichi shobō, 1982.

Tamamuro Fumio. "Meiji ki no shūkyō seisaku." In *Kyōdoshi kenkyū kōza*, Vol. 6, *Meiji zenki kyōdoshi kenkyū*, edited by Wakamori Tarō, 196–216. Tokyo: Asakura shoten, 1972.

———. *Shinbutsubunri*. Tokyo: Kyōikusha, 1979.

Tanaka Sen'ya. *Tanaka Sen'ya Nikki*. Saitama: Saitama shinbun shuppansha, 1977.

Tokushige Asakichi. *Ishin seiji shūkyōshi kenkyū*. Tokyo: Rekishi toshosha, 1974.

Toyota Takeshi. *Nihon shūkyō seido shi no kenkyū*. Rev. ed. Tokyo: San'ichi shobō, 1973.

Tsuji Zennosuke. *Meiji Bukkyōshi no mondai*. Tokyo: Ritsubun shoin, 1945.

Tsuji Zennosuke, and Murakami Sensei, eds. *Meiji ishin shinbutsubunri shiryō*. 7 vols. Tokyo: Meichō shuppan, 1970.

Umeda Toshihiko. *Nihon shūkyō seido shi*. 3 vols. Tokyo: Tōsen shuppansha, 1971.

Uno Masato. "Chiiki shakai ni okeru Shintō kyōha no denpa to teichaku." *Shintō kyōgaku* 94 (July 1979): 60–82.

———. "Tokoyo Nagatane kōjutsu monjinra hikki, 'Shinkyō soshiki monogatari.'" *Nihon bunka kenkyūjo kiyō* 52 (May 1983): 179–272.

Urakawa Wasaburō. *Urakami Kirishitanshi*. Osaka: Zenkoku shobō, 1927.

Wach, Joachim. *The Comparative Study of Religions*. Edited and with an introduction by Joseph M. Kitagawa. New York: Columbia University Press, 1958.

Waldman, Marilyn R. "Tradition as a Modality of Change: Islamic Examples." *History of Religions* 25 (May 1986): 318–40.

Watanabe Hironao. *Kusa no ne no sakebi*. Kesenuma City, Miyagi Prefecture: Airinsha, 1980.

Weinstein, Stanley. "Iwashimizu Hachiman Shrine." In *Encyclopedia of Japan*, Vol. 3, p. 363. Tokyo: Kōdansha, 1983.

———. "Tsurugaoka Hachiman Shrine." In *Encyclopedia of Japan*, Vol. 8, p. 116. Tokyo: Kōdansha, 1983.

———. "Usa Hachiman Shrine." In *Encyclopedia of Japan*, Vol. 8, p. 181. Tokyo: Kōdansha, 1983.

Woodward, William P. *The Allied Occupation of Japan 1945–1952 and Japanese Religions*. Leiden: E. J. Brill, 1972.

Yamada Jitsuo. "Junkyō no yōsō to sono mondaisei." *Konkōkyōgaku* 14 (1974): 55–94.

———. "Shintō Mihashira kyōkai no seiritsu to hokai." *Konkōkyōgaku* 18 (1978): 1–28.

Yamada Morii. *Asahi no yado nikki, Kawagoe Hikawa Jinja Shikan Yamada Morii nikkishū*. Kawagoe City: Privately published, 1979.

Yamamoto Nobuyoshi and Imano Toshihiko. *Kindai kyōiku no tennōsei ideorogii*. Tokyo: Shinsensha, 1973.

———. *Taishō, Shōwa kyōiku no tennōsei ideorogii*. Tokyo: Shinsensha, 1976.

Yamanashi shinbun.

Yamazumi Masami. *Kyōiku chokugo*. Tokyo: Asahi shinbunsha, 1980.

Yanagita Kunio. "Shintō shikan." In *Teihon Yanagita Kunio shū*, edited by Teihon Yanagita Kunio shū hensaniinkai, Vol. 10, pp. 315–96. Tokyo: Chikuma shobō, 1982.

_____. "Shintō to minzokugaku." In *Teihon Yanagita Kunio shū*, edited by Teihon Yanagita Kunio shū hensaniinkai, Vol. 10, pp. 315–96. Tokyo: Chikuma shobō, 1982.

Yasukuni kōshiki sanpai o hihan suru. Tokyo: Shinkyō shuppansha, 1985.

Yasumaru Yoshio. *Kamigami no Meiji ishin*. Iwanami shinsho 103. Tokyo: Iwanami shoten, 1980.

Yoneji Minoru. "Meiji shoki ni okeru sonraku shozai jinja to kokka tōsei." *Nihon joshi daigaku kiyō* 19 (1970): 51–95.

_____. "Saishi soshiki to ujiko seido." In *Nihon minzoku bunka taikei*, Vol. 9, *Koyomi to saiji*, edited by Miyata Noboru, pp. 395–440. Tokyo: Shōgakkan, 1984.

_____. *Sonraku saishi to kokka tōsei*. Tokyo: Ochanomizu shobō, 1974.

Yoshii Yoshiaki. *Jinja seido shi no kenkyū*. Tokyo: Yūzankaku, 1935.

Zenkoku shinshoku kaikaihō.

Index

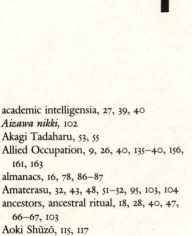

DATE DUE
